DIVISIA MONETARY AGGREGATES AND ECONOMIC ACTIVITIES IN ASIAN DEVELOPING ECONOMIES

To Juwana, Anam Shah, Ridhwan, Anwar and Amirul

Divisia Monetary Aggregates and Economic Activities in Asian Developing Economies

MUZAFAR SHAH HABIBULLAH, PhD
Associate Professor
Department of Economics
Universiti Putra Malaysia
Malaysia

LONDON AND NEW YORK

First published 1999 by Ashgate Publishing

Reissued 2018 by Routledge
2 Park Square, Milton Park, Abingdon, Oxon, OX14 4RN
711 Third Avenue, New York, NY 10017, USA

Routledge is an imprint of the Taylor & Francis Group, an informa business

Copyright © Muzafar Shah Habibullah 1999

All rights reserved. No part of this book may be reprinted or reproduced or utilised in any form or by any electronic, mechanical, or other means, now known or hereafter invented, including photocopying and recording, or in any information storage or retrieval system, without permission in writing from the publishers.

Notice:
Product or corporate names may be trademarks or registered trademarks, and are used only for identification and explanation without intent to infringe.

Publisher's Note
The publisher has gone to great lengths to ensure the quality of this reprint but points out that some imperfections in the original copies may be apparent.

Disclaimer
The publisher has made every effort to trace copyright holders and welcomes correspondence from those they have been unable to contact.

A Library of Congress record exists under LC control number: 99073315

ISBN 13: 978-1-138-33139-6 (hbk)
ISBN 13: 978-1-138-33141-9 (pbk)
ISBN 13: 978-0-429-44732-7 (ebk)

Contents

List of Tables vii

Acknowledgements x

Preface xii

PART ONE **Financial Liberalisation and Monetary Aggregates in Asian Developing Economies** 1

1 Financial Development and Economic Growth in Asian Developing Countries 3

2 Monetary Aggregates and the Effectiveness of Monetary Policy in Financial Liberalised Developing Economies: Application of the Liquidity Constraint Approach 41

PART TWO **Divisia Money, Inflation and Income: Empirical Evidence for Asian Developing Countries** 65

3 Rationale for Divisia Monetary Aggregates in 'Deregulated' Asian Developing Countries 67

4 The P-Star Model Approach: Linking Divisia Money and
   Prices in the Asian Countries   112

5 Divisia Money and Income in the Asian Countries   141

Bibliography   *176*

List of Tables

1.1	Liberalisation of interest rates in the Asian countries	25
1.2	Selected measures of monetisation and financial deepening in Asian countries, 1966-94	27
1.3	Macroeconomic stability in Pre-Reform and Post-Reform era in ASEAN, selected African and Latin American countries	30
1.4	Results of unit root tests	31
1.5	Results of Johansen cointegration tests	33
1.6	Summary of cointegration results for different measure of financial development and economic growth	35
1.7	Results of Granger causality tests between financial development and real output as measure for economic growth	36
1.8	Results of Granger causality tests between financial development and real output per capita as measure for economic growth	38

1.9	Summary of Granger causality tests results for different measure of financial development and economic growth indicators	40
2.1	Results of unit root tests	60
2.2	Results of Euler equation (2.19)	61
2.3	Comparative estimates of λ among Asian developing countries	62
2.4	Results of regressions between λ and financial liberalisation indicators	63
3.1	Information used to construct Divisia aggregates	91
3.2	Simple-sum and Divisia monetary aggregates for the Asian developing countries	96
3.3	Tests of Granger causality from money to output (real income)	111
4.1	Dickey-Pantula integration tests results	132
4.2	Summary of the order of integration	135
4.3	Results of cointegration tests	136
4.4	The P-Star models from the error-correction mechanisms	137
4.5	The P-Star models from the error-correction mechanisms	138
4.6	The P-Star models from the error-correction mechanisms	139
4.7	Results of forecast-encompassing tests for narrow versus broad Divisia money	140

5.1	Results of HEGY tests for seasonal unit roots	165
5.2	Tests for cointegration at frequency zero: The long-run	168
5.3	Tests for cointegration at frequency ½: Biannual cycle	169
5.4	Tests for cointegration at frequency ¼ (and ¾): Annual cycle	170
5.5	Results of seasonal error-correction models	171
5.6	Results of seasonal error-correction models	172
5.7	Results of seasonal error-correction models	173
5.8	Results of seasonal error-correction models	174
5.9	Summary of results of long-run relationships between Divisia money and income at different frequencies	175

Acknowledgements

This book is based on part of my PhD thesis submitted to the University of Southampton in February 1998. I am especially indebted to my supervisor Dr. Peter Smith, who has been extremely supportive in every way throughout my entire graduate career and my pleasant stay in the United Kingdom. His valuable advice, comments and suggestions at every stage of my work are deeply appreciated. I am also very grateful to Professor George McKenzie who generously gave much of his time and for his continuous interest in the progress of my research. Many thanks are also due to my external examiner, Dr. Peter N. Smith from the University of York, who has spent invaluable time reading, making suggestions and giving comments on my work.

During the course of my research work, I have benefited from the insights of seminar participants at the Department of Economics workshop in November 1996. Useful comments were also made by delegates at the 1997, Sixth Tun Razak Conference, Ohio University, Ohio, USA.

I must admit that it is unlikely that this work would have been completed were it not for the continuous support I received from many persons. I wish to thank my parents, my in-laws, my supervisor Dr. Peter Smith, my colleagues Mohammed Yusoff, Ahmad Zubaidi and Zawawi, and my friends Philip, Sofri and Rahim.

Last, but not least, my greatest indebtedness and gratitude is to my beautiful wife, Juwana, for her love, understanding, patience, support and continuous encouragement. To her and our sons Anam Shah, Ridhwan, Anwar and Amirul, this effort is dedicated.

Needless to say, I should finally emphasize that I am solely responsible for any errors and omissions.

Preface

In a recent issue of *Monetary Trends* published by the Federal Reserve Bank of St. Louis, using more than one hundred years of data, Dewald (1997) makes an observation on the association between the growth of M2 and inflation and the growth of GNP in the United States. Dewald (1997: p. 1) concludes that, '...every major acceleration in M2 growth historically has been associated with a major acceleration in inflation; and every major deceleration in M2 growth, with a major deceleration in inflation. Thus, it would be a mistake if noisy short-term movements in M2 and inflation persuaded decision-makers that money doesn't matter anymore. Since the long run consists of an accumulation of short runs, it follows that sustained M2 growth is worth noting in formulating monetary policy. Keeping longer-term M2 growth and nominal GNP growth in line with longer-term real GNP growth remains a guide for a low inflation environment. It is unequivocally supported by the historical record'.

This book has dealt with the above proposition that 'money matters' for monetary policy actions in ten 'deregulated' Asian developing countries. The selected Asian developing countries included in the study were Indonesia, Malaysia, Myanmar, Nepal, the Philippines, Singapore, South Korea, Sri Lanka, Taiwan and Thailand. During the periods of 1970s through 1990s, these Asian countries have experienced changes in the financial environment which among others include interest rates deregulation, relaxation of exchange control, free entry of foreign banks, financial innovations, adoption of flexible exchange arrangements, elimination of credit ceilings, privatization of government owned-banks etc.

From the experience of the developed countries, financial liberalisation has important implications for the role of monetary aggregates as intermediate targets and/or indicators for monetary policy purposes. As a result of far-reaching financial innovation in domestic and international markets, the previously close relationships between real and monetary variables have become less stable, and the use of monetary aggregates as guides for monetary policy action encounters numerous problems. Consequently, monetary aggregates have been downgraded from intermediate targets to information variables. Similar trends have also been observed in the Asian developing countries where the relationship between narrow money M1 and nominal income was less stable, and as a result the central bank chose to emphasis broader monetary aggregates for policy purposes.

On this basis, this book provides empirical evidence on the relationships between the monetary aggregates and nominal income and the price level for the Asian developing countries. It is divided into two parts. Part one describes and tests the implications of financial development and deregulation on the effectiveness of monetary aggregate as guide for monetary policy actions. Part two provides evidence on the potential role of Divisia monetary aggregate as financial indicator or information variable in the design of formulating monetary policy actions for the 'deregulated' Asian developing countries.

The evidence of this book suggests that, despite the occurrence of financial liberalisation, the monetary aggregates have close relationships with nominal income and the price level in the Asian developing economies investigated. Furthermore, this book offers one of the first attempt to evaluate the usefulness of Divisia monetary aggregate as alternative to the conventional Simple-sum aggregate as financial indicator for a group of developing countries.

PART ONE

Financial Liberalisation and Monetary Aggregates in Asian Developing Economies

PART ONE

Financial Liberalisation and Monetary Aggregates in Asian Developing Economies

1 Financial Development and Economic Growth in Asian Developing Countries

Introduction

It is well known that the developing countries in the 1960s and early 1970s have corresponded to what McKinnon (1973) and Shaw (1973) described as 'financially repressed economies'. According to McKinnon, pervasive government intervention and involvement in the financial system through the regulatory and supervisory network, particularly in controlling interest rates and the allocation of credit, tends to distort financial markets. This situation will adversely affect saving and investment decisions of market participants and lead to fragmentation of financial markets and financial disintermediation. The result is a financially repressed economy. McKinnon recommends that the authority liberalise the regulatory regime by allowing interest rates to attain their true equilibrium level and by determining credit allocation on the basis of viability and productivity of projects. McKinnon contends that higher positive real interest rates are necessary to encourage agents to accumulate real money balances, increase financial intermediation and unification of financial markets, thereby ensuring an efficient utilization of resources for economic growth.[1]

The recommendations made by McKinnon are well taken by majority of the developing countries of the Latin America, Africa and Asia. Many of these developing countries attempted to increase the role of market forces in the determination of interest rates, the allocation of credit and the overall scale of financial intermediation in the late 1970s and the 1980s. However, the results of the process of financial liberalisation in many developing countries have varied from a disastrous one to a successful transition to a more efficient and market-oriented financial systems. On one hand, the Southern Cone region of Latin America-Argentina, Chile and Uruguay experienced bank panics and collapses as a result of financial liberalisation (Diaz-Alejandro, 1985). Other countries in this region, in particular, Colombia, Brazil and Mexico have abandoned financial liberalisation programmes (Fry, 1989).

On the other hand, financial liberalisation in a number of Asian countries has helped make financial systems more efficient and has enhanced the effectiveness and flexibility of monetary policies. In the early 1960s, the financial system of almost all countries in Asia were characterized by one or more of a range of restrictive financial measures, including interest rate regulations, selective credit allocation controls, explicit and implicit taxes on financial institutions, government ownership of financial institutions, segmentations and international capital controls, among others. However, such features have either become less distinct or completely removed as deregulation, market-orientation and internationalisation of banking and finance have proceeded at a rapid pace since the early 1980s.

Financial Liberalisation in the Asian Countries

The purpose of financial liberalisation is to enhance the development of an efficient financial system through a greater reliance on market forces as well as to improve the effectiveness of monetary policy. This development, often referred to as the process of financial deepening, involves the design and implementation of policies to increase the monetisation of the economy, to foster and develop a sound and diversified financial structure with coordinated money and capital markets and maintain monetary stability (Bank Negara Malaysia, 1994). In the Asian countries, the key reforms were aimed at liberalising interest rates, reducing control on credit, enhancing competition and efficiency in the financial system, strengthening the supervisory framework and promoting the growth and deepening of financial markets. The effort towards liberalisation also includes the relaxation of restrictions on international capital flows and a shift toward a more flexible exchange rate arrangement (Tseng and Corker, 1993).

Interest Rate Liberalisation

The implementation of financial liberalisation varied widely across these countries in terms of both the pace and scope of reforms (see Table 1.1). The liberalisation of interest rates was a prominent feature of the financial reforms implemented by the Asian countries during the 1980s. The objectives of interest rate liberalisation are to promote savings and efficient investment and to deepen financial markets. Positive real interest rates (as pointed out by McKinnon (1973)) favour financial over non-financial savings, leading to the deepening of financial markets. In turn, greater financial intermediation tends to ensure that more productive investments are financed. Positive real interest rates, therefore, contribute to economic growth by promoting financial deepening and improving the productivity of investment.

Interest rates were fully deregulated in Indonesia, the Philippines and Sri Lanka in the early 1980s. Deregulation in Indonesia was initiated in January 1978 where rates on time deposits of less than 3 months maturity are not controlled. However, in June 1983, the government removed controls over interest rates on deposits and loans of government owned banks and eliminated credit ceilings on all banks. The Philippines initiated an ambitious program of financial reform which focused primarily upon institutional change but also had the goal of interest rate liberalisation. Interest rate ceilings on deposits and term loans were removed in July 1981 and on short-term loans in June 1983. For Sri Lanka, the removal of the restrictions on interest rates was an important event in its financial reform. Its first stage of deregulation was initiated in September 1977 whereby the National Savings Bank (NSB, a government owned bank) was induced to raise its deposit rates very sharply. NSB which accounted for the bulk of financial savings in Sri Lanka influenced the rates offered by other banks. These reforms in turn led to upward revision in the deposit and lending rates of the commercial banks. In the second stage of deregulation, in June 1984, the bank was allowed the freedom to fix its own deposit and lending rates.

In Korea, interest rates were partially deregulated. In July 1984, banks were permitted to vary their lending rates within a limited range according to the borrowers' creditworthiness. The removal of interest rate restrictions only took place in December 1988, whereby all interest rates on loan from banks and non-bank financial institutions were fully liberalized. Interest rates on certificates of deposits, repurchase agreements, commercial paper, financial debentures, and corporate bonds have been fully deregulated. Yields on fund type instruments were also liberalised. As for deposits, only interest rates on a few deposits with long maturities have been liberalised. Interest rates of time deposits with maturities of more than two years at banks, postal savings, credit unions and mutual credits were liberalised.

But, in April 1989, the December 1988 deregulation exercises were reversed. However, in November 1991, another phase of deregulation began where rates on deposits with more than 3 years were liberalised. In November 1993, rates on deposits of more than 2 years were liberalised, and rates on all bank lending were also liberalised. In November 1994, rates on deposits of more than 1 year were finally liberalised.

Malaysia's Central Bank introduced a new interest rate scheme for the commercial bank in October 1978. Accordingly, commercial banks were free to quote the interest rate payable on deposits and lending rates. However, with effect from November 1983, all interest rates on loans and advances have been tied to the base lending rates of the two largest commercial banks. In fact the deposit rates of the banks and finance companies became linked to the deposit rates of the two leading domestic banks (namely, Malayan Banking Berhad and Bank Bumiputra Malaysia Berhad) with effect from October 1985. In February 1987, all deposit rates at financial institutions were fully liberalised. However, it was only in February 1991 that interest rates on loans became free from the administrative control of the Central Bank.

For Nepal, deregulation of interest rates only took place in the second half of the 1980s. From May 1986, the commercial bank and other financial institutions are partially allowed to fix interest rate subject to a minimum rate on deposits and maximum lending rate. However, complete liberalisation of interest rate structure of commercial banks and financial institutions took place in August 1989.

Interest rates in Thailand have been geared towards a liberal regime since the early 1980s. One of the first and most important steps towards this flexibility was the freeing of ceiling rates on loans. Accordingly, the ceiling on lending rates of financial institutions was freed from 15.0 percent per annum limit imposed since 1924. In June 1989, a ceiling of deposit rates for deposits of more than one year was announced. In March

1990, the ceilings on time deposits of less than one year maturity were terminated. From January 1992, ceilings on savings deposit rates were also abolished, thus, completely eliminating all deposit rates ceilings for commercial banks. On the other hand, ceilings on lending rates were abolished in June 1992.

Singapore and Myanmar are two extreme cases in the context of financial reforms among the Asian countries. Singapore, on one hand, has abolished the cartel system of determining interest rates since July 1975. From this date, banks were free to quote their own rate of interest. On the other hand, Myanmar which was basically a planned economy prior to 1988, maintained a highly regulated financial system. An important step towards financial deregulation was the revision of interest rates in September and October 1989. The Central Bank's bank rate was increased from 4 percent to 11 percent, that of Treasury bills from 1 percent to 4 percent, and those of Treasury bonds from 2.5/3.0 percent to 10/10.5 percent. At the same time, rates on call deposits and fixed deposits were also increased. The complete liberalisation of interest rate is, however, uncertain in the near future in Myanmar. This is best described by Lwin (1993: p. 302), 'interest rates will be subject to ceilings to be imposed by the Central Bank for all banks establised in the country. Moreover, these banks were required to maintain a reserve ratio of 35 percent of their liabilities. As Myanmar is in transition to a market economy and as the financial market is yet to be developed, deregulation of interest rates, less reliance on banks' reserve requirements and the introduction of open market operations by the Central Bank is not yet considered for the moment'.

Other Financial Reforms: Increasing Competition and Efficiency

Apart from the above important reform, other financial reforms introduced by the countries of the Asian countries include reductions in capital controls and adoptions of flexible exchange rate arrangements, relaxation of entry barriers for foreign banks, elimination of ceilings on bank credits, reduction in reserve requirements, elimination of compulsory credit allocation to priority sectors, privatization of government-owned banks and so on. These reforms were intended to increase competition in the banking sector in the provision of services to customers, to improve the payments system, to encourage savings through the banking system and to improve credibility and stability of the financial system.[2] Furthermore, according to Schmidt-Hebbel *et al.* (1996), financial reforms and the consequent increase in geographical density of financial institutions, the range of financial instruments, and the quality of financial regulation and supervision, typically lead to financial deepening that will be reflected in a permanent increase in the stocks of financial savings.

Financial Deepening and Monetisation in the Asian Countries

Shaw (1973) defines financial deepening as the phenomenon in which the financial sector grows at a rate faster than the real sector of an economy. Although there is no ideal method to measure the process of financial deepening, the popular indicator cited in the literature is the financial interrelations ratio (see Goldsmith, 1969). The financial interrelations ratio is defined as the ratio of total financial assets to national income, either in terms of the absolute change or the percentage change, both being good measures of the extent of financial deepening. The income elasticity of net issues, that is, the ratio of the percentage growth in financial assets to the percentage growth in national income (namely, gross national product) is easier to interprete. A value greater than unity for these ratios indicates financial deepening.

The process of monetisation refers to the size as well as the composition of the stock of money (money supply) in an economy. According to Chandavarkar (1977: p. 665), 'monetisation involves the extension through time and space of the use of money in all its aspect- namely, as a medium of exchange, a unit of account, and a store of value- to the non-monetised (subsistence and barter) sector. The monetisation ratio, that is, the proportion of the total goods and services of an economy that is monetised, in the sense of being paid for in money by the purchaser, is one of the most important characteristics of the level and course of economic development'.

Chandavarkar further notes that the difference between monetisation and financial intermediation is that the latter refers to the process of mediation through institutions and instruments between primary savers and lenders and ultimate borrowers and is measured by the financial interrelations ratio. Thus, it connotes financial deepening rather than widening (enlargement of the money exchange economy), which is the phenomenon expressed in the term 'monetisation'. Goldsmith (1969) proposes the ratio of money supply to national income, money supply per capita and total bank deposits per capita as measures of the degree of monetisation. The rapid pace of monetisation can also be shown by ratios of currency/M1 and M2/M1.

The selection of indicators in Table 1.2 summarises the development of monetisation and financial deepening in the Asian countries. As shown in Table 1.2, the degree of monetisation in the Asian countries has been significant over the 1956-94 period. The use of money (M1), relative to GNP (gross national product), has stabilised in most of the Asian countries, and declined in Myanmar, Singapore, Sri Lanka, and Thailand. But increasing use of broad money (M2) is evident in all the Asian countries, as shown by the consistent rise in their M2/M1 and M2/GNP ratios during the periods, reflecting the movement towards higher level of monetised economy. During the deregulation period of 1986-94, Thailand registered the highest M2/M1 ratio of 7.46, followed by Korea (4.00), Singapore (3.75), Malaysia (3.61), Philippines (3.38) and Indonesia (3.34). Other Asian countries show a ratio of less than 3.00. During the same period, other indicators of monetisation, the holdings of money per capita and total bank deposits per capita, suggest that Singapore and Taiwan have significantly higher levels of monetisation relative to those in the remaining eight Asian countries.

In Table 1.2, we also present the relationship between total assets of the financial system and national income, which can be used to measure the stage of financial intermediation in a country. More interestingly, the dominance of the banking system (comprising only the Central Bank and commercial banks) in all the Asian financial system was particularly marked, ranging from 0.54 for Nepal to 2.50 for Singapore. On the other hand, the income elasticity of assets of financial institutions to national income is just as revealing. As indicated in Table 1.2, the income elasticity of financial assets during the deregulation era was way above unity for all the Asian countries. The income elasticity of financial asset in Malaysia which was 1.53 during the period 1971-94, is one of the highest among the Asian countries.

Financial Liberalisation and the Real Sector

Does financial liberalisation matter for economic growth? Proponents of the McKinnon (1973) and Shaw (1973) approach strongly advocate the efficacy of financial development in contributing significantly to the real growth of developing economies. They contend that the banking system is invariably growth-inducing and that only when it is repressed, would it fail to make a positive contribution or act as an obstacle to real growth. McKinnon points out that in a repressed economy, the only source of funds for investment is from 'self-finance'. Potential investors must accumulate savings (money balances) prior to their investment. In a financial system where positive real interest rates prevail, the process of accumulating money will be more significant and subsequently, total investment will also increase. Shaw (1973: p. 3) emphasizes that 'the financial sector of the economy does matter in economic development if it is repressed and distorted it can intercept and destroy impulses to development'. In like manner, Cameron (1972: p. 24) concludes that 'if the banking system is 'tilted' by the unwise legislation and policy, it can distort and even thwart the growth of the economy'. Thus, according to their view, without these distortions and deviations from the free-market system, the banks will have the largest impact on developing economies.

Empirical evidence on numerous developing countries surveyed by Fry (1988) and more recently by Odedokun (1996), support the view that there is a direct association between financial and real development as a result of financial liberalisation. In a more recent study of the Asia-Pacific economies, Fry (1996) indicates the importance of financial liberalisation in promoting economic growth. Fry (1996: p. 24) concludes that 'undistorted financial and foreign exchange markets have stimulated investment and export growth. High investment and rapid export growth has accelerated output growth. Higher output growth rates and undistorted financial and foreign exchange markets raise both saving and investment ratios. The evidence presented in this paper suggests that financial conditions established by government policies played an important role in producing virtuous circles of high saving, investment, output growth and export growth found in the Pacific Basin'. A comprehensive study by the World Bank (1989) on developing countries that have embarked on financial liberalisation programs supports the contention that 'financial liberalisation matters for economic growth'. The World Bank (1989: p. 30) reports that, 'faster growth, more investment and greater financial depth all come partly from higher saving. In its own right, however, greater financial depth also contributes to growth by improving the productivity of investment. Investment productivity is significantly higher in the faster growing countries, which also have deeper financial systems.

This suggests a link between financial development and growth'. The World Bank's report further stressed that this is workable as a result of the positive real interest rates that favour financial saving over other forms of saving which promotes financial deepening.

Lessons from ASEAN Financial Liberalisation

The success of the 1960s reforms in South Korea and Taiwan has encouraged other developing countries to emulate the financial liberalisation programme adopted by the two countries. In fact in the 1970s several countries in Latin America, Africa and Asia have liberalised interest rate control, some at a rapid pace and others following a more cautious approach by adopting a gradual liberalisation process. However, the success of financial liberalisation among these countries is mixed. In some cases, the results of financial liberalisation have been disastrous; elsewhere financial liberalisation has acted as a growth-promoting factor. Argentina, Chile and Uruguay have experienced bank panics and financial collapses and Colombia, Brazil and Mexico have abandoned their financial liberalisation programmes. Countries in Africa, namely Gambia, Ghana, Kenya and Malawi have not been successful either (see Sek and Nil, 1993). In Asia, the countries of the ASEAN region have benefited greatly from the financial liberalisation exercises.

The success of the countries in Asia and the failure of majority of the countries in Latin America and Africa has resulted in great debate about the McKinnon approach towards economic development. Many have argued that in his seminal book, McKinnon underscored the importance for a country to maintain macroeconomic stability while implementing financial reform. The World Bank (1989: p. 11) reports that, 'in East Asia the newly industrialised economies and several others have pursued sound macroeconomic policies and maintained the competitiveness of the exports. They have generally adapted well to the shocks of the 1970s and early 1980s. The populous economies of South Asia have also achieved good results. Their success has more to do with macroeconomic stability, prudent fiscal and external borrowing policies and rural modernisation than with internationally competitive trade policies'. McKinnon (1988) admits the pitfall of financial liberalisation and warns that the premature opening of the capital account of the balance of payments may undermine the liberalisation process by giving rise to either inflation or appreciation in the home country currency that would be harmful to the export sector. Villanueva and Mirakhor (1990) point out that for a weak economy, financial liberalisation should be undertaken gradually, and in the event of economic difficulties, postponing the removal of interest rate regulations may be appropriate until the monetary situation has been stabilised and banking supervision strengthened. Arestis and Demetriades (1993) emphasize the timing of financial liberalisation, that is, instead of being concerned with the issue of whether to liberalise, policy makers in developing economies should only be concerned with the issue of when to liberalise.

Cho and Khatkhate (1989a) have noted nine lessons that can be drawn from financial liberalisation. However, the most important lesson that has been cited in the literature is the initial economic condition of a country as a key prerequisite for successful financial liberalisation. Many countries that have failed the financial liberalisation exercise have one thing in common, that is, the need for a stable macroeconomic environment has not been met satisfactorily. So what lessons can we learn from the success of ASEAN financial liberalisation? Did the member countries of ASEAN meet this criterion during the process of liberalisation? Table 1.3 gives a summary of the changes in some of the key macroeconomic indicators prior to liberalisation and after the removal of interest rate regulations in the ASEAN countries.[3] For comparative purposes, we have also included four African countries and three Latin American countries.

Prior to the reform period, the economic performance of the ASEAN member countries was mixed although generally satisfactory. Singapore had the highest real growth in GNP registering more than 10 percent on average per year. This is followed by Indonesia, Malaysia and Thailand which average about 6 to 8 percent per year preceding the reform period. On the other hand, the growth in real GNP for the Philippines averages less than 5 percent. Other countries of Africa (Kenya and Malawi) and the Latin America have also registered a real growth of GNP of less than 5 percent per year preceding to financial reform. However, Gambia and Ghana experienced the worst, in that negative real growth in GNP was plaguing the economy for at least 3 years before the reform period.

Price stability is one of the most important macroeconomic stability indicator. The differences in the inflation rate between the ASEAN, African and Latin American countries have been markedly significant. Malaysia, Singapore and Thailand are considered stable economies with relatively low inflation rates.[4] The inflation rate of other countries like Indonesia, the Philippines, Gambia, Kenya and Malawi ranges from 11 percent to 16 percent. On the other hand, Ghana and Uruguay experienced inflation rates of more than 60 percent, while Argentina and Chile registered inflation rates of about 200 percent and 100 percent respectively.

The post-reform scenarios are rather interesting. In most countries of the ASEAN, African and Latin American, there is an improvement in the economic performance in terms of the growth in real GNP after the implementation of financial liberalisation. This is notably shown by Gambia and Ghana where their growth in real GNP has been remarkable, from a negative growth prior to reform to positive growth rate after the reform. On the other hand, Philippines and Argentina experienced negative growth for the period after the reform. As for the inflation rate, a majority of the countries in Table 1.3 experienced a very high rate of inflation, ranging from 13 percent in Kenya to 268 percent in Argentina. Among the ASEAN member countries, the inflation rate of 17 percent on average for the period 1984-88 in the Philippines is rather high compared with other countries in the region. On the other hand, the inflation rate in the four remaining countries of ASEAN is relatively stable and has been contained due to good macroeconomic management.

The expected immediate effect of the removal of interest rate regulations on a repressed economy is the achievement of a positive real interest rate. However, without sustaining economic growth and containing inflation, a reasonable positive real interest rate may be difficult to achieve and maintain, given the need for the banking sector to operate high lending/deposits spreads under inflationary conditions, high liquidity and high reserve requirements (Seck and Nil, 1993). Furthermore, very high positive real interest rates can be destructive. Fry (1996) points out that higher positive real interest rates can produce an epidemic effect by turning profitable and solvent firms into insolvency. Fry further notes that distorted financial conditions (that is, excessively high real interest rates) appear to be just as debilitating as financial repression. In Table 1.3, we observe that the effect of financial liberalisation on real interest rates has been very positive indeed, at least for the ASEAN member countries, except the Philippines. Prior to the reform period, all of the countries in Table 1.3 experienced negative real interest rates as a result of a repressed economy. However, for the ASEAN countries, notably Indonesia, Malaysia, Singapore and Thailand, a positive real interest rate has been achieved and maintained for at least five years after the reform. On the other hand, the Philippines and other African and Latin American countries experienced negative real interest rates, mostly due to high inflation rates in these countries.

The above analysis suggests that macroeconomic stability (in particular, price stability) is an important platform for achieving successful financial liberalisation. Indonesia, Malaysia, Singapore and Thailand have demonstrated that in economies with stable growth and inflation, the success of financial liberalisation will be greatly enhanced. In contrast, in the Philippines, the financial liberalisation programmes have been a failure. Although the Philippines economy in the 1970s was relatively stable, the severe macroeconomic setback in the mid 1980s has been blamed for the failure of the financial liberalisation exercise. In the first half of 1980s, Philippine has been plagued with a confidence crisis as a result of the Dewey See scandal in 1981, political turmoil as a result of the assassination of Benigno Aquino in 1983, major devaluations, capital flight and foreign exchange crisis in 1984 and the economic recession in 1985. These events combined to halt and substantially reverse the process of financial deepening. The net result of the strains placed on the Philippine financial system by the convergence of both international and domestic destabilising factors was that between 1981 and 1987, 182 smaller financial institutions ceased trading. These had covered 7.6 percent of deposit money bank assets. In addition, the authorities had to intervene in support of two large government and five private banks that were also facing financial difficulties. According to the World Bank (1993), by 1986, the Philippines central bank assistance to financial institutions amounted to 19.1 billion pesos or 3 percent of GDP.[5] However, the Philippines economy started to recover in the late 1980s and early 1990s.

Financial Liberalisation and Economic Growth: Some Empirical Evidence

A Review of Related Studies

Capital formation has been widely accepted as a prerequisite for economic growth (Lewis, 1955; Nurkse, 1962). The role of financial sector has been well recognised in the development literature. The seminal work of Patrick (1966) has resulted in widespread investigations into the role of the financial sector as an engine for economic growth. Patrick points out two possible relationships between financial development and economic growth. First, as the economy grows, it generates demand for financial services which he called a 'demand-following' phenomenon. According to this view, the lack of financial institutions in developing countries is an indication of lack of demand for their services. Second, the establishment and the widespread expansion of financial institutions in an economy may actively promote development, which Patrick called 'supply-leading' phenomenon. This latter view which has been dubbed the 'financial-led' growth hypothesis has been popular among governments in several developing countries as a means to promoting development.[6]

Moreover, there are two views in which the financial system can be manipulated for enhancing economic growth. The struturalist school recommends an expansion in the structure of the financial system, such as an increase in the number of financial institutions. This school also encourages an increase in the array of financial instruments made available to the public (Goldsmith, 1969; Patrick, 1966). Neo-liberals on the other hand, advocate the liberalization of the financial system, by which they mean the relaxation of controls imposed on the financial systems by the monetary authorities (McKinnon, 1973; Shaw, 1973). Neo-liberals believe that administratively determined (as opposed to market-determined) low rates of interest may not encourage savings. Without savings there cannot really be any investment. Thus, according to this school, the freeing of interest rates is the key to capital formation and growth.

Goldsmith (1969), McKinnon (1973), Shaw (1973), Fry (1988) and more recently King and Levine (1993) are among others who have provided evidence that financial development is a prerequisite for economic growth. Nevertheless, other researchers are skeptical with respect to the financial-led growth hypothesis. Dornbusch and Reynoso (1989) have questioned the conclusions of the previous influential studies and argue that the evidence in support of the financial-led growth paradigm is 'episodic' and a 'vast exaggeration'. We believe that there are at least three reasons why the financial-led growth hypothesis is rejected in more recent studies. First, the conclusions reached by previous influential studies are subject to what Granger and Newbold (1977) dubbed as 'spurious regression results'. Traditionally, it has been general practice to regress one integrated series against another integrated series. However, Granger and Newbold have warned against using integrated series as it will invalidate the statistical tests on which hypotheses are commonly tested, and frequently leads to the acceptance of a spurious regression.

More recently, Engle and Granger (1987) have introduced the cointegration methodology to avoid spurious regression problems. The cointegration approach provides a way in which the long-run information of the integrated series in levels is conserved into equations that comprise stationary components (called the error correction model) that give valid statistical inferences. Secondly, as noted by Fry (1996: p. 1), 'whatever positive effects of financial liberalisation were detected in the 1970s appear to have become smaller over time'. Several factors could contribute to the diminishing effect of financial liberalisation on economic growth. For example, it may be that other forms of financial repression exist in the economy, or that there are financial distortions in the form of high real interest rates and black market exchange rates. There may also be a 'crowding-out effect' from other macroeconomic policies (World Bank, 1989; Fry, 1996).

Since the seminal article of Engle and Granger (1987), the method of cointegration has been a popular approach used in testing economic hypotheses; among others are the financial-led hypothesis, export-led hypothesis, law of one price, purchasing power parity, capital mobility, Wagner's law and so on. However, testing for the financial-led hypothesis using the cointegration approach is of recent application. Demetriades and Hussein (1996), Arestis and Demetriades (1996), Murinde and Eng (1994) and Thornton (1996) are among the few studies that have tested the financial-led hypothesis on several Asian countries. Using annual data from 1965 to 1992, Demetriades and Hussein found that among the Asian countries covered under the study, only in the case of Sri Lanka did the evidence support the financial-led growth hypothesis. For Pakistan, their result indicates that economic growth causes financial development. Further, Demetriades and Hussein's study suggests that bidirectional causal relationships are evident for India, South Korea and Thailand. In another related study, Arestis and Demetriades further support the evidence that the relationships between financial development and economic growth for India and South Korea is bidirectional.

Murinde and Eng tested the financial-led hypothesis on Singapore using quarterly data for the period 1979:1 to 1990:4. Using an array of financial indicators, they found that the results strongly support the financial-led hypothesis for Singapore. On the other hand, Thornton provides some empirical evidence on the supply-leading hypothesis in several Asian countries. Using annual data as far back as 1950s to 1990, Thornton found that the financial-led hypothesis was supported by monetary data of Nepal, the Philippines and Thailand. The demand-following hypothesis was supported by Myanmar and South Korean monetary data. However, a bidirectional relationship between the monetisation variable and economic growth is evident for Malaysia. For India and Sri Lanka, the results suggest that there is no causal relationship between economic growth and the financial indicator.

Method of Estimation

Since our interest is to determine the long-run relationships between financial development indicators and economic growth, the first step is to verify the order of integration of each of the series involves.[7] In this study, we employed two measures of economic growth, that is, real output measured by GDP deflated by GDP deflator (LRY), and real output per capita (LRYK). We used three measures for financial development indicator - ratio of money stock (M2) to income (LM2Y), ratio of total deposits to income (LDEPY) and total domestic credit to income (LDCY). The standard procedure for determining the order of integration of a time series is the application of augmented Dickey-Fuller test (Dickey and Fuller, 1981) which requires regressing Δy_t on a constant, a time trend, y_{t-1} and several lags of the dependent variables to render the disturbance term white-noise. Table 1.4 presents the augmented Dickey-Fuller (ADF) tests for all series involved in the analysis in logarithmic form in levels and first-differences. Our results indicate that non-stationarity cannot be rejected for the levels at the 5 percent significance level base on the ADF test. When the series are differences, non-stationarity can be rejected for all series. The ADF statistic suggest that all five series are integrated of order one, whereas the first-differences are integrated of order zero. Therefore, all series is best characterized as difference-stationary process instead of trend-stationary process, and in our case each series need to be differenced once to achieve stationarity.

After determining that the series are of the same order of integration, we test whether the linear combination of the series that are non-stationary in levels are cointegrated. It has been a standard practice to use the Engle and Granger (1987) two-step procedure to test for cointegration. However, more recently the Engle-Granger estimation procedure has been criticized for being static and suffers from several econometric problems. First, as Banerjee *et al.* (1986) noted that even though the two-step procedure produces super consistent parameter estimates, for small sample, the bias on the parameter estimates can be quite severe. Second, when cointegration between variables are not unique, the Engle-Granger two-step procedure is less satisfactory. The estimates are not invariant to the chosen normalization, that is which variable to be used as regressor and which to be used as regressand. Finally, using OLS estimates, as regressing integrated series will invalidates statistical inferences (see Perman, 1991).

As an alternative to the Engle-Granger two-step procedure, the Johansen (1988) maximum likelihood estimation procedure for cointegration is appropriate which does not suffer from any of the above mentioned problems. Detailed discussion of the Johansen technique has been discussed in Dickey *et al.* (1991), Cuthbertson *et al.* (1992) and Charemza and Deadman (1992). However, a brief discussion of the Johansen technique is as follows. We begin with the following k-lag vector autoregressive (VAR) representation

$$X_t = \alpha + \Pi_1 X_{t-1} + \Pi_2 X_{t-2} + ... + \Pi_k X_{t-k} + \mu_t \quad (t=1, 2,...T) \quad (1.1)$$

where X_t is a *px1* vector of nonstationary I(1) variables, α is a *px1* vector of constant terms, $\Pi_1, \Pi_2...\Pi_k$ are *pxq* coefficient matrices and μ_t is a *px1* vector of white Gaussian noises with mean zero and finite variance. Equation (A1) can be reparameterised as

$$\Delta X_t = \alpha + \Gamma_1 \Delta X_{t-1} + \Gamma_2 \Delta X_{t-2} + ... + \Gamma_{k-1} \Delta X_{t-k+1}$$
$$+ \Pi_k X_{t-k} + \mu_t \quad (1.2)$$

where $\Gamma_i = -I + \Pi_1 + \Pi_2 + ... + \Pi_I$ (for i=1, 2,...k-1) and Π is defined as

$$\Pi = -I + \Pi_1 + \Pi_2 + ... + \Pi_k. \quad (1.3)$$

Johansen (1988) shows that the coefficient matrix Π_k contains the essential information about the cointegrating or equilibrium relationship between the variables in the data set. The rank of the matrix Π_k indicates the number of cointegrating relationships existing between the variables in X_t. In this study, for a two case variables, X_t = (financial development and economic growth) and so p=2. Therefore, then the hypothesis of cointegrating between money and income is equivalent to the hypothesis that the rank of $\Pi_k=1$. If the rank=0, then the two variables are not cointegrated.

In estimating a two-variables case using the Johansen procedure, we begin with the following least square estimating regressions

$$\Delta X_t = \alpha_1 + \sum_{i=1}^{k-1} \Gamma_i \Delta X_{t-i} + \omega_{1t} \qquad (1.4)$$

$$X_{t-k} = \alpha_2 + \sum_{i=1}^{k-1} \Gamma_i \Delta X_{t-i} + \omega_{2t} \qquad (1.5)$$

Define the product moment matrices of the residuals as $S_{ij} = T^{-1} \sum_{t=1}^{T} \varpi_{it}\varpi_{jt}'$ for i,j=1,2. Johansen (1988) shows that the likelihood ratio test statistic for the hypothesis of at most r equilibrium relationships is given by

$$-2\ln Q_r = -T \sum_{i=r+1}^{p} \ln(1-\lambda_i) \qquad (1.6)$$

where $\lambda_1 > \lambda_2 > ... \lambda_p$ are the eigenvalues that solve the following equation

$$|\lambda S_{22} - S_{21} S_{11}' S_{12}| = 0. \qquad (1.7)$$

The eigenvalue are also called the squared canonical correlations of ϖ_{2t} with respect to ϖ_{1t}. The limiting distribution of the $-2\ln Q_r$ statistic is given in terms of a p-r dimensional Brownian motion process, and the quantiles of the distribution are tabulated in Johansen (1988) for p-r = 1,...,5 and in Osterwald-Lenum (1992) for p-r = 1,...10.

Equation (1.6) is usually called the trace test statistic which can be rewritten as follows

$$L_{trace} = -T \sum_{i=r+1}^{p} \ln(1-\lambda_i) \qquad (1.8)$$

where $\lambda_{r+1},...\lambda_p$ are the p-r smallest squared canonical correlation or eigenvalue. The null hypothesis is at most r cointegrating vectors. The other test for cointegration is the maximal eigenvalue test based on the following statistic

$$L_{max} = -T.\ln(1-\lambda_{r+1}). \tag{1.9}$$

where λ_{r+1} is the $(r+t)^{th}$ largest squared canonical correlation or eigenvalue. The null hypothesis is r cointegrating vectors, against the alternative of r+1 cointegrating vectors.

Results of the Cointegration Tests

Table 1.5 reports the Johansen cointegration tests. Since the Johansen tests are sensitive to the lag length used, we have presented the lag length of 2 through 5 in the VAR analysis. We observe that the results of the trace test indicate that the null hypothesis of at most one cointegrating vector (r≤1) cannot be rejected depending on the lag length and the measurements of economic growth and financial development indicators used.[8] For example, Nepal and Philippine clearly indicate the choice of measurement of economic growth used. For Nepal, cointegration between financial development and economic growth are detected at lags 2 and 3 for all three measures of financial development with real output but not when real output per capita is used. Similar results are also shown by Philippine where cointegration are detected at lag 5 between LRY and LM2Y and LDEPY. On the other hand, for Taiwan the reverse is true. Cointegration between financial development and economic growth are detected at lag 3 for LM2Y and at lag 3 and 5 for LDEPY when real output per capita is used. We summarised all these results in Table 1.6. It is interesting to note that we can only find cointegration between financial development and economic growth after we experimented with various measures of financial development and economic growth indicators and also the number of lag length used in the VAR analysis. Thus, our results suggest that there is a long-run relationship between financial development and economic growth in the Asian countries investigated.

Our next task is to determine the causal direction between the two variables in question. Does financial development led economic growth or otherwise? In other words, we are testing whether monetary data in the Asian countries support the 'supply leading' or 'demand following' hypotheses? We do this using the standard Granger causality test. However, for a given set of I(1) variables that are cointegrated, causality tests conducted in first difference vector autoregressive (VAR) framework will be misspecified unless the lagged residual (error-correction coefficient) from the cointegrating regression is also included in the VAR specification. For the following bivariate vector error-correction models (VECM)

$$\Delta y_t = \alpha_0 + \sum_{i=1}^{k} \alpha_i \Delta y_{t-i} + \sum_{i=1}^{k} \beta_i \Delta x_{t-i} + \gamma_1 ecm_{t-1} + \varepsilon_{1t} \quad (1.10)$$

$$\Delta x_t = \delta_0 + \sum_{i=1}^{k} \delta_i \Delta x_{t-i} + \sum_{i=1}^{k} \phi_i \Delta y_{t-i} + \gamma_2 ecm_{t-1} + \varepsilon_{2t} \quad (1.11)$$

where ecm_{t-1} is the lagged residual from the cointegration between y_t and x_t in level. Granger (1988) points out that based on equation (1.10), the null hypothesis that x_t does not *Granger cause* y_t is rejected not only if the coefficients on the x_{t-i} are jointly significantly different from zero, but also if the coefficient on ecm_{t-1} is significant. The VECM also provides for the finding that x_t *Granger cause* y_t, if ecm_{t-1} is significant even though the coefficients on x_{t-i} are not jointly significantly different from zero. Furthermore, the importance of α's and β's represent the short-run causal impact, while γ gives the long-run impact. In determining whether y_t *Granger cause* x_t, the same principle applies with respect to equation (1.11).

The results of the Granger causality tests are reported in Tables 1.7 and 1.8 with real output and real output per capita as the measures for economic growth respectively. If we take the case of Indonesia as an example, from column 7, for lag 3 in Table 1.7, we find that financial development (measured by LDCY) does not *Granger cause* economic growth can be rejected as shown by the significant of the ecm term although the joint test are not significantly different from zero. In column 8, the null hypothesis that economic growth does not *Granger cause* financial development cannot be rejected since neither the ecm term nor the joint test are not significantly different from zero. We therefore conclude that this evidence support the 'supply leading' hypothesis. On the other hand, for lag 5 (column 7 and 8), the evidence suggest that the relationship between LRY and LDCY are bidirectional for Indonesia. In Table 1.9, we have summarised all the results for the Granger causality tests. It is clear from these results that the direction of causality between financial development and economic growth has been bidirectional. For Malaysia, Myanmar, Nepal, South Korea, Sri Lanka, Taiwan and

Thailand, two-way causality dominated the relationship between financial development and economic growth. However, for Indonesia and Singapore, the evidence strongly suggest that the data support the 'supply leading' hypothesis.

Conclusions

It has long been recognised that financial markets play a central role in economic development. Cameron-McKinnon-Shaw have provided a recipe for the developing countries to achieve fast growth. The removal of interest rate regulations and the subsequent success of South Korea's and Taiwan's economies has put the financial liberalisation programme advocated by McKinnon into the limelight. Not surprisingly, the majority of the developing countries in Africa, Asia and Latin America embarked on financial liberalisation programmes by removing interest rate controls. However, the result have been rather alarming, and have brought chaos to many of the developing countries. In Latin America, the financial liberalisation exercises have not been successful-bank panics, financial collapses and the ultimate abandonment of the financial liberalisation exercise were experienced by those countries. In Africa, financial liberalisation has not been successful either. However, it is in the Asian region that financial liberalisation programme has been a sucess. Particularly, in the ASEAN region, Economic growth has been sustained, inflation has been contained and positive real interest rates were recorded in these countries. Macroeconomic stability has been singled out as a prime condition for successful financial liberalisation. Macroeconomic stability measured by the level of inflation rate will reflect the appropriate monetary and fiscal policies (good management) adopted by a country. The low inflation environment will be conducive for the development of the financial markets during the financial liberalization process.

The importance of financial development for promoting economic growth was supported by the data of the ten Asian countries analysed. Our results indicates that there is a long-run between financial development and economic growth in ten of the Asian developing countries investigated. Our Granger causality results clearly suggest that the relationship between financial development and economic growth in the majority of the Asian developing countries has been bidirectional. In other words, this implies that financial development and economic growth are reciprocal to each other. However, only in the cases of Indonesia and Singapore that the data support the 'supply leading' hypothesis that finance led economic growth. Nevertheless, as pointed by Arestis and Demetriades (1996), these evidences (bidirectional and supply leading) support the case where the financial system in developing countries are characterised by 'bank-based' financial system. In a 'bank-based' system, borrowers rely heavily on bank loans rather than on equity since capital market in the majority of the Asian developing countries are at their infancy stage. As banks exercise an important monitoring role, banks, therefore, play an important role in the process of economic development.

Notes

1. In contrast, Dornbusch and Reynoso (1989) argue that the evidence in support of the financial repression paradigm as 'episodic' and a 'vast exaggeration'. However, Thornton (1991) points out that the argument made by Dornbusch and Reynoso is unfair. He argues that although the evidence is by no means unanimous, there is considerable amount of evidence in support of the 'financial repression' paradigm. Fry (1988) provides survey of countries that are consistent with the McKinnon view of financial liberalisation. McKinnon (1988) himself recognises the pitfalls to financial liberalisation. The new view is that sequencing the liberalisation of financial markets is important for successful financial liberalisation process.
2. For further discussions on financial deregulation in the Asian countries, see for example Adhikary (1989a) and Talib (1993).
3. The Association of South-East Asian Nations (ASEAN) was formed in 1967 with the signing of the ASEAN Declaration. Brunei joined in January 1984 and Vietnam in July 1995 as the sixth and seventh member of the Association. For the purposes of this paper, ASEAN will refer only to the original five, since Brunei and Vietnam are recent members and furthermore because of data unavailability on boths economies. The member countries of ASEAN (except the Philippines) comprise an important group of actors among those the World Bank has labelled 'High Performing Asian Economies' (World Bank, 1995). The Philippines, on the other hand, has been described as one of the 'Asian Third Generation NIEs' together with India and China (see McGiven, 1996). Indonesia, Malaysia and Thailand have

also been labelled as the 'Asian Second Generation NIEs'. The 'Asian First Generation NIEs' comprise Hong Kong, Singapore, South Korea and Taiwan (also popularly known as the Four Tigers or Four Little Dragons).

4. Although for the three years preceding the implementation of financial liberalization, Singapore's inflation rate was almost 15 percent, this is due mostly to the effect of the first oil shock of 1973.

5. Financial distress is not uncommon to other ASEAN member countries. In Indonesia two banks experienced difficulties between 1990-92. In Malaysia, between 1985-88, 24 deposit-taking cooperative, 4 banks and 4 finance companies were in financial difficulties. In Singapore in 1982, commercial banks showed signs of financial distress whereby domestic commercial banks' non-performing loans rose to about $200 million or 0.63 percent of GDP. In Thailand, between 1985-87, 50 finance companies and 5 commercial banks were in financial difficulties (see World Bank, 1993). However, as a result of prudential supervision and regulations, the situation of financial instability in each country was quickly arrested and as a result the effects on the economy were much less severe.

6. For a comprehensive study on financial development-economic growth nexus in developing countries, see Gupta (1984) and Jung (1986).

7. All annual data covering from the period 1950 to 1994 were collected from various issues of the International Financial Statistics published by International Monetary Fund.

8. Similar results were obtained from the maximal eigenvalue statistics.

Table 1.1
Liberalisation of interest rates in the Asian countries

Countries	Year	Features of interest rate regulations
Indonesia	1978	State banks, private and foreign banks are allowed to set their own interest rate on time deposits with maturities not exceeding 3 months.
	1983	Deregulation of state banks' interest rates on most categories of deposits and on all loans except for high priority loans.
Malaysia	1978	Financial institutions were free to quote deposits and lending rates, except lending rates for priority sectors.
	1983	All interest rates on loans and advances other than those prescribed by maximum ceiling rates and law, has been tied to base lending rates of the respective largest commercial banks.
	1987	All financial institutions are free to determine their deposit rates.
	1991	All financial institutions are free to set its lending rates based on its own cost of funds.
Myanmar	1989	Deregulation on interest rate structure whereby interest rate were increased on Treasury bills, Central Bank's bank rate, Treasury bonds, call deposit rate and interest on loans to farmers.
Nepal	1984	Financial institutions were granted freedom to manage their deposit rates with a narrow range of one to one and a half percentage points after maintaining the minimum rate as prescribed by the Nepal Rastra Bank (NRB, the Central Bank).
	1986	Financial institutions were granted the freedom to offer higher rate than the minimum rate as prescribed by the NRB.
	1989	Interest rates were completely liberalized and financial institutions were allowed to fix their own deposit and lending rates.
Philippines	1981	Lifted the ceilings on interest rates on deposit and loans, except those with maturities of less than two years.
	1983	Complete removal of the remaining interest rate ceilings on deposits and loans.

Sources: Talib (1993), Adhikary (1989a), Lee (1992) and de Brouwer (1995).

Table 1.1 (continued)

Countries	Year	Features of interest rate regulations
Singapore	1975	The cartel system of determining interest rates is abolished. Banks are free to quote their own rates of interest.
South Korea	1984	Interest rates on deposits and loans of banking institutions can be decided freely within the guidelines set by the Governor of the Bank of Korea.
	1988	Deregulation of all lending rates, some money market instruments and some long-term deposit rates.
	1991	Rates on deposits of more than 3 years liberalised. Short-term rates on bank overdraft loans liberalised.
	1993	Rates on deposits of more than 2 years liberalised. Rates on all bank lending liberalised.
	1994	Rates on deposits of more than 1 year liberalised.
Sri Lanka	1977	The National Savings Bank (NSB, government owned bank) was induced to raise its deposit rates. These reforms in turn led to upward revision on the deposits and lending rates of the commercial banks.
	1984	Financial institutions was given the freedom to fix their own deposits and lending rates.
Taiwan	1980	Association of Banks could propose a range of lending and deposits rate to the Central Bank for approval. The maximum deposit rates was still determine by the Central Bank. Interest rate in money market and NCDs (negotiable certificate of deposits) are not subject to the limitation of the maximum deposit rates.
	1985	The lending rate has been completely free. The maximum deposit rate is still controlled by the Central Bank.
	1989	Bank's ceiling and floor limits on deposit and lending rates have been abolished.
Thailand	1980	Lending rates of financial institutions was freed from 15.0 percent per annum limit imposed since 1924.
	1989	Ceiling on commercial bank's time deposit rates of over one year maturity was abolished.
	1990	Ceiling on time deposit rate of less than one year maturity was abolished.
	1992	Ceiling on savings deposit and lending rates were abolished.

Sources: Talib (1993), Adhikary (1989a), Lee (1992) and de Brouwer (1995).

Table 1.2
Selected measures of monetisation and financial deepening in Asian countries, 1966-94

Financial indicators	Indonesia 1966-75	Indonesia 1976-85	Indonesia 1986-94	Malaysia 1966-75	Malaysia 1976-85	Malaysia 1986-94	Myanmar 1966-75	Myanmar 1976-85	Myanmar 1986-94	Nepal 1966-75	Nepal 1976-85	Nepal 1986-94
M1/GNP	0.08	0.11	0.12	0.18	0.20	0.23	0.23	0.21	0.21	0.09	0.12	0.14
M2/GNP	0.11	0.19	0.40	0.37	0.57	0.81	0.25	0.27	0.30	0.12	0.24	0.32
M2/M1	1.33	1.73	3.34	2.02	2.91	3.61	1.11	1.29	1.44	1.36	2.00	2.35
Currency/M1	0.60	0.45	0.41	0.50	0.47	0.41	0.83	0.91	0.91	0.69	0.64	0.69
M2 per capita (US$)	12	82	239	180	924	1985	22	44	175	10	31	55
Per capita total bank deposits (US$)	8	61	211	145	803	1668	6	14	58	4	21	40
Total financial assets/GNP	0.29	0.48	0.86	0.65	1.19	2.17	0.51	1.44	1.84	0.19	0.39	0.54
Assets/GNP:												
Central Bank	0.15	0.22	0.26	0.17	0.23	0.40	0.39	0.34	0.45	0.12	0.18	0.24
Commercial banks	0.14	0.26	0.60	0.40	0.72	1.23	0.13	1.10	1.39	0.07	0.21	0.30
Total banking system	0.29	0.48	0.86	0.57	0.95	1.63	0.51	1.44	1.84	0.19	0.38	0.54
		1971-94			1971-94			1971-94			1971-94	
Income elasticity of net issues:												
Financial system,		1.24			1.53			1.15			1.38	
of which;												
Central Bank		1.05			1.46			0.89			1.20	
Commercial banks		1.37			1.50			1.76			1.62	
Total banking system		1.24			1.47			1.15			1.37	

Source: International Monetary Fund, International Financial Statistics and author's calculations.
Note: For Myanmar, period ended 1993.

Table 1.2 (continued)

Financial indicators	Philippines			Singapore			South Korea			Sri Lanka		
	1966-75	1976-85	1986-94	1966-75	1976-85	1986-94	1966-75	1976-85	1986-94	1966-75	1976-85	1986-94
M1/GNP	0.10	0.08	0.08	0.27	0.25	0.24	0.11	0.11	0.10	0.17	0.14	0.13
M2/GNP	0.21	0.23	0.27	0.61	0.66	0.89	0.29	0.34	0.39	0.25	0.29	0.31
M2/M1	1.98	2.74	3.38	2.29	2.63	3.75	2.59	3.28	4.00	1.51	2.18	2.40
Currency/M1	0.52	0.53	0.67	0.44	0.51	0.46	0.45	0.46	0.41	0.53	0.50	0.54
M2 per capita (US$)	54	127	205	829	4243	12503	94	556	2276	44	77	146
Per capita total bank deposits (US$)	59	148	180	744	4249	12889	82	578	2524	28	62	113
Total financial assets/GNP	0.58	0.94	0.99	0.97	1.90	2.63	0.64	1.05	1.45	0.54	0.74	0.72
Assets/GNP:												
Central Bank	0.16	0.29	0.41	0.07	0.38	0.54	0.16	0.20	0.24	0.24	0.30	0.25
Commercial banks	0.34	0.54	0.49	0.86	1.42	1.97	0.38	0.66	0.70	0.24	0.37	0.44
Total banking system	0.50	0.82	0.90	0.92	1.80	2.50	0.53	0.86	0.93	0.48	0.67	0.69
		1971-94			1971-94			1971-94			1971-94	
Income elasticity of net issues:												
Financial system, of which;		1.20			1.41			1.26			1.11	
Central Bank		1.25			2.50			1.04			1.04	
Commercial banks		1.23			1.31			1.20			1.23	
Total banking system		1.22			1.41			1.16			1.14	

Source: International Monetary Fund, International Financial Statistics and author's calculations.

Table 1.2 (continued)

Financial indicators	Taiwan 1966-75	Taiwan 1976-85	Taiwan 1986-94	Thailand 1966-75	Thailand 1976-85	Thailand 1986-94
M1/GNP	0.18	0.27	1.47	0.14	0.10	0.09
M2/GNP	0.44	0.74	1.47	0.30	0.43	0.70
M2/M1	2.46	2.70	3.16	2.24	4.34	7.46
Currency/M1	0.34	0.27	0.18	0.62	0.67	0.69
M2 per capita (US$)	316	1759	12449	69	278	1116
Per capita total bank deposits (US$)	244	1290	9617	53	250	1062
Total financial assets/GNP	1.09	1.55	2.59	0.58	0.89	1.36
Assets/GNP:						
Central Bank	0.32	0.35	0.63	0.21	0.20	0.23
Commercial banks	0.63	0.96	1.55	0.31	0.52	0.86
Total banking system	0.94	1.31	2.18	0.52	0.72	1.09
Income elasticity of net issues:		1971-94			1971-94	
Financial system,		1.39			1.38	
of which;						
Central Bank		1.24			1.06	
Commercial banks		1.45			1.46	
Total banking system		1.37			1.34	

Source: International Monetary Fund, International Financial Statistics and author's calculations.
Note: For Taiwan, period starts 1970.

Table 1.3
Macroeconomic stability in Pre-Reform and Post-Reform era in ASEAN, selected African and Latin American countries

Countries	Reform start date	Pre-Reform	real GDP (percent)	Inflation (percent)	Real interest rate (percent)	Post-Reform	real GDP (percent)	Inflation (percent)	Real interest rate (percent)
ASEAN:									
Indonesia	1983	1978-82 (5)	6.8	12.8	-3.8	1984-88 (5)	5.2	7.7	10.1
Malaysia	1978	1973-77 (5)	8.0	8.0	-0.3	1979-83 (5)	7.2	5.9	3.3
Philippines	1983	1978-82(5)	4.7	13.3	-1.1	1984-88 (5)	-0.0	17.4	-1.3
Singapore	1975	1970-74 (5)	11.5	9.3	-3.8	1976-80 (5)	8.6	3.8	3.3
Thailand	1980	1975-79 (5)	8.0	7.0	0.0	1981-85 (5)	5.5	5.0	6.6
Africa:									
Gambia	1985	1980-84 (5)	-1.5	11.3	-3.4	1986-90 (5)	8.2	22.5	-8.3
Ghana	1983	1978-82 (5)	-0.7	63.3	-51.8	1984-88 (5)	4.7	29.2	-12.8
Kenya	1986	1981-85 (5)	4.4	13.4	-1.9	1987-91 (5)	4.5	13.4	-1.8
Malawi	1988	1983-87 (5)	3.1	16.6	-4.4	1989-93 (5)	3.9	15.9	-0.8
Latin America:									
Argentina	1979	1974-78 (5)	1.7	200.4	-16.6	1980-84 (5)	-0.4	268.1	-59.9
Chile	1974	1969-73 (5)	1.6	103.8	na	1975-79 (5)	3.4	150.4	-83.5
Uruguay	1977	1972-76 (5)	2.4	76.5	-46.3	1978-82 (5)	2.0	45.6	2.6

Sources: IMF, International Financial Statistics and authors' calculations.
Notes: The number in parentheses is the number of years preceding or after the implementation of reform over which data are averaged. na denotes not available.

Table 1.4
Results of unit root tests

Country	Series in levels	Weighted symmetric t:α (lag)	Dickey-Fuller t:α (lag)	Phillips-Perron t:α (lag)	Country	Series in levels	Weighted symmetric t:α (lag)	Dickey-Fuller t:α (lag)	Phillips-Perron t:α (lag)
Indonesia	LRY	-0.94(9)	-2.94(3)	-7.38(3)	Malaysia	LRY	1.75(5)	-1.91(3)	-15.80(3)
	LRYK	-1.01(9)	-1.97(7)	-7.18(7)		LRYK	1.39(2)	-2.89(3)	-11.10(3)
	LM2Y	-1.44(7)	-3.61*(8)	-19.45(8)		LM2Y	-2.76(2)	-2.53(2)	-12.40(2)
	LDEPY	-1.71(5)	-2.67(8)	-10.44(8)		LDEPY	-3.36*(2)	-3.95*(3)	-18.18(3)
	LDCY	-1.16(3)	-1.95(2)	-20.11(2)		LDCY	-0.59(2)	-2.17(2)	-5.85(2)
Myanmar	LRY	-2.15(2)	-3.14(8)	-9.60(8)	Nepal	LRY	-0.13(2)	0.41(4)	-0.22(4)
	LRYK	-2.24(2)	-3.58*(8)	-10.14(8)		LRYK	-0.84(2)	0.24(2)	-2.16(2)
	LM2Y	-2.14(2)	-2.97(2)	-10.96(2)		LM2Y	-1.10(2)	-0.34(5)	-8.08(5)
	LDEPY	-2.56(2)	-2.42(2)	-9.44(2)		LDEPY	-1.05(2)	-0.09(7)	-8.26(7)
	LDCY	-1.62(3)	-2.52(3)	-4.89(3)		LDCY	-0.94(9)	-0.91(9)	-5.71(9)
Philippines	LRY	0.36(4)	-0.96(3)	-2.36(3)	Singapore	LRY	-1.20(2)	-2.89(4)	-3.40(4)
	LRYK	-0.60(2)	-1.22(3)	-3.47(3)		LRYK	-1.40(2)	-2.25(4)	-4.43(4)
	LM2Y	-2.46(2)	-2.28(3)	-13.08(3)		LM2Y	-1.92(2)	-1.68(4)	-6.67(4)
	LDEPY	-2.50(3)	-2.08(3)	-9.93(3)		LDEPY	-1.95(2)	-1.84(3)	-6.23(3)
	LDCY	-2.66(5)	-0.85(9)	-5.87(9)		LDCY	-1.25(2)	-0.79(2)	-6.97(2)
South Korea	LRY	-0.30(2)	-3.32(2)	-6.76(2)	Sri Lanka	LRY	-2.22(2)	-1.89(2)	-8.20(2)
	LRYK	0.00(2)	-1.79(2)	-5.49(2)		LRYK	-2.16(2)	-2.53(2)	-9.48(2)
	LM2Y	-1.98(3)	-1.10(8)	-4.51(8)		LM2Y	-2.74(3)	-2.51(3)	-12.56(3)
	LDEPY	-1.46(2)	-0.89(8)	-4.06(8)		LDEPY	-2.25(4)	-2.53(4)	-11.74(4)
	LDCY	-2.48(2)	-0.66(9)	-21.07(9)		LDCY	-1.49(4)	-1.48(3)	-7.94(3)
Taiwan	LRY	0.05(6)	-1.99(3)	-21.95*(3)	Thailand	LRY	-1.68(2)	-2.56(3)	-7.03(3)
	LRYK	-2.30(9)	-4.43*(3)	-26.95*(3)		LRYK	-0.61(2)	0.02(9)	-0.39(9)
	LM2Y	-2.16(6)	-2.96(2)	-19.86(2)		LM2Y	-1.74(2)	-1.77(4)	-4.86(4)
	LDEPY	-2.33(6)	-2.47(2)	-19.69(2)		LDEPY	-2.24(2)	-2.10(3)	-11.43(3)
	LDCY	-2.67(2)	-1.62(3)	-14.02(3)		LDCY	-2.36(3)	-2.67(7)	-10.51(7)

Notes: LRY = real output, LRYK = real output per capita, LM2Y = ratio of broad money M2 to income, LDEPY = ratio of money less currency to income, LDCY = ratio of domestic credit to income. Asterisk (*) denotes statistically significant at 5 percent level.

Table 1.4 (continued)

Country	Series in first-differences	Weighted symmetric t:α (lag)	Dickey-Fuller t:α (lag)	Phillips-Perron t:α (lag)	Country	Series in first-differences	Weighted symmetric t:α (lag)	Dickey-Fuller t:α (lag)	Phillips-Perron t:α (lag)
Indonesia	LRY	-1.93(2)	-2.71(2)	-17.26*(2)	Malaysia	LRY	-1.03(2)	-3.81*(2)	-29.91*(2)
	LRYK	-1.72(2)	-2.56(2)	-16.13*(2)		LRYK	-0.18(7)	-3.15*(2)	-29.47*(2)
	LM2Y	-1.89(6)	-4.85*(2)	-21.84*(2)		LM2Y	-3.62*(2)	-3.41*(2)	-45.92*(2)
	LDEPY	-3.12*(4)	-4.49*(2)	-23.03*(2)		LDEPY	-3.18*(5)	-5.12*(3)	-41.07*(3)
	LDCY	-1.00(2)	-3.12*(8)	-21.88*(8)		LDCY	-3.46*(2)	-3.82*(2)	-39.67*(2)
Myanmar	LRY	-2.68*(2)	-3.24*(9)	-40.83*(9)	Nepal	LRY	-0.77(5)	-1.14(5)	-50.23*(5)
	LRYK	-2.67*(2)	-2.83*(2)	-46.37*(2)		LRYK	-2.77*(2)	-2.64(2)	-38.90*(2)
	LM2Y	-4.27*(2)	-4.09*(2)	-52.25*(2)		LM2Y	-0.86(5)	-2.78(4)	-36.97*(4)
	LDEPY	-3.89*(2)	-3.69*(2)	-40.06*(2)		LDEPY	-3.94*(2)	-1.43(6)	-38.28*(6)
	LDCY	-3.66*(2)	-3.68*(2)	-29.80*(2)		LDCY	-1.61(8)	-3.04*(3)	-21.18*(3)
Philippines	LRY	-2.85*(2)	-2.99*(2)	-18.32*(2)	Singapore	LRY	-2.70*(2)	-3.05*(3)	-21.53*(3)
	LRYK	-3.12*(2)	-3.24*(2)	-19.91*(2)		LRYK	-2.76*(2)	-2.43(4)	-21.15*(4)
	LM2Y	-3.82*(2)	-4.02*(2)	-33.32*(2)		LM2Y	-3.28*(2)	-2.41(3)	-25.94*(3)
	LDEPY	-4.01*(2)	-4.08*(2)	-36.93*(2)		LDEPY	-3.01*(2)	-2.59(3)	-21.86*(3)
	LDCY	-2.44(2)	-3.54*(9)	-29.05*(9)		LDCY	-1.69(2)	-3.05*(2)	-22.47*(2)
South Korea	LRY	-2.57*(2)	-2.91*(2)	-29.61*(2)	Sri Lanka	LRY	-4.12*(2)	-3.90*(2)	-43.51*(2)
	LRYK	-2.34*(2)	-2.50(2)	-35.91*(2)		LRYK	-3.99*(2)	-3.79*(2)	-42.76*(2)
	LM2Y	-3.23*(3)	-2.33(7)	-21.79*(7)		LM2Y	-4.42*(2)	-4.53*(2)	-34.79*(2)
	LDEPY	-2.22(7)	-2.37(7)	-39.92*(7)		LDEPY	-3.30*(4)	-4.60*(2)	-35.01*(2)
	LDCY	-3.92*(2)	-3.37*(9)	-35.20*(9)		LDCY	-3.24*(3)	-3.90*(2)	-28.56*(2)
Taiwan	LRY	-0.07(2)	-5.69*(2)	-16.98*(2)	Thailand	LRY	-2.82*(3)	-3.29*(2)	-51.69*(2)
	LRYK	-0.56(2)	-3.47*(9)	-16.38*(9)		LRYK	-2.40(3)	-2.81(2)	-48.49*(2)
	LM2Y	-2.30(5)	-3.04*(5)	-51.84*(5)		LM2Y	-4.14*(2)	-3.42*(3)	-38.47*(3)
	LDEPY	-2.34(5)	-3.01*(2)	-60.27*(2)		LDEPY	-4.76*(2)	-3.45*(3)	-37.52*(3)
	LDCY	-4.04*(3)	-3.84*(3)	-34.54*(3)		LDCY	-2.97*(2)	-2.27(5)	-25.45*(5)

Notes: LRY = real output, LRYK = real output per capita, LM2Y = ratio of broad money M2 to income, LDEPY = ratio of money less currency to income, LDCY = ratio of domestic credit to income. Asterisk (*) denotes statistically significant at 5 percent level.

Table 1.5
Results of Johansen cointegration tests

Countries	Trace statistics							
	k=2		k=3		k=4		k=5	
	$H_0:r\leq 1$	$H_0:r=0$	$H_0:r\leq 1$	$H_0:r=0$	$H_0:r\leq 1$	$H_0:r=0$	$H_0:r\leq 1$	$H_0:r=0$

(a) Variables included in cointegrating vector: LRY, LM2Y

Indonesia	17.51**	5.92**	11.38	1.50	8.99	2.63	9.77	1.48
Malaysia	13.65*	2.25	20.15**	4.09**	18.33**	5.64**	15.84**	3.12*
Myanmar	14.58*	0.05	10.71	0.01	15.13*	0.00	10.66	0.03
Nepal	21.44**	2.35	16.71**	1.62	11.64	1.16	6.40	0.09
Philippines	9.06	2.38	10.16	1.90	9.13	1.79	17.15**	2.36
Singapore	26.37**	0.63	6.08	1.05	12.18	1.35	10.95	3.37*
South Korea	8.94	0.00	10.76	0.02	20.51**	0.03	9.47	0.18
Sri Lanka	8.23	0.01	6.06	0.09	5.99	0.12	8.01	0.14
Taiwan	4.90	1.08	8.09	2.61	5.21	1.42	6.60	2.41
Thailand	4.37	1.24	17.43**	4.81**	13.69*	3.33*	11.80	3.65*

(b) Variables included in cointegrating vector: LRY, LDEPY

Indonesia	24.68**	6.56**	10.42	1.34	9.82	2.49	9.42	2.64
Malaysia	11.39	0.89	14.59*	1.44	8.92	0.67	5.35	0.06
Myanmar	10.81	0.22	9.28	1.07	10.90	1.16	9.41	3.11*
Nepal	20.48**	0.51	15.84**	0.05	12.22	0.06	7.35	0.82
Philippines	9.87	2.85*	10.93	2.34	10.57	2.85*	18.83**	2.53
Singapore	22.58**	1.29	6.21	0.79	11.40	0.84	10.98	4.16**
South Korea	10.41	0.21	9.67	0.15	20.56**	0.22	10.63	0.65
Sri Lanka	10.22	0.03	7.71	0.10	10.56	0.43	11.17	0.30
Taiwan	6.97	1.31	14.35*	3.96**	17.13**	7.20**	10.64	3.86**
Thailand	10.26	0.00	12.09	0.01	10.77	0.14	39.10**	0.05

(c) Variables included in cointegrating vector: LRY, LDCY

Indonesia	13.15	1.61	16.05**	1.67	9.81	2.36	17.63**	1.71
Malaysia	11.28	0.00	7.95	0.03	8.89	0.00	4.72	0.00
Myanmar	12.96	0.01	15.00*	0.57	23.29**	0.09	8.64	0.10
Nepal	21.71**	0.04	15.52**	0.17	7.43	0.04	8.74	0.55
Philippines	12.09	4.96**	25.49**	5.25**	24.96**	4.65**	23.67**	4.84**
Singapore	14.39*	1.65	6.04	1.51	10.82	3.94**	16.53**	5.07**
South Korea	12.73	0.35	7.01	0.10	9.89	0.00	7.90	0.00
Sri Lanka	4.28	0.66	6.26	0.52	16.64**	2.06	29.31**	3.49*
Taiwan	4.56	0.00	3.81	0.04	8.63	2.21	3.88	0.23
Thailand	11.63	0.01	21.89**	0.01	15.08*	0.01	20.93**	4.11**

Notes: LRY = real output, LM2Y = ratio of broad money M2 to income, LDEPY = ratio of money less currency to income, LDCY = ratio of domestic credit to income. k is the number of lag length in VAR. The 5 percent and 10 percent critical values are: trace: $r\leq 1$, 15.41 (5 percent) and r=0, 3.76 (5 percent); $r\leq 1$, 13.33 (10 percent) and r=0, 2.69 (10 percent); and max: r=1, 14.07 (5 percent) and r=0, 3.76 (5 percent); r=1, 12.07 (10 percent) and r=0, 2.69 (10 percent). See Table 1 in Osterwald-Lenum (1992). Asterisks (**), (*) denote statistically significant at 5 percent and 10 percent level respectively.

Table 1.5 (continued)

Countries	Trace statistics							
	k=2		k=3		k=4		k=5	
	$H_0: r \leq 1$	$H_0: r=0$	$H_0: r \leq 1$	$H_0: r=0$	$H_0: r \leq 1$	$H_0: r=0$	$H_0: r \leq 1$	$H_0: r=0$

(a) Variables included in cointegrating vector: LRYK, LM2Y

Indonesia	19.76**	4.58**	15.46**	0.84	11.56	1.78	9.75	0.63
Malaysia	21.11**	3.29*	30.62**	4.74**	28.60**	2.30	15.10*	2.80*
Myanmar	16.36**	0.20	11.73	0.27	14.77*	0.32	11.27	0.48
Nepal	9.60	0.95	9.73	0.27	5.60	0.05	6.68	0.12
Philippines	6.32	1.60	7.00	1.14	5.98	0.90	10.42	1.85
Singapore	24.20**	0.77	6.69	1.45	14.72*	2.38	12.54	4.50**
South Korea	9.98	0.00	12.77	0.05	17.51**	0.03	14.66*	0.12
Sri Lanka	7.63	0.23	6.44	0.06	5.71	0.12	8.55	0.18
Taiwan	8.88	0.07	16.44**	0.15	9.70	0.21	10.00	0.54
Thailand	8.86	3.38*	26.08**	5.61**	22.33**	9.93**	23.12**	5.51**

(b) Variables included in cointegrating vector: LRYK, LDEPY

Indonesia	25.18**	5.92**	14.24*	1.08	10.62	1.50	10.10	1.29
Malaysia	13.27	0.43	19.78**	0.54	8.72	0.06	9.54	0.00
Myanmar	10.88	0.86	8.89	1.94	10.21	2.02	10.49	4.74**
Nepal	7.41	0.47	6.30	0.10	3.65	0.32	5.60	1.14
Philippines	7.52	1.99	8.39	1.47	7.77	1.63	11.86	1.91
Singapore	21.85**	1.35	6.65	1.56	14.18*	1.92	13.03	5.82**
South Korea	10.03	0.15	12.58	0.02	16.10**	0.00	16.43**	0.36
Sri Lanka	9.39	0.21	8.41	0.04	9.02	0.01	10.34	0.06
Taiwan	9.00	0.26	17.48**	0.00	13.12	0.00	14.74*	0.08
Thailand	9.14	0.40	10.95	0.27	9.72	3.74*	22.43**	0.84

(c) Variables included in cointegrating vector: LRYK, LDCY

Indonesia	18.47**	1.02	20.75**	0.19	11.23	0.05	10.56	0.46
Malaysia	17.40**	1.03	7.85	0.01	10.24	0.84	4.23	0.12
Myanmar	16.42**	0.74	20.94**	2.15	25.04**	1.79	9.76	1.01
Nepal	6.95	0.02	4.84	0.34	2.76	0.14	5.13	0.93
Philippines	12.07	4.86**	23.25**	5.20**	22.44**	4.54**	21.32**	5.17**
Singapore	14.56*	1.84	6.52	2.30	13.57*	5.97**	18.26**	4.93**
South Korea	11.40	1.62	8.61	0.38	7.47	0.31	11.22	0.02
Sri Lanka	5.40	0.78	5.40	0.15	15.87**	1.20	26.83**	1.75
Taiwan	11.79	1.98	7.70	1.40	8.58	0.28	5.27	1.39
Thailand	13.54*	2.73*	23.92**	3.54*	18.32**	3.13*	33.20**	12.45**

Notes: LRYK = real output per capita, LM2Y = ratio of broad money M2 to income, LDEPY = ratio of money less currency to income, LDCY = ratio of domestic credit to income. k is the number of lag length in VAR. The 5 percent and 10 percent critical values are: trace: r≤1, 15.41 (5 percent) and r=0, 3.76 (5 percent); r≤1, 13.33 (10 percent) and r=0, 2.69 (10 percent); and max: r=1, 14.07 (5 percent) and r=0, 3.76 (5 percent); r=1, 12.07 (10 percent) and r=0, 2.69 (10 percent). See Table 1 in Osterwald-Lenum (1992). Asterisks (**), (*) denote statistically significant at 5 percent and 10 percent level respectively.

Table 1.6
Summary of cointegration results for different measure of financial development and economic growth

Countries	LRY versus			LRYK versus		
	LM2Y	LDEPY	LDCY	LM2Y	LDEPY	LDCY
Indonesia	-	-	[3,5]	[3]	[3]	[2,3]
Malaysia	[2]	[3]	-	[4]	[3]	[2]
Myanmar	[2,4]	-	[3,4]	[2,4]	-	[2,3,4]
Nepal	[2,3]	[2,3]	[2,3]	-	-	-
Philippines	[5]	[5]	-	-	-	-
Singapore	[2]	[2]	[2]	[2,4]	[2,4]	[2]
South Korea	[4]	[4]	-	[4,5]	[4,5]	-
Sri Lanka	-	-	[4]	-	-	[4,5]
Taiwan	-	-	-	[3]	[3,5]	-
Thailand	-	[5]	[3,4]	-	[5]	-

Source: Table 1.5.
Note: Figures in square brackets indicate the lag length at which cointegration between financial development and economic growth were established.

Table 1.7
Results of Granger causality tests between financial development and real output as measure for economic growth

Countries	k	LM2Y				LDEPY			
		F=/=>Y		Y=/=>F		F=/=>Y		Y=/=>F	
		t_{ecm}	F-test	t_{ecm}	F-test	t_{ecm}	F-test	t_{ecm}	F-test
Indonesia	2	-	-	-	-	-	-	-	-
	3	-	-	-	-	-	-	-	-
	5	-	-	-	-	-	-	-	-
Malaysia	2	-0.99	0.05 [0.94]	3.34**	0.16 [0.84]	-	-	-	-
	3	-	-	-	-	-2.45**	2.61 [0.06]*	2.98**	0.31 [0.81]
	4	-	-	-	-	-	-	-	-
Myanmar	2	1.92*	2.61 [0.08]*	3.04**	0.24 [0.78]	-	-	-	-
	3	-	-	-	-	-	-	-	-
	4	1.88*	1.48 [0.23]	2.72**	1.30 [0.28]	-	-	-	-
Nepal	2	4.56**	0.46 [0.63]	-1.71*	0.05 [0.94]	4.61**	0.04 [0.95]	-1.27	0.35 [0.70]
	3	3.80**	0.24 [0.86]	-1.85*	0.03 [0.99]	3.88**	0.09 [0.96]	-1.59	0.15 [0.92]
Philippines	5	-1.55	1.29 [0.29]	2.27**	0.39 [0.84]	-1.86*	1.15 [0.35]	2.22**	0.67 [0.64]
Singapore	2	-5.67**	1.10 [0.34]	-0.12	1.11 [0.34]	-4.99**	0.21 [0.81]	0.37	0.10 [0.90]
	4	-	-	-	-	-	-	-	-
South Korea	4	-1.63	0.21 [0.92]	3.86**	2.70 [0.05]*	-1.93*	0.02 [0.99]	3.43**	2.05 [0.11]
	5	-	-	-	-	-	-	-	-
Sri Lanka	4	-	-	-	-	-	-	-	-
	5	-	-	-	-	-	-	-	-
Taiwan	3	-	-	-	-	-	-	-	-
	5	-	-	-	-	-	-	-	-
Thailand	3	-	-	-	-	-	-	-	-
	4	-	-	-	-	-	-	-	-
	5	-	-	-	-	-0.23	3.34 [0.02]**	3.01**	1.54 [0.21]

Notes: t_{ecm} denotes the t-statistic of the ecm term. F-test is the F-statistic for the test of joint significance of lagged x_t or y_t in respective VECM equations. Figures in square brackets are p-values. Asterisks (**) and (*) denote statistically significant at 5 percent and 10 percent level respectively.

Table 1.7 (continued)

Countries	k	LDCY			
		F=/=>Y		Y=/=>F	
		t_{ecm}	F-test	t_{ecm}	F-test
Indonesia	2	-	-	-	-
	3	-3.49**	1.34 [0.29]	1.70	1.69 [0.20]
	5	-2.98**	1.52 [0.25]	1.90*	0.93 [0.49]
Malaysia	2	-	-	-	-
	3	-	-	-	-
	4	-	-	-	-
Myanmar	2	-	-	-	-
	3	0.92	3.60 [0.02]**	3.34**	0.34 [0.79]
	4	1.95*	3.33 [0.02]**	3.38**	0.88 [0.48]
Nepal	2	4.94**	1.69 [0.20]	0.08	4.99 [0.01]**
	3	3.70**	0.99 [0.41]	0.31	2.52 [0.08]*
Philippines	5	-	-	-	-
Singapore	2	-3.43**	0.13 [0.87]	-1.42	1.26 [0.30]
South Korea	4	-	-	-	-
	5	-	-	-	-
Sri Lanka	4	-1.05	2.12 [0.10]	3.61**	7.84 [0.00]**
	5	-	-	-	-
Taiwan	3	-	-	-	-
	5	-	-	-	-
Thailand	3	-6.80**	5.92 [0.00]**	2.73**	1.86 [0.13]
	4	1.45	3.02 [0.04]**	2.49**	4.26 [0.01]**
	5	-	-	-	-

Notes: t_{ecm} denotes the t-statistic of the ecm term. F-test is the F-statistic for the test of joint significance of lagged x_t or y_t in respective VECM equations. Figures in square brackets are p-values. Asterisks (**) and (*) denote statistically significant at 5 percent and 10 percent level respectively.

Table 1.8
Results of Granger causality tests between financial development and real output per capita as measure for economic growth

Countries	k	LM2Y t_{ecm}	LM2Y F=/=>Y F-test	LM2Y t_{ecm}	LM2Y Y=/=>F F-test	LDEPY t_{ecm}	LDEPY F=/=>Y F-test	LDEPY t_{ecm}	LDEPY Y=/=>F F-test
Indonesia	2	—	—	—	—	—	—	—	—
	3	-3.57**	2.13[0.13]	-0.24	1.32[0.29]	-3.43**	1.86[0.17]	0.43	1.45[0.26]
	5	—	—	—	—	—	—	—	—
Malaysia	2	—	—	—	—	—	—	—	—
	3	-4.19**	1.72[0.17]	4.07**	0.99[0.42]	-4.35**	5.39[0.00]**	2.91**	0.18[0.90]
Myanmar	2	1.75*	2.70[0.08]*	3.36**	0.13[0.87]	—	—	—	—
	3	—	—	—	—	—	—	—	—
Nepal	4	1.68	1.63[0.19]	2.76**	1.05[0.39]	—	—	—	—
	2	—	—	—	—	—	—	—	—
	3	—	—	—	—	—	—	—	—
Philippines	5	—	—	—	—	—	—	—	—
Singapore	2	-5.27**	1.02[0.37]	-0.21	0.96[0.39]	-4.85**	0.61[0.54]	0.08	0.00[0.99]
	4	-3.14**	0.49[0.74]	0.22	2.24[0.10]	-2.99**	0.29[0.87]	0.81	2.02[0.13]
South Korea	4	-2.54**	0.27[0.89]	2.79**	0.92[0.46]	-2.84**	0.08[0.98]	2.12**	0.25[0.90]
Sri Lanka	5	-1.48	0.18[0.96]	2.95**	1.34[0.27]	-1.82*	0.09[0.99]	2.88**	1.14[0.36]
	4	—	—	—	—	—	—	—	—
	5	—	—	—	—	—	—	—	—
Taiwan	3	-3.04**	0.75[0.52]	1.16	7.60[0.00]**	-3.36**	0.29[0.82]	1.52	7.43[0.00]**
	5	—	—	—	—	-3.16**	0.27[0.92]	0.12	3.67[0.01]**
Thailand	3	—	—	—	—	—	—	—	—
	4	—	—	—	—	—	—	—	—
	5	—	—	—	—	-4.42**	1.61[0.19]	2.24**	1.67[0.17]

Notes: t_{ecm} denotes the t-statistic of the ecm term. F-test is the F-statistic for the test of joint significance of lagged x_t or y_t in respective VECM equations. Figures in square brackets are p-values. Asterisks (**) and (*) denote statistically significant at 5 percent and 10 percent level respectively.

Table 1.8 (continued)

Countries	k	LDCY F=/=>Y		LDCY Y=/=>F	
		t_{ecm}	F-test	t_{ecm}	F-test
Indonesia	2	-4.27**	1.02 [0.37]	0.56	0.15 [0.85]
	3	-4.66**	2.69 [0.07]*	0.92	2.24 [0.12]
	5	-	-	-	-
Malaysia	2	-2.86**	0.51 [0.59]	3.25**	0.30 [0.74]
	3	-	-	-	-
	4	-	-	-	-
Myanmar	2	1.18	0.46 [0.63]	3.69**	1.18 [0.31]
	3	0.52	3.63 [0.02]**	4.20**	0.94 [0.42]
	4	1.58	3.04 [0.03]**	3.78**	0.96 [0.43]
Nepal	2	-	-	-	-
	3	-	-	-	-
Philippines	5	-	-	-	-
Singapore	2	-3.54**	0.08 [0.91]	-1.18	0.94 [0.40]
	4	-	-	-	-
South Korea	4	-	-	-	-
	5	-	-	-	-
Sri 'Lanka	4	-1.50	2.32 [0.07]*	3.54**	7.86 [0.00]**
	5	-1.82*	2.09 [0.09]*	4.84**	4.66 [0.00]**
Taiwan	3	-	-	-	-
	5	-	-	-	-
Thailand	3	-	-	-	-
	4	-	-	-	-
	5	-	-	-	-

Notes: t_{ecm} denotes the t-statistic of the ecm term. F-test is the F-statistic for the test of joint significance of lagged x_t or y_t in respective VECM equations. Figures in square brackets are p-values. Asterisks (**) and (*) denote statistically significant at 5 percent and 10 percent level respectively.

Table 1.9
Summary of Granger causality tests results for different measure of financial development and economic growth indicators

Countries	k	LRY versus			LRYK versus		
		LM2Y	LDEPY	LDCY	LM2Y	LDEPY	LDCY
Indonesia	2	-	-	-	-	-	SL
	3	-	-	SL	SL	SL	SL
	5	-	-	BD	-	-	-
Malaysia	2	DF	-	-	-	-	BD
	3	-	BD	-	-	BD	-
	4	-	-	-	BD	-	-
Myanmar	2	BD	-	-	BD	-	DF
	3	-	-	BD	-	-	BD
	4	BD	-	BD	DF	-	BD
Nepal	2	BD	SL	BD	-	-	-
	3	BD	SL	BD	-	-	-
Philippines	5	DF	BD	-	-	-	-
Singapore	2	SL	SL	SL	SL	SL	SL
	4	-	-	-	SL	SL	-
South Korea	4	DF	BD	-	BD	BD	-
	5	-	-	-	DF	BD	-
Sri Lanka	4	-	-	DF	-	-	BD
	5	-	-	-	-	-	BD
Taiwan	3	-	-	-	BD	BD	-
	5	-	-	-	-	BD	-
Thailand	3	-	-	BD	-	-	-
	4	-	-	BD	-	-	-
	5	-	BD	-	-	BD	-

Sources: Tables 1.7 and 1.8.
Notes: SL = supply leading causality; DF = demand following causality; BD = bidirectional causality.

2 Monetary Aggregates and the Effectiveness of Monetary Policy in Financial Liberalised Developing Economies: Application of the Liquidity Constraint Approach

Introduction

Financial liberalisation has been a common feature in developing countries in the late 1970s and the 1980s. However, during the 1960s and most of the 1970s, the majority of the Asian countries had tightly regulated and administratively controlled financial systems prior to financial reform. Such common characteristics were manifested in interest rate restrictions, segmented financial markets and institutions, underdeveloped money and capital markets, credit allocation and control mechanisms and a variety of international capital and exchange controls. Among these financial distortions, interest rate ceilings on deposits and lending were important features. But, as a result of rapid advancement in technology and communication and the globalisation in the financial markets worldwide, there is a need for the developing countries to be more flexible and responsive to the needs of their national and international economies in the 1970s and 1980s. As a result, many Asian developing countries liberalised their financial system as early as the late 1970s.

The first step in deregulating the financial system in the developing countries is the abolition of interest rate control on deposit and lending. McKinnon (1973) advocates that real positive interest rates will lead to the accumulation of financial savings, increase financial intermediation and enhance the efficient allocation of resources for economic growth. There is an abundance of literature which suggests that financial intermediation plays an important role in economic growth.[1] Furthermore, Fry (1996) points out that a conducive financial environment which is characterised by lack of financial distortions will lead to high economic growth.

Financial liberalisation has resulted in the development of a more sophisticated financial system not only in the developed countries but also in the developing countries. The emergence of financial intermediaries, new financial instruments, more developed money and capital markets and other financial innovations are some of the interesting by-products of financial liberalisation. However, more recently financial liberalisation has been associated with undesirable macroeconomic outcomes. Blundell-Wignall et al. (1990) have pointed out that financial liberalisation will reduce liquidity constraints on consumption. With financial deregulation, households will be able to increase their consumption based on expected earnings and future wealth and relative prices. Current income and current liquid wealth are no longer relevant factors for spending decisions. As a result, permanent income and expected wealth are likely to be more closely associated with spending decisions. Consequently, the relationship between money supply (a major component of liquid wealth) and nominal demand will be affected and ultimately the effectiveness of monetary policy will be reduced.

The purpose of this chapter is to investigate whether financial liberalisation has reduced liquidity constraints in the Asian countries. In several of the developed countries, empirical studies have indicated that liquidity constraints have declined in importance during the 1980s, as financial systems have been deregulated (see Blundell-Wignall et al., 1995). Following the work of Campbell and Mankiw (1991) and Blundell-Wignall et al. (1995), we explore this idea by investigating whether the fraction of liquidity constrained consumers vary over time.[2] Generally, a reduction in the fraction of liquidity constrained consumers signifies that liquidity constraints have been reduced as a result of financial liberalisation.

The Implications of Liquidity Constraints for Monetary Aggregates

In a regulated financial environment, households often face limits on borrowing, that is, they are subject to liquidity constraints. Constrained households want to consume more but are prevented from doing so by restrictions on their ability to borrow through credit rationing. This limitation implies that consumption could be shifted into the future through saving, or consumption may have to await increases in actual income. Therefore, consumption is more sensitive to current income in a regulated financial market. Empirical studies have shown that with heavily regulated financial markets, consumption ought to track current income closely. In other words, consumption seems to respond to predictable changes in current income, that is, there is evidence of 'excess sensitivity'. Excess sensitivity has been associated with the existence of liquidity constraints. The findings by Blundell-Wignall *et al.* (1995) and Campbell and Mankiw (1991) that excess sensitivity of current consumption to disposable income in the OECD countries suggests the existence of liquidity constraints. Nevertheless, Blundell-Wignall *et al.* found that in several of the OECD countries liquidity constraints have been declining over time as a result of financial liberalisation.

Thus, one important implication of financial liberalisation is to reduce liquidity constraints. As a result of financial deregulation, borrowing constraints are lifted. Households will be able to smooth their consumption relative to income through borrowing and thus increase their debt.[3] Households that are not liquidity constrained base their consumption plan not only on current income but also on their future earnings and expected wealth. Thus, the effect of financial deregulation is that consumption should become more sensitive to factors such as wealth, future income (permanent income) and relative financial prices. As a result, the link between consumption and current income has become weaker in countries following the liberalisation of financial markets (see Blundell-Wignall *et al.*, 1995).

The ability of households to borrow and adjust their financial portfolios has important implications for monetary aggregates and consequently for the conduct of monetary policy. In periods of liquidity constraints the relationship between consumption and current income is closely linked. Since all spending decisions will be based on current income, we should expect that there to be a stable relationship between money supply and current income. In deregulated financial markets, households will be able to increase their wealth - both financial (interest-bearing financial instruments and equities) and non-financial wealth (for example, housing). In the absence of interest rate ceilings, credit restrictions and exchange controls, commercial banks and non-bank financial intermediaries will be able to innovate and offer new 'attractive' financial instruments and also set competitive rates on their deposits. In the process, it is likely that there will be a shift out of asset components in the monetary aggregates to other interest-bearing financial assets offered in the markets. This reallocation of financial portfolios is not limited to liabilities of banks and non-banks financial institutions but also extends to the stock and housing markets. On the other hand, consumption choices will be based on future income and also wealth. In order to increase their current consumption, households will increase their borrowing (using available financial or physical assets as collateral), adjust their financial portfolios or relinquish part of their accumulated wealth. As a result of financial liberalisation consumption becomes more sensitive to wealth and the relationship between consumption and current income will be weakened. Consequently, we should observe that the relationship between monetary aggregates and current income will also be weakened in financially liberalised economies (see Blundell-Wignall *et al.*, 1990). In other words, the behaviour of income velocity in financially liberalised economies cannot be explained by the standard money demand determinants (current income and interest rate only) without taking into account factors such as the role of the stock market, housing market, exchange rates, among others.

For example, Field (1984) found that an estimate of the dollar volume of trading on the New York Stock Exchange (NYSE) was both positive and significant in a money demand function for the United States in the period 1919-1929. Furey's (1993) study found that the estimates and forecasts of the U.S. money demand function suggest that fluctuations in the dollar volume of financial market trading significantly affects money demand. Fase and Winder (1996) have shown that incorporating wealth effects (proxied by net financial wealth) in the money demand function seem to mitigate the volatility of the monetary growth in the Netherlands.[4] Palley (1995) has included both the value of transactions on the NYSE and sales of family houses in money demand function and found that both variables improve the forecast of both M1 and M2 demand for the United States. In another study, Choudhry (1996) points out that a long-run money demand function for the United States and

Canada can only be satisfactorily estimated after the inclusion of real stock prices.

Friedman (1988) suggests the importance of the stock market in explaining the behaviour of income velocity in the United States for the period of 1970-1986. Friedman found that income velocity is positively related to the real stock price (lagged three quarters) and negatively related to the contemporaneous real stock price. The positive relation reflect a wealth effect and the negative a substitution effect. Similar results are obtained by McCornac (1991) using Japanese data from 1975 to 1988. In another study, Levi *et al.* (1996: p. 30) conclude that, 'The improvement in the explanation of the income velocity of money we have achieved in this paper has potentially important implications for helping unravel the 'velocity puzzle' of the 1980s. The large swings in housing and stock market transactions, wealth and returns during that decade could be responsible for some of the changes in velocity which have hitherto been unexplained. The results suggest that events in the housing and stock markets could help resolve at least part of the velocity puzzle. Certainly, there is reason to pay more attention to the housing and stock markets when studying the behaviour of money demand or monetary velocity'.

Lehmussaari (1990) points out that the deregulation of financial markets in the Nordic countries[5] has opened new opportunities for household borrowing, leading to a surge in household demand for credit, as pent-up demands were freed and households sought to rearrange their portfolios. For example, in Sweden, deregulation of banks' lending rates and the lifting of loan ceilings on banks and finance companies in 1985 has resulted in the increase of households' borrowing for the purchase of assets like real estate and common stocks (see Agell and Berg, 1996). Thus, we would expect that in the period of financial liberalisation, the stable relationship between money supply and income will be affected. However, as pointed out by Blundell-Wignall *et al.* (1990), monetary aggregates will only be relevant to current income under liquidity constraints.

Liquidity Constraints and Financial Liberalisation: Some Empirical Evidence

Numerous studies have been conducted to determine λ, that is the fraction of consumers who are liquidity constrained. However, only a few studies have attempted to relate λ to financial liberalisation. These studies include Jappelli and Pagano (1989), Bayoumi and Koujianou (1990), Campbell and Mankiw (1991) and Blundell-Wignall *et al.* (1995). Jappelli and Pagano examined the implications of liquidity constraints between Sweden, Italy, Spain and Greece with imperfect capital markets and Japan, United States and United Kingdom that are characterised by well developed and highly competitive capital markets. Except for Sweden (λ was not significantly different from zero), the values of λ parameter were relatively high for Greece (0.54), Italy (0.58) and Spain (0.52), and lower for Japan (0.34), United Kingdom (0.40) and United States (0.21).[6] Jappelli and Pagano further conclude that the inability to borrow from the capital markets will result in high excess sensitivity of consumption to current income.

Bayoumi and Koujianou (1990) considered the effect of financial liberalisation in reducing liquidity constraints in six industrialised countries,[7] estimating all functions using the Generalised Method of Moments (GMM). Their estimate of the λ parameter recorded that except for Sweden which was not significantly different from zero, Canada and United Kingdom have the lowest estimate of the proportion of liquidity constrained consumption with an estimated λ of 0.18. This is followed by United States (0.27), France (0.32) and Japan (0.51). Bayoumi and Koujianou investigated the effect of financial liberalisation on consumption using a dummy variable. This dummy was set to zero prior to deregulation, and from the start of deregulation, the value was made to increase in equal increments to unity after two and a half years. For all six countries, the fraction of consumption that is liquidity constrained was found to decline after deregulation.

Campbell and Mankiw (1991) used the Instrumental Variables (IV) procedure to estimate λ for the same six developed countries.[8] In the majority of cases, the estimates of λ are both economically and statistically significant. Except for Japan (λ is unidentified), the estimates of λ range from 0.2 for Canada, through 0.35 for Sweden and the United States, to 0.97 for France. For the United Kingdom, λ is estimated at 0.35 for seasonally adjusted quarterly data and 0.65 when annual differences of seasonally unadjusted data are used. To determine the effect of financial liberalisation on λ, Campbell and Mankiw allow (i) λ to be a linear function of a time trend, and (ii) for a one-time shift in λ. However, their results failed to support the idea that liquidity constraints have declined over time.

Blundell-Wignal et al. (1995) examined whether excess sensitivity of consumption to current income has fallen over time as a result of financial liberalisation in eight OECD countries.[9] Blundell-Wignal et al. estimated two models - the standard Euler equation and an error-correction model. To allow for the effect of financial liberalisation, both models were estimated for different sub-samples - 1960s/70s and 1980s/90s. In the majority of cases, except for Australia and Germany, liquidity constraints were found to have declined over time as a result in financial deregulation in these countries.

More recently, Chyi and Huang (1997) have attempted to investigate the effect of financial deregulation on the estimates of λ for five Asian countries, namely; Japan, South Korea, the Philippines, Taiwan and Thailand. Their results suggest that in most cases the λ estimates for the five Asian nations are generally substantial (range between 0.54 to 0.73), and are generally higher than those of the OECD countries found in the previous studies. However, their study does not find evidence of a decline in λ for all five Asian countries investigated.

Testing for Liquidity Constraints

In testing for liquidity constraints, we follow the consumption model of testing for life-cycle permanent-income hypothesis introduced by Hall (1978). Hall proposed an approach of modelling consumption that obeys the first-order condition for optimal choice of a fully rational and forward-looking representative consumer - called the 'Euler equation approach'. The Euler equations are preferred to the traditional consumption function (or its ECM specification) because it is not vulnerable to the Lucas critique. Favero (1993) points out that the estimation of the Euler equation does not require the specification of the marginal processes for the expected variables in order to obtain closed form solutions. Furthermore, Campbell and Mankiw (1989) have shown that the fraction of aggregate consumption which is liquidity constrained can be estimated directly from the Euler equation.

According to Hall, the consumption equation for a consumer can be obtained from the first-order conditions of an intertemporal maximization problem under the following assumptions: (i) consumers can freely borrow and lend at the same rate of interest, (ii) consumers form expectations rationally, (iii) consumers have identical, time-separable preferences, with a quadratic utility function, and (iv) consumers cannot die in debt. Using these assumptions, the consumer's problem is then to

$$\text{Max } E_0 \sum_{t=1}^{T} [1/(1+\delta)]^t U(C_t) \qquad (2.1)$$

$$\text{s.t. } A_{t+1} = (1+i)(A_t + Y_t - C_t), \text{ for } t = 1,...,T-1. \qquad (2.2)$$

$$A_T \geq 0 \qquad (2.3)$$

where E is the mathematical expectation, conditional on information known at the beginning of the period; T is the length of life, δ is the constant rate of time preference, C is consumption, Y is disposable income, A_t is asset holdings and i is the constant rate of return on assets. For a quadratic utility function, $U_t = -(\alpha - C_t)^2$, the first-order condition for the consumer's maximization problem is

$$C_t = \{1-[(1+\delta)/(1+i)]\}\alpha + [(1+\delta)/(1+i)]C_{t-1} + \varepsilon_t, \text{ for } t = 1,...,T. \qquad (2.4)$$

where ε_t is the error term uncorrelated with all variables known to the consumer at time t-1. Equation (2.4) can be rewritten in a compact form as follows,

$$C_t = a_0 + a_1 C_{t-1} + \varepsilon_t \qquad (2.5)$$

where $a_0 = \{1-[(1+\delta)/(1+i)]\}$ and $a_1 = [(1+\delta)/(1+i)]$.

Equation (2.5) has been used in numerous empirical studies to test the life cycle-permanent income hypothesis (see Speight, 1990; Deaton, 1992). The implication of this life cycle-permanent income hypothesis (LC-PI) is that only consumption lagged one period should have a nonzero coefficient in a regression of current consumption on variables entering the lagged information set. However, in most cases, the LC-PI hypothesis has been rejected. Liquidity constraints have been recognised as one of the reasons for rejecting the LC-PI hypothesis.

Hall and Mishkin (1982) have pointed out that the population can be divided into two groups of consumers who share $1-\lambda$ and λ of total disposable income. The first group, who receive $1-\lambda$ of the total income behave according to the LC-PI hypothesis, that is, according to equation (2.5). Consumers in the second group are assumed to be liquidity constrained and therefore spend their entire disposable income. Consumption for the first group of consumers is represented as follows

$$C_{1t} = a_0 + a_1 C_{1t-1} + \varepsilon_t \qquad (2.6)$$

Consumption for the second group of consumers is

$$C_{2t} = Y_{2t} = \lambda Y_t \qquad (2.7)$$

where Y_{2t} is disposable income for consumers in the second group and Y_t is disposable income for both groups.

Using equations (2.6) and (2.7), total consumption (C_t) for both groups is

$$C_t = a_0 + a_1 C_{1t-1} + \varepsilon_t + \lambda Y_t \qquad (2.8)$$

Adding $(\lambda a_1 Y_{t-1} - \lambda a_1 Y_{t-1})$ to the right hand side of equation (2.8), we have

$$C_t = a_0 + a_1 C_{1t-1} + \varepsilon_t + \lambda Y_t + \lambda a_1 Y_{t-1} - \lambda a_1 Y_{t-1} \qquad (2.9)$$

Since $\lambda Y_t = C_{2t}$, we substitute C_{2t-1} for λY_{t-1} in equation (2.9), and we have

$$C_t = a_0 + a_1 C_{1t-1} + \lambda Y_t + a_1 C_{2t-1} - \lambda a_1 Y_{t-1} + \varepsilon_t \qquad (2.10)$$

Rearranging the term in equation (2.10), we have

$$C_t = a_0 + a_1 C_{1t-1} + \lambda Y_t - a_1 \lambda Y_{t-1} + \varepsilon_t \qquad (2.11)$$

and

$$C_t = a_0 + a_1 C_{1t-1} + \lambda (Y_t - a_1 Y_{t-1}) + \varepsilon_t \qquad (2.12)$$

Equation (2.12) imposes a nonlinear constraint on a_1. According to Jappelli and Pagano (1989), the fraction of consumers who are liquidity constrained and who do not behave according to the LC-PI hypothesis is represented by λ. Furthermore, if $a_1 = 1$, equation (2.12) becomes the following equation in first-differences

$$\Delta C_t = a_0 + \lambda \Delta Y_t + \varepsilon_t \tag{2.13}$$

where Δ is the first difference operator.

Equation (2.13) forms a linear consumption function. However, Campbell and Mankiw (1989, 1991) prefer a log-linear consumption function as the processes driving aggregate consumption and income seem to be log-linear rather than linear. To arrive at a log-linear consumption function, following Campbell and Mankiw (1991), we assume a representative agent having the following power utility

$$u(C_t) = C_t^{1-\gamma}/(1-\gamma) \tag{2.14}$$

where γ is the coefficient of relative risk aversion and $\sigma = 1/\gamma$ is the intertemporal elasticity of substitution. The first-order condition for optimal consumption choice is given by,

$$1 = E_t[\beta R_{t+1}(C_{t+1}/C_t)^{-\gamma}] \tag{2.15}$$

for any random asset return R_{t+1}. According to Hansen and Singleton (1983), the Euler equation simplifies to,

$$E_{t-1}\Delta c_t = \mu^* + \sigma E_{t-1} r_t \tag{2.16}$$

where μ^* is a constant and lowercase letters indicate the logs of variables. Campbell and Mankiw replace equation (2.16) for expected consumption growth and arrive at the following expressions

$$E_{t-1}\Delta c_t = \lambda E_{t-1}\Delta y_t + (1-\lambda)[\mu^* + \sigma E_{t-1} r_t] \tag{2.17}$$

and equivalently we can have

$$\Delta c_t = \mu + \lambda \Delta y_t + \theta r_t + e_t \tag{2.18}$$

where $\mu=(1-\lambda)\mu^*$, $\theta=(1-\lambda)\sigma$, and the error term e_t is the innovation between time t-1 and time t in households' assessment of the total permanent income. Since e_t is an innovation, it is orthogonal to any variable that is in households' information set at time t-2 or earlier. If expected real interest rates are constant, equation (2.18) becomes[10]

$$\Delta c_t = \mu + \lambda \Delta y_t + e_t \qquad (2.19)$$

which is analogous to equation (2.13).

Recent econometric procedure has recognised that the least squares estimates of equation (2.19) may suffers from the so-called spurious regression problem which was highlighted earlier by Granger and Newbold (1974) as consumption and income contain unit roots. Furthermore, if consumption and income are both integrated series of the same order and are cointegrated, equations (2.19) is misspecified if the residual one lagged period (usually known as the error-correction term) from the cointegrating regression between consumption and income is omitted. Alternatively, the following error-correction model for consumption can be used to estimate λ,

$$\Delta c_t = a_0 + \lambda \Delta y_t + b_1 ecm_{t-1} + \varepsilon_t \qquad (2.20)$$

where ecm_{t-1} term is the residual of regressing c_t on a constant and y_t. According to Kremers *et al.* (1992), estimating equation (2.20) is a form of a direct testing for cointegration between consumption and income. The coefficient of the ecm_{t-1} term, with a negative sign and significantly different from zero denotes that consumption and income are cointegrated. If the ecm_{t-1} term is not significantly different from zero, equation (2.19) is appropriate to represent the data that contain integrated series.

Data and Empirical Results

The Asian countries included in the study are Indonesia, Malaysia, Myanmar, Nepal, Philippines, Singapore, South Korea, Sri Lanka, Taiwan and Thailand. The model is estimated country by country using annual data and the sample period covering from 1950 to 1994.[11] The variables included are: (a) real private consumption per capita to measure household consumption,[12] (b) real income per capita to measure disposable income, where income is measured by GDP[13] and (c) All nominal variables are deflated using the Consumer Price Index (CPI). Data were collected from various issues of International Financial Statistics published by International Monetary Fund. All variables were transformed into logarithms.

For each country, equation (2.19) was estimated using Instrumental Variable (IV) method.[14] OLS estimation is not appropriate in this case because the error term e_t is not orthogonal to Δy_t, although it is orthogonal to the lagged variables. However, when using the IV procedure, we need to define the instruments. Campbell and Mankiw (1990) have pointed out that any lagged stationary variables are potentially valid instruments since they are orthogonal to e_t. However, the potential instruments must be correlated with Δy_t. If the instruments are not a good predictor of Δy_t, then there are no instruments that are orthogonal to e_t but correlated with Δy_t, and the procedure breaks down. Furthermore, the instruments used should be dated $t-2$ or earlier to deal with a time-aggregation problem due to the use of time averaged data instead of data at isolated points in time. Villagomez (1997) points out that the delays in the publication of important economic data in developing countries justify lagging the instruments two periods. Following Campbell and Mankiw (1991) and Agell and Berg (1996), the instruments set used in the study include lagged two to four periods of first-differences of real private consumption per capita, real output per capita, real export per capita, population and lagged two period of the consumption-income ratio.

Before estimating equation (2.19), we examine the time series properties of all the series involved in the analysis. Our unit root tests presented in Table 2.1, suggest that all the series seem to be I(1) and hence are said to be stationary in their first-differenced form. An important implication of an integrated series is that equation (2.19) is said to be misspecified if the residual lagged one period (usually known as the error-correction term, ecm_{t-1}) of the cointegrating regression between c_t and y_t is omitted. Kremers et al. (1992) suggested testing for cointegration between c_t and y_t directly by estimating equation (2.19) augmented with ecm_{t-1} as an additional variable.

Table 2.2 reports the final IV regression results for equation (2.19). Only in the case of Thailand do we find the ecm_{t-1} term is significantly different from zero, suggesting that c_t and y_t are cointegrated. For the remainder of the Asian countries, our initial IV regression results including the ecm_{t-1} term were not significantly different from zero and therefore were subsequently excluded from the final regression equation. In Table 2.2, we show that instrument set B for Singapore, instrument set C for South Korea and instrument set A for the remainder of the Asian countries were used to ensure that the null hypothesis of no serial correlation is not rejected. In all cases the Sargan test suggests that the null hypothesis that the instruments are uncorrelated with the error term is not rejected. Our LM test for first-order serial correlation suggests that the null of no serial correlation cannot be rejected. All the ten Asian developing countries passes the Arch and normality tests except for Malaysia, Myanmar and the Philippines in which the normality of the residuals is rejected at the five percent level.[15] From Table 2.2, our estimates of λ, that is, the fraction of consumers who are liquidity constrained, range between 0.53 and 0.91 for the Asian countries investigated.

In Table 2.3, these results are comparable with the estimates for the developing countries obtained by Speight and White (1995) which range between 0.38 and 1.12, Villagomez (1997) which range between 0.37 and 1.26, and with Chyi and Huang (1997) which range between 0.54 and 0.73. Our results therefore implies that the permanent-income hypothesis is rejected for all these countries. Our results are consistent with the findings of Thornton and Molyneux's (1996) study that the rational expectation permanent-income hypothesis (REPIH) is rejected for the developing countries.[16] Thus, our study has confirmed that the rejection of the REPIH in the developing countries is due to the presence of liquidity constraints. Our estimates of the liquidity constrained consumers can be as low as 53 percent of the population as in the Philippines, to as high as 91 percent of the population as in Nepal and South Korea.

Did λ Change During the Deregulation Era?

If the financial liberalisation process seen in financial markets has caused liquidity constraints to be progressively relaxed (thus weakening the relation between monetary aggregates and income), then estimating equation (2.19) for successive time periods should indicate a reduction in the λ parameter. Most of the Asian countries in our sample have undergone substantial financial liberalisation in the late 1970s and early 1980s.[17] As a result of financial liberalisation, liquidity constraints will be progressively relaxed and there should be a reduction in the λ parameter in financially deregulated economies. In other words, there should be an inverse relationship between λ and financial liberalisation (or financial development).

In the present study, we estimate the following three models to investigate the relationship between λ and financial liberalisation (or financial development);

$$\Delta c_t = \mu + \lambda'\Delta y_t + \delta_0(\text{Dummy}*\Delta y_t) + \omega_{1t} \qquad (2.21)$$

$$\lambda_t = \alpha_1 + \delta_1 t + \omega_{2t} \qquad (2.22)$$

$$\lambda_t = \alpha_2 + \delta_2 fd_t + \omega_{3t} \qquad (fd_t = m2y_t, depy_t \text{ and } dcy_t) \qquad (2.23)$$

In equation (2.21), the variable, Dummy, equals 1 from the date interest rate deregulation starts and zero before. The parameter λ' has the interpretation of the fraction of liquidity constrained consumers prior to the introduction of interest rate deregulation, and the sum of λ' and δ_0 indicates the fraction of liquidity constrained consumers after deregulation. It is expected that δ_0 should be negative and significantly different from zero (see Patterson and Pesaran, 1992). In estimating equation (2.21), variable Dummy*Δy_t, should be included in the instrument set for IV estimation. In equation (2.22), we allow λ to be a linear function of a time trend.[18] The time trend is to proxy for financial innovation and sophistication in each country (see Campbell and Mankiw, 1991). It is expected that λ should be declining over time and the coefficient δ_1 should be negative and significantly different from zero. On the other hand, in equation (2.23), if liquidity constraints are relaxed in a financially liberalised economy, the relationship between λ and indicators of financial development (fd) should be inverse. We have experimented with three measures of financial development, namely, the money supply M2 to GDP ratio (m2y), total deposits to GDP ratio (depy) and total domestic credit to GDP ratio (dcy).[19]

In Table 2.3, columns 2 and 3 show the IV regression results for equation (2.21). Columns 4, and 5 through 7 report the OLS regression results for equations (2.22) and (2.23) respectively.[20] Our main interest is to determine whether the proxies for financial liberalisation are significantly different from zero in each regression equation estimated. Generally, in most cases the proxies for financial liberalisation indicators are either not significantly different from zero or significantly different from zero but with a positive sign such as in the cases of Malaysia and Thailand. Only in the case of South Korea do we find evidence that suggests financial liberalisation has resulted in reducing liquidity constraints as shown by the inverse relationship (significantly different from zero) between λ and $\Delta m2y$ and $\Delta depy$.

Conclusions

Financial liberalisation has been recognised as an important step towards achieving economic progress by allowing financial markets to be determined by market forces. The proliferation of financial intermediaries, financial instruments and the development of money and capital markets will enhance the formation of an efficient and sophisticated financial system. Nevertheless, one important implication for financial liberalisation is to reduce liquidity constraints. As a result of financial deregulation, households will be able to smooth their consumption relative to income through borrowing as borrowing constraints are lifted. The ability of households to borrow and adjust their financial portfolios has important implications for monetary aggregates and consequently for the conduct of monetary policy. In order to increase their current consumption, households will increase their borrowing (using available financial or physical assets as collateral) or adjust their financial portfolios or relinquish part of their accumulated wealth. As a result of financial liberalisation consumption becomes more sensitive to wealth and the relationship between consumption and current income will be weakened. Consequently, we should observe that the relationship between monetary aggregates and current income will also be weakened in financially liberalised economies.

The purpose of the present study is to investigate whether financial liberalisation has reduced liquidity constraints in the Asian countries. To do this, we have estimated an Euler equation model to determine whether the estimates of λ's have been reduced in the deregulation era. The empirical evidence indicates that the fraction of liquidity constrained consumers in the Asian countries are quite substantial, exceeding 50 percent in all cases. Generally, the results suggest that liquidity constraints have not been reduced as a result of financial liberalisation in the Asian countries. However, our results indicate that the speed of financial liberalisation process adopted by each country does matter. On one hand, Indonesia, the Philippines, Sri Lanka and Singapore which completely deregularised lending and deposits rates by the early 1980s, show that the fraction of liquidity constrained consumers range between 0.5 for the Philippines to 0.8 for Sri Lanka (an average of $\lambda = 0.6$). On the other hand, the remainder of the Asian countries which have adopted a gradual form of liberalisation process, register λ between 0.5 for Malaysia to 0.9 for Nepal and South Korea (an average of $\lambda = 0.7$). This means that countries which rapidly liberalised their financial markets have tended to register fewer liquidity constrained consumers. Thus, this would suggest that a country which has experienced a longer post-liberalisation period will have provided more time for the consumers, policy makers and the financial markets to respond and interact, and consequently this will have led to lower the numbers of liquidity constrained consumers in the population.

Despite these differences, there is no indication that financial liberalisation has relaxed liquidity constraints in the Asian countries. There are several reasons as to why this might occur in the Asian region. First, the financial liberalisation era is too short to significantly affect the behaviour of the consumer and the financial markets. Blundell-Wignal *et al.* (1995) have pointed out that, even in the developed economies, twelve years of data is insufficient to assess the implication of financial liberalisation on liquidity constraints. Second, the requirement for 'down payment' in order to qualify for a mortgage loan or a hire purchase loan will restrict consumer borrowing. Thus, households wishing to own a house (car, washing machine, television etc) must accumulate a down payment in order to qualify for a mortgage loan (hire purchase loan).[21] Third, a common practice by the lending institutions that could impede the ability of consumer to borrow is the use of payment-to-income rule. This means that applications for loans are likely to be disapproved if the ratio of total loan payments to income breaches a ceiling. For example, if the repayment ceiling is 40 percent of the income, this implies that in order to qualify for a loan with a monthly repayment of $400, a monthly income of $1000 is sufficient. However, if the total debt is $600 (i.e. $400 plus any other debt of $200), then the loan will be disapproved.[22] Finally, discrimination of financial services practice by lending institutions can also restrict consumer borrowing.[23] Different racial background, gender and political-business-link has been some of the main factors for banks to refuse loans. Given the multi-racial and multi-cultural background of each of the Asian countries, this kind of credit restraint is rather rampant. It is believe that in Indonesia, Malaysia, South Korea, Taiwan and Thailand, potential borrower with 'political connection' can have easy access to obtain credit. On the other hand, racial discrimination in bank lending is widely practised in Indonesia, Malaysia and Singapore.

Nevertheless, our results suggest that an important policy implication for these countries is that the use of monetary aggregates as indicators for monetary policy can be effective in the presence of liquidity constraints. Since financial liberalisation has not weakened the relationship between monetary aggregates and income in the Asian developing countries, the use of monetary aggregates to predict future growth in income will be effective. This would also imply that the behaviour of income velocity in the Asian countries is adequately explained by the standard money demand function with income and the interest rate as its determinants.

Notes

1. See Fry (1997) for a survey of studies that support the role of financial development and economic growth.
2. The fraction of liquidity constrained consumers is usually denoted by parameter λ.
3. Empirical studies have indicated that savings has fallen as a result of financial liberalisation due to the reduction in liquidity constraint (see Bayoumi, 1993; and Jappelli and Pagano, 1989). This is another undesirable effect of financial liberalisation.
4. In Fase and Winder's (1996) study, net financial wealth is defined as the differential between total assets (the sum of M3, government bonds, other capital market investments and gross foreign assets) and total liabilities (credit plus gross foreign liabilities) of the non-monetary private sector.
5. The Nordic countries comprise Denmark, Finland, Norway and Sweden.
6. These results were obtained from their Non-Linear Instrumental Variable (NLIV) method of estimation. Their estimate using Full Information Maximum Likelihood (FIML) were similar.
7. These six countries were Canada, France, Japan, Sweden, United Kingdom and United States.

8. These countries were Canada, France, Japan, Sweden, United Kingdom and United States.
9. These countries were Australia, Canada, France, Germany, Italy, Japan, United Kingdom and United States.
10. Numerous studies have indicated that this basic standard Euler equation model is robust to the inclusion of other variables. The λ estimates generally remain unaffected by the addition of real interest rates or nominal interest rates or lagged dependent variable or the error-correction term. Among others, see for example, Agell and Berg (1996), Blundell-Wignal *et al.* (1995) and Chyi and Huang (1997). Furthermore, data on interest rates for most of the developing countries are not readily available, in particular for the early periods of 1950s to 1970s.
11. Sample periods for each country are: Indonesia (1966-1994), Malaysia (1958-1994), Myanmar (1950-1994), Nepal (1958-1994), Philippines (1950-1994), Singapore (1960-1994), South Korea (1953-1994), Sri Lanka (1950-1994), Taiwan (1950-1994) and Thailand (1952-1994).
12. The relevant theoretical variable is household consumption on non-durable and services. However, since data for most Asian developing countries do not distinguish between the different components of consumption, we have used real total private consumption as a proxy for household consumption. For example, see Speight and White (1995) and Villagomez (1997).
13. Since private income data for most Asian developing countries are not available, we follow Campbell and Mankiw (1989) using GDP as a proxy for private income. Campbell and Mankiw point out that the use of GDP to measure y_t does not invalidate the instrumental test procedure and the potential loss of the test's power appears not to be a problem.
14. GR-squared denotes generalised R-squared. The Sargan instrument test is asymptotically distributed as χ-square, and we report the probability value at which we can reject the null that the instruments are uncorrelated with the error term. LM is the Lagrange multiplier tests for first-order serial correlation. Arch (1) is the first-order autoregressive conditional heteroscedasticity test of Engle (1982). Norm (2) is a test for the normality of the residuals based on Jarque and Bera (1980). These tests are asymptoticlly distributed as χ-square.

15. Caution is thus needed when interpreting the results for Malaysia, Myanmar and the Philippines.
16. The countries included in their study were Indonesia, Malaysia, Philippines, Singapore, Korea and Thailand. However, the REPIH was supported only in the case of Singapore.
17. The prominent feature of the financial liberalisation programmes in the Asian countries are the deregulation of interest rates on deposits and lendings. Interest rates deregulation were first initiated in each countries as follows: Indonesia (1978), Malaysia (1978), Myanmar (1989), Nepal (1984), Philippines (1981), Singapore (1975), South Korea (1984), Sri Lanka (1977), Taiwan (1980) and Thailand (1980). See Chapter 1 for further discussion on financial liberalisation in these countries.
18. Following Vaidyanathan (1993), equations (2.19) or (2.20) were used to calculate λ for each country.
19. Vaidyanathan (1993) uses M2 to GDP ratio (m2y) to proxy for financial liberalisation. We follow Arestis and Demetriades (1996) in using total deposits to GDP ratio (depy) and total domestic credit to GDP ratio (dcy) as additional indicators for financial liberalisation in the present study. All three ratios were transformed into logarithm.
20. Since our unit root tests suggest that levels of m2y, depy and dcy are non-stationarity, these three proxies for financial liberalisation indicators were estimated in their first-differenced form.
21. For example, in the United States, most lending institutions require between 5 percent and 20 percent of the purchase price of the home put down in advance of the purchase (see Engelhardt, 1996). In Malaysia, 10 percent down payment is require for the purchase of a house, and 20 - 30 percent down payment for the purchase of a car.
22. See Wilcox (1989) for further discussion on the effect of payment-to-income policy on liquidity constraints in the United States.
23. The whole issue of the Journal of Financial Services Research (1997) was devoted to the discussions and empirical analysis of discrimination of financial services in the United States.

Table 2.1
Results of unit root tests

Variables	Indonesia	Malaysia	Myanmar	Nepal	Philippines	Singapore	South Korea	Sri Lanka	Taiwan	Thailand
A. Integration tests on levels of series										
c_t	-2.95 (3)	-3.17 (1)	-3.38 (2)	-2.78 (1)	-1.92 (1)	-3.10 (1)	-2.84 (1)	-2.06 (1)	-3.31 (4)	-1.93 (3)
y_t	-2.40 (1)	-2.66 (1)	-2.81 (1)	-0.68 (2)	-1.42 (1)	-3.19 (3)	-3.06 (1)	-2.45 (1)	-3.43 (4)	-1.55 (1)
B. Integration tests on first-differences of series										
Δc_t	-3.22 (1)*	-3.90 (1)*	-5.52 (1)*	-6.39 (1)*	-4.40 (1)*	-3.87 (1)*	-4.40 (1)*	-3.55 (1)*	-3.16 (2)*	-3.79 (1)*
Δy_t	-3.07 (2)*	-5.28 (1)*	-4.61 (1)*	-7.53 (1)*	-4.24 (1)*	-3.85 (3)*	-4.16 (1)*	-3.24 (1)*	-3.42 (2)*	-3.62 (1)*
C. Integration tests on residuals of cointegrating regression: $c_t = a + by_t + e_t$										
e_t	-0.89 (1)	-2.23 (1)	-2.45 (3)	-1.97 (1)	-2.03 (1)	-2.35 (1)	-3.60 (1)*	-4.71 (2)*	-1.28 (1)	-2.05 (1)

Notes: The relevant tests are derived from the OLS estimation of the following augmented Dickey-Fuller (ADF) regression: $\Delta y_t = a + bt + \beta y_{t-1} + \sum_{i=1}^{n} d_i \Delta y_{t-i} + v_t$, where Δ is the difference operator, t is a linear time trend and v is the disturbance term. The hypothesis that a series contains a unit root is tested by $H_0 : \beta = 0$ while the hypothesis that the series is non-stationary with a stochastic trend rather than a deterministic time trend is tested by $H_0 : b = -\beta$. Rejection of the latter hypothesis suggests the existence of a deterministic trend. τ_τ is the t-statistic for testing the significance of β when a time trend is included in the above equation while τ_μ when time trend is excluded. The lag length n, was chosen based on Schwarz Bayesian Criterion (SBC). The calculated statistics are those computed in MacKinnon (1991). The critical values at 5 percent are -3.62 (Indonesia), -3.56 (Malaysia, Nepal), -3.53 (Myanmar, Philippines, South Korea, Sri Lanka, Taiwan, Thailand), -3.57 (Singapore) for τ_τ. When testing for first-differences of the series, time trend was dropped from the above regression equation. The critical values for τ_μ at 5 percent level are -3.00 (Indonesia), -2.96 (Malaysia, Nepal), -2.94 (Myanmar, Philippines, South Korea, Sri Lanka, Taiwan, Thailand), and -2.97 (Singapore). The critical values for cointegration tests at 5 percent level are -3.61 (Indonesia), -3.53 (Malaysia, Nepal), -3.50 (Myanmar, Philippines, South Korea, Sri Lanka, Taiwan, Thailand), and -3.55 (Singapore).

Table 2.2
Results of Euler equation (2.19)

Countries	First-stage regression R-squared	Constant	Δy_t	ecm_{-1}	GR-squared	Sargan test	LM χ^2 (1)	Arch χ^2 (1)	Norm χ^2 (2)
A. Instruments lists: Δc_{t-2} Δc_{t-3} Δc_{t-4} Δy_{t-2} Δy_{t-3} Δy_{t-4} $(c-y)_{t-2}$ Δx_{t-2} Δx_{t-3} Δx_{t-4} Δpop_{t-2} Δpop_{t-3} Δpop_{t-4}									
Indonesia	0.591	0.0017 (0.0962)	0.7368 (3.0311)*	-	0.294	12.22 [0.427]	1.217 [0.270]	0.022 [0.881]	4.602 [0.100]
Malaysia	0.488	0.0090 (0.8752)	0.5473 (3.1204)*	-	0.245	7.520 [0.821]	3.248 [0.072]	0.541 [0.462]	6.383 [0.041]*
Myanmar	0.450	0.0068 (0.5747)	0.8889 (4.040)*	-	0.300	6.001 [0.916]	1.406 [0.236]	0.058 [0.810]	7.809 [0.020]*
Nepal	0.685	0.0033 (0.3083)	0.9145 (5.2488)*	-	0.534	2.466 [0.998]	2.093 [0.148]	1.780 [0.182]	0.366 [0.833]
Philippines	0.372	0.0027 (0.5094)	0.5321 (2.9852)*	-	0.189	6.079 [0.912]	0.060 [0.805]	0.106 [0.745]	15.35 [0.000]*
Sri Lanka	0.582	0.0073 (0.7772)	0.8167 (4.0923)*	-	0.305	8.663 [0.731]	0.195 [0.658]	2.742 [0.098]	0.127 [0.938]
Taiwan	0.425	0.0088 (0.7652)	0.6940 (3.9854)*	-	0.300	12.04 [0.442]	3.352 [0.067]	1.648 [0.199]	0.378 [0.828]
Thailand	0.507	0.0114 (1.4629)	0.6223 (4.3421)*	-0.7049 (3.1997)*	0.415	6.360 [0.848]	0.091 [0.763]	0.079 [0.779]	5.257 [0.072]
B. Instruments lists: Δc_{t-2} Δc_{t-3} Δc_{t-4} Δy_{t-2} Δy_{t-3} Δy_{t-4} $(c-y)_{t-2}$ Δpop_{t-2} Δpop_{t-3} Δpop_{t-4}									
Singapore	0.372	0.0045 (0.2919)	0.6068 (3.0614)*	-	0.250	2.275 [0.986]	3.816 [0.051]	1.684 [0.194]	3.498 [0.174]
C. Instruments lists: Δy_{t-2} Δy_{t-3} Δy_{t-4} $(c-y)_{t-2}$ Δx_{t-2} Δx_{t-3} Δx_{t-4} Δpop_{t-2} Δpop_{t-3} Δpop_{t-4}									
South Korea	0.180	-0.0056 (0.2746)	0.9148 (3.6849)*	-	0.279	1.954 [0.992]	2.419 [0.120]	0.629 [0.428]	2.937 [0.230]

Source: Habibullah and Smith (1999).

Notes: The estimation method is the Instrumental Variable (IV) procedure. All instrument sets include a constant. Variables c, y, $(c-y)$, x and pop are real private consumption per capita, real income per capita, consumption-income ratio, real exports per capita and population respectively. The ecm_{t-1} term is the residual lagged one period from the cointegrating regression between c_t and y_t. Figures in parentheses (.) and square brackets [.] are t-statistics and p-values respectively. Asterisk (*) denotes statistically significant at five percent level.

Table 2.3
Comparative estimates of λ among Asian developing countries

Countries	This study (1998)	Speight and White (1995)	Villagomez (1997)	Chyi and Huang (1997)
Model used	Basic Euler equation	Augmented Euler equation with interest rate and public consumption	Augmented Euler equation with interest rate	Augmented Euler equation with interest rate
Data used	Annual (1950-1994)	Annual (1950-1988)	Annual (1970-1989)	Annual (1961-1990)
No. of countries covered	10	9	16	5
Method of estimation	IV	IV	IV	IV
Range of λ's	0.53 - 0.91	0.38 - 1.12	0.37 - 1.26	0.54 - 0.73
Asian:				
Indonesia	0.73	-	0.68/0.73	-
Malaysia	0.54	-	0.64/0.46	-
Myanmar	0.88	-	-	-
Nepal	0.91	-	-	-
Philippines	0.53	-	0.75/0.65	0.73
Singapore	0.60	-	0.68/0.44	-
South Korea	0.91	-	0.45/0.85	0.60
Sri Lanka	0.81	0.82	0.54/0.49	-
Taiwan	0.69	-	-	0.54
Thailand	0.62	-	0.60/0.61	0.71

Sources: Table 2.2 of this study, Table 2 in Speight and White (1995), Table 2 in Villagomez (1997), and Table 4 in Chyi and Huang (1997). The countries included in Speight and White's study were Cyprus, Dominican Republic, Ecuador, Greece, Guatemala, Honduras, Mexico, Nigeria, Sri Lanka, Turkey and Venezuela. The countries included in Villagomez's study were Brazil, Chile, Colombia, Greece, Indonesia, Korea, Malaysia, Mexico, Pakistan, Philippines, Singapore, Sri Lanka, Thailand, Turkey, Uruguay and Venezuela. The countries included in Chyi and Huang (1997) were Japan, South Korea, the Philippines, Taiwan and Thailand.

Table 2.4
Results of regressions between λ and financial liberalisation indicators

Countries	Equation (2.21)		Equation (2.22)	Equation (2.23)		
	Δy_t	Dummy*Δy_t	t	$\Delta m2y$	$\Delta depy$	Δdcy
Indonesia	0.5147	0.2670	0.0017	-0.0357	-0.0562	0.0014
	(1.7924)	(0.9632)	(1.1808)	(0.2911)	(0.5209)	(0.0284)
Malaysia	0.4138	0.2886	0.0828	6.9251	2.7330	0.4976
	(2.5538)*	(1.3445)	(2.5934)*	(1.4039)	(0.5923)	(0.1610)
Myanmar	0.6451	0.5501	-0.0705	-6.6905	-6.7157	-2.4963
	(2.5449)*	(1.2946)	(0.4873)	(0.5631)	(0.7986)	(0.2336)
Nepal	0.9514	-0.0824	-0.1905	-1.8699	0.6594	5.6332
	(6.0479)*	(0.2437)	(1.6069)	(0.1884)	(0.0842)	(1.1749)
Philippines	0.8013	-0.3309	-0.0215	2.0256	2.2256	-0.8777
	(2.8242)*	(0.7977)	(0.4574)	(0.3208)	(0.4394)	(0.2599)
Singapore	0.6355	0.0752	0.1277	35.292	22.992	-9.1237
	(3.4590)*	(0.4962)	(0.6420)	(1.0173)	(0.7718)	(0.8244)
South Korea	0.8385	0.0259	0.0069	-1.4887	-1.1760	-0.6090
	(3.3631)*	(0.1495)	(0.9352)	(2.5922)*	(2.8513)*	(1.6492)
Sri Lanka	0.8969	-0.1475	0.0097	-2.0688	2.0642	-2.7582
	(3.6242)*	(0.4711)	(0.2989)	(0.4112)	(0.4973)	(0.9308)
Taiwan	0.6264	0.3930	0.0696	-20.950	-1.9353	18.396
	(3.6891)*	(1.8232)	(0.8543)	(1.6113)	(0.2181)	(1.5279)
Thailand	0.6249	-0.0761	-0.0082	-0.6898	-0.2671	2.6496
	(3.8653)*	(0.4823)	(0.8167)	(0.2834)	(0.1254)	(2.0500)*

Source: Habibullah and Smith (1999).
Note: Asterisk (*) denotes statistically significant at 5 percent level.

PART TWO

Divisia Money, Inflation and Income: Empirical Evidence for Asian Developing Countries

3 Rationale for Divisia Monetary Aggregates in 'Deregulated' Asian Developing Countries

Introduction

The question of the appropriate empirical definition of money is one of the most debatable and unsettled issues in economics. Proponents of the medium of exchange function of money prefer the narrow concept of money which includes currency and demand deposits. On the other hand, the proponents of the store of value of money favour a broader concept of money which include currency, demand deposits and other interest-bearing financial assets in the financial system. In fact, monetary authorities all over the world have used alternative measures of money with respect to both approaches to defining money-the medium of exchange and store of value approaches. A recent survey by Kumah (1989) indicates that in general, the measurement of money used by monetary authorities for over 150 countries is limited to M1, M2 and M3, depending on the level of development or monetisation of the financial system.

Gurley and Shaw (1960) argue that as the financial sector develops, new financial intermediaries emerge, offering varieties of interest-bearing financial assets with various maturity dates, and these financial assets should be added as components of money, giving a broader concept of monetary aggregates. Kumah (1989) observes that this has been the trend for the countries surveyed where broader measures of money are emphasized. However, more recently, the practice of adding the components of financial assets together without appropriately taking into consideration the weight of each assets component has been criticised by Barnett (1980). According to Barnett, the traditional 'simple-sum' monetary aggregates are calculated on the assumption that their components received equal weights of one and are therefore considered to be perfect substitutes. This would mean that the elasticity of substitution between any pair of components is infinite. This is contrary to the voluminous studies existing in the literature. For example, studies by Chetty (1969), Moroney and Wilbratte (1976) and Boughton (1981) showed that financial assets are less than perfect substitutes. They argued that each monetary asset has a certain degree of 'moneyness' associated with it. The key observation is that in monetary aggregation, it is not which assets are to be included in the measure of money stock which is important, but rather how much of each monetary asset is to be included. This points to the conclusion that each component should be given a different weight when adding the various components of financial assets to arrive at the official monetary aggregates.

Barnett (1980) goes further in pointing out that the Simple-sum monetary aggregate is an incorrect measurement of the flow of monetary services of a nation. For example, in determining the services of the transportation sector, it is illogical to add the physical units of trains, taxis, buses to come up with an aggregate flow of transportation services. This is inconsistent with economic theory. A meaningful economic measure would be a weighted-sum aggregate, with weights reflecting relevant value-shares. The same principle ought to apply to monetary aggregation. Barnett offers the Divisia monetary aggregate as an alternative to the Simple-sum aggregate. The Divisia aggregate was derived theoretically from economic aggregation theory and first-order conditions for utility optimization and has been found to be appropriate to measure the flow of monetary services of a country.[1]

The most important contribution of Divisia monetary measurement is towards an appropriate indicator for monetary policy purposes. Barnett and his associates have emphasized that the Simple-sum measure will badly distort monetary aggregates. Since the traditional monetary aggregates are 'accounting' measures, they are not suitable to measure 'money is what money does', that is providing services to the holder. Friedman and Schwartz (1970: p. 151-152) observe that 'this (simple summation) procedure is a very special case of the more general approach discussed earlier. In brief, the general approach consists of regarding each asset as a joint product having different degrees of 'moneyness', and defining the quantity of money as the weighted sum of the aggregate value of all assets, the weights for individual assets varying from zero to unity with a weight of unity assigned to that asset or assets regarded as having the largest quantity of 'moneyness' per dollar of aggregate value. The procedure we have followed implies that all weights are either zero or unity. The more general approach has been suggested frequently but experimented with only occasionally. We conjecture that this approach deserves and will get much more attention than it has so far received'.

Earlier, Fisher (1922: p. 29) pointed out that 'the simple arithmatic average produces one of the very worst of index numbers, and if this book has no effect than to lead to total abandonment of the simple arithmatic type of index number, it will have served a useful purpose'. Fisher further strongly advises that this index should not be used under any circumstances because it possessed two undesirable properties, that is, 'bias and freakishness'.

Indeed, the early 1980s witnessed a growing interest in the concept of weighted monetary aggregates which was first inspired by an early work by Chetty (1969). Apart from Chetty (1969), other alternative weighted monetary aggregates were proposed by Roper and Turnovsky (1980), Spindt (1985), Rotemberg et al. (1995) and Barnett (1980).[2] However, in most empirical studies, Barnett's (1980) Divisia aggregate has emerged as the most popular approach adopted in the literature. In these studies the relative performance of the Divisia aggregates is compared to the traditional Simple-sum aggregates in order to evaluate whether the former are a better monetary indicator than the latter. This is important because if an aggregate is found to have a closer and more predictable link to economic activity, it could be useful for monetary policy purposes.

In 1980s, most developed countries abandoned their monetary targeting[3] due to financial innovation which has made the relationship between money (Simple sum) and income unpredictable. However, the unstable relationship between money and income found by previous influential studies has been questioned recently. Studies using Divisia aggregates alter significantly the conclusion of instability between money and income made by previous studies. Studies by Swofford and Whitney (1991) and Chou (1991) on United States monetary data; Spencer (1994) and Belongia and Chrystal (1991) for United Kingdom; Ishida (1984) and Suzuki (1987) for Japan; Horne and Martin (1989) for Australia; Yue and Fluri (1991) for Switzerland; Fase (1985) for the Netherlands; McCann and Giles (1989) for New Zealand and Serletis and King (1993) for Canada. All these studies support the alleged superiority of Divisia monetary aggregates to the standard Simple-sum aggregates.

On the other hand, there are evidence that the Simple-sum monetary aggregate performed better than the Divisia aggregate. Among others, these studies include Fackler *et al.* (1990) and Thornton and Yue (1992) for the United States; Driscoll *et al.* (1985) for Austria; Issing *et al.* (1993) for Germany; Kitchen (1985) and Bailey *et al.* (1982) for the United Kingdom. The diversities of results for the United States and United Kingdom is rather disturbing. Fackler *et al.* (1990) pointed out that the conflicting results arise because of the potential problems in the construction of the Divisia aggregates. In particular, deriving the correct measurement of user cost is not an easy task. Batchelor (1988) is skeptical about the superiority of the Divisia aggregate. Batchelor (1988: p. 22) notes that 'the fact that a properly weighted monetary aggregate behaves differently from the traditional unweighted aggregates does not of course mean a fortiori that it will prove to be useful as a monetary indicator in a situation where the other aggregates have failed. It is still possible that the empirical relationships on which the theory of monetary targetry is based-in particular, the existence of predictable trends in monetary velocity-are false'.

Nonetheless, Batchelor (1988) notes that the main contribution of the Divisia aggregate is that it represents the appropriate measure of money against such theory can be tested. Therefore, whether or not Divisia aggregate performed better than the Simple-sum aggregate is, ultimatedly, an empirical question (Fackler *et al.*, 1990). The contention made by Fackler *et al.* (1990) is not without support. More recently, Chrystal and MacDonald (1994) investigate the role of Divisia aggregate for the United States, United Kingdom, Australia, Germany, Switzerland, Canada and Japan and find support for the Divisia aggregate as opposed to the Simple sum aggregate in these developed countries. They pointed out that in the United States, the credibility of the Simple sum aggregate has been greatly undermined compared to the Divisia aggregate even during the period in which financial innovation is greatest. Chrystal and MacDonald's (1994) main conclusion is very clear indeed. Chrystal and MacDonald (1994: p. 74-76) note that 'there has been a major measurement error in virtually all of the previous literature on money. Instability in empirical relationships has been primarily due to the fact that Simple sum measures of money are not admissible aggregates on index-theoretic grounds. Hence, this suggests that the problems with tests of money in the economy in recent years may be more due to bad measurement theory rather than to an instability in the link between the true money and the economy. Rather than a problem associated with the Lucas Critique, it could instead be a problem stemming from the Barnett Critique'. In supporting the used of Divisia measures of money, Belongia (1996) asserts that many of the monetary puzzles of the 1980s would have been resolved if Divisia monetary aggregates would have been used. Belongia (1996: p. 1082) argues that 'the results show that basic inferences about the direction, magnitude and significance of money growth on economic activity can depend crucially on the chosen measure. Because simple-sum indexes violate basic theoretical principles, the sensitivity of empirical results illustrated here offers practical evidence against further use of the reported simple-sum monetary aggregates'.

Despite the theoretical implication of the Divisia approach as an appropriate measurement of monetary services, the investigation has been mostly limited to developed countries. An empirical testing of the performance of Divisia aggregate in developing countries, therefore, can be useful in ascertaining the robustness of the conclusion derived for the developed countries. As yet there has been no attempt to address this issue, particularly for developing countries that have undergone rapid financial liberalization. This study intends to fill that gap in the literature.

The Relevance of Divisia Money in Asian Countries

It has been observed that there has been a lack of empirical research in determining the role of Divisia monetary aggregates in developing economies.[4] One of the probable reasons is that the Divisia money works well in developed market-oriented financial system economies. Even there, it has been found that the Divisia money aggregate does not perform better than the Simple-sum aggregate in some of the developed countries.[5] Thus, why should this deter research in developing countries? Judd and Scadding (1982) have pointed that the construction of a Divisa monetary aggregate depends critically on the measurement of user costs of the relevant monetary components. Judd and Scadding (1982: p. 1011-1012) concluded that 'the Divisia approach is perhaps most useful for a world in which interest rates on monetary assets are unregulated so that reliable measures of user costs are easily calculated. Hence it promises to become increasingly important if the current trend towards interest rate deregulation continues'.

However, since late 1970s and early 1980s, the Asian economies have witnessed a significant financial deepening and disintermediation in the financial system. With changes in financial markets of the developing countries including the deregulation of financial institutions and innovations in financial instruments, the new development in the theory and practice of monetary aggregation pioneered by Barnett and his colleagues may have some relevance for the developing Asian countries.

There are important developments in the financial system of the Asian countries that qualify for the rationale for the used of Divisia monetary aggregates. In the 1980s, the majority of the Asian countries has experienced substantial structural changes and rapid growth in the financial system. The financial system has undergone a radical transformation from a relatively simple structure of the early 1960s, comprising the Central Bank and small financial intermediaries, into a more sophisticated financial system characterised by the prevalence of finance companies, merchant banks, commercial banks, discount houses, development finance institutions, capital market institutions, commodity market institutions, new thrift and trust institutions, among others. Parallel to the increase in the sophistication of the financial system, there is evidence that financial innovations and deregulation have become more frequent issues in the Asian financial markets. Among the major innovations was the liberalisation of interest rates, relaxation of exchange control, foreign exchange dealings by financial institutions, computerised cheque clearing system, electronic banking, new financial instruments (example, negotiable certificate of deposits, bankers acceptance and repurchase agreement arrangement (repos)), etc.[6]

Although the implementation of financial liberalisation varied widely across these countries in terms of both the pace and scope of reforms, however, the liberalisation of interest rates was a prominent feature of the financial reforms implemented by the Asian countries during the 1980s. Interest rates on deposits were fully deregulated in Indonesia, the Philippines and Sri Lanka in the early 1980s. As for Malaysia, Nepal, South Korea, Taiwan and Thailand, majority of the deposit rates were liberalised in the late 1980s. While Singapore liberalised her financial system as early as 1975, on the other hand, Myanmar has 'partially' deregulated her financial system in late 1989. An important implication of this event is that the liberalisation of interest rates will enable the computation of user costs and this situation will not limit the usefulness of Divisia monetary aggregates for these Asian countries.

Our main questioned is: Is there a role for Divisia monetary aggregates in a changing financial environment or 'deregulated' Asian countries as predicted by Judd and Scadding (1982)? Nevertheless, a study by Subrahmanyam and Swami (1991) for India, found that although the Indian economy experienced a significant financial deepening and disintermediation, Simple-sum monetary aggregates were more informative than the Divisia aggregates. On the other hand, Huang *et al.* (1992) study's of the Taiwanese economy suggest that there are potential roles for Divisia money as a useful aggregate for monetary policy purposes in Taiwan. Therefore, given a new financial environment, the feasibility and usefulness of the Divisia monetary aggregates needs to be examined rigorously in the context of the Asian countries.

Alternative Procedures for Monetary Aggregation

Monetary aggregates are important and essential to policy makers and researchers. To the policy makers, the need for such aggregates may arise in designing policies to curb inflation, influence economic growth and employment. On the other hand, the researchers may use these aggregates in estimating a money demand function or a complex macro model of an economy. Traditionally, Simple-sum monetary aggregates have been used for these purposes. In recent years, these aggregates have been criticised as being inferior and (are therefore considered as) potentially inappropriate measures of 'money'. Barnett (1980) argues that the Simple-sum procedure which imposes restrictions of perfect substitutability on the components of monetary assets, and hence can be aggregated linearly is unacceptable. Existing literature on the substitutability between money and near-monies indicates that the assumption of perfect substitutability is violated. In other words, these asset components have low elasticity of substitution.

Barnett (1980, 1983) points out that when asset components are not perfect substitutes, non-linear aggregation is required to approximate these aggregates with different weights attached to each component asset. To overcome these deficiencies, several procedures for constructing weighted monetary aggregates have been introduced in the literature.

Alternative procedures to the construction of weighted monetary aggregates can be classified into three broad categories or approaches, namely; the regression model approach, the asset substitution approach and the index number approach.

The Regression Model Approach

A simple regression model approach was proposed by Timberlake and Forston (1967) and Laumas (1968) in which multiple regression analysis was used to measure the degree of moneyness of the asset components. The parameter estimates will indicate the degree of moneyness or weight of the component assets. For example, Laumas (1968) estimates the following equation

$$Y_t = \alpha + \beta M_t + \theta S_t \qquad (3.1)$$

and rewritten in the following form

$$Y_t = \alpha + \beta[M_t + (\theta/\beta)S_t] \qquad (3.2)$$

where Y is income, M is currency and demand deposits and S is saving deposits. Parameters α, β and θ are to be estimated. The degree of moneyness was to be indicated by the regression coefficients of M and S. If $0<\theta/\beta<1$, then S would have some degree of moneyness. If $\theta/\beta=1$, then M and S would have the same degree of moneyness. On the other hand, if $\theta/\beta<0$, then S would be an investment, that is, the holding of M would have to be lowered to acquire S.

A dynamic regression model was proposed by Clements and Nguyen (1980). In this approach, information about the characteristics of the monetary aggregates is obtained by empirically estimating the parameters of a price equation consisting of various monetary asset components. The price equation is derived based on the money market clearing conditions. In this model, Clements and Nguyen (1980) estimate the following price equation

$$\Delta \ln P_t = \lambda_1 \Delta \ln C_t + \lambda_2 \Delta \ln F_t + \lambda_3 \Delta \ln S_t$$
$$- \alpha \Delta \ln Y_t - \beta \Delta \ln r_t + \theta \Delta \ln P_{t-1} \qquad (3.3)$$

where P is the price level. C, F and S are currency and demand deposits, fixed deposits and saving deposits respectively. Y is income and r is the interest rate. Parameters to be estimated are denoted as λ's, α, β and θ. The lagged dependent variable P_{t-1} is added to induce dynamics into the process. In this model, the parameter estimates of the price equation represent the liquidity of moneyness of each component in which those components which have a larger effect on prices receive a larger weight in the liquidity measure of money.

Recently, a vector autoregression (VAR) approach for constructing weighted monetary aggregates has been proposed by Roper and Turnovsky (1980). According to this approach, the optimal monetary aggregate (M) is the one which minimises the forecast variance in the target variable nominal income. Thus,

$$M_t = \sum_{i=1}^{N} \phi_{it} m_{it} \qquad (3.4)$$

where m_{it} is the i-th monetary asset and ϕ_i is the optimal weight for the i-th asset and must satisfy the adding up property, $\Sigma \phi_{it} = 1$. In order to derive the optimal weight to be attached to each of the component assets, Roper and Turnovsky estimate an (unrestricted) vector autoregressive model (VAR) where each endogenous variable is expressed as a function of the lagged values of all variables in the model.

However, Barnett (1990) has reservations in using the above approaches. According to Barnett, the monetary aggregates constructed from the above approaches do not represent a measurement of monetary services or liquidity of an economy. Since the derivation of these aggregates does not follow from microeconomic theory, Barnett (1990) notes that 'this aggregate does not "exist" since it is not produced from blockwise separability of any structural function'.

The Asset Substitution Approach

The asset substitution approach was based on the pioneering work of Chetty (1969). According to Chetty, the method of aggregation used is by estimating the cross-elasticity of substitution between that asset and a reference asset that is designated to be the most liquid asset. The estimates of the weights were derived from the marginal conditions of the maximised utility function subject to the budget constraint. In this respect, Chetty was the first to use microeconomic aggregation theory to define money. In fact, Chetty was the first to estimate a neoclassical aggregator function embedded within a constrained optimization decision. In his analysis, Chetty utilised the Constant Elasticity of Substitution (CES) utility function as the aggregator function.

Chetty (1969) considers the following utility function of a consumer

$$U = (\alpha M^{-\rho} + \beta T^{-\rho})^{-1/\rho} \qquad (3.5)$$

where M and T are money holdings and time deposits respectively. The budget constraint is given by

$$Mo = M + T/(1 + r) \qquad (3.6)$$

where Mo is consumer's total cash holdings. The consumer's utility maximisation subject to the budget constraint yields the following equation

$$[(\alpha/\beta)(M/T)]^{-(1+\rho)} = 1 + r \qquad (3.7)$$

For estimation purposes, taking logarithms and rearranging terms we have

$$\ln (M/T) = -[1/(1 + \rho)]\ln (\beta/\alpha)$$
$$+ [1/(1 + \rho)]\ln [1/(1 + r)] \qquad (3.8)$$

Having obtained the parameter estimates of ρ, β and α (assumed to be unity), the new monetary aggregate (M*) is derived by substituting these values in equation (3.5). Therefore,

$$M^* = (M^{-\rho} + \beta T^{-\rho})^{-1/\rho} \qquad (3.9)$$

However, Chetty's model is only appropriate for a two-period world. Furthermore, in Chetty's model, the 'prices', $[1/(1 + r)]$ are not the user cost. Barnett (1990) has pointed out that without the user cost, one cannot derived a useful monetary aggregate based on microeconomic aggregation theory. For a multi-period world, Barnett (1980) extended Chetty's model by deriving the Jorgensonian user cost (equivalent rental price) of the monetary assets from a rigorous Fisherine intertemporal consumption expenditure allocation model.

The Index Number Approach

The index number approach in deriving weighted monetary aggregates was first proposed by Barnett (1980). The index number approach to monetary aggregation does not require the assumption of substitutability between components (Barnett, 1983; Barnett *et al.* 1992). This implies that the weighted aggregate does not depend on the aggregator function. Upon the derivation of user cost of monetary assets, Barnett was able to link index number theory with monetary aggregation theory. Barnett proposes two quantity indices that are relevant to monetary aggregation, that is, the Fisher Ideal index and Divisia index in discrete time. The application of index number theory to monetary economics was made possible after a stimulating paper by Diewert (1976), in which he defines a class of superlative index numbers. The seminal work by Diewert has bridged the gap between index number theory and aggregation theory.

Diewert (1976) constructed the theory of superlative index numbers in discrete time and defines an index number to be 'superlative' if it is exact for some aggregator function which can provide a second-order approximation to any linearly homogeneous aggregator function. An index number is exact if it exactly equals the aggregator function whenever the data is consistent with microeconomic maximising behaviour. Diewert (1976) has proved that both Fisher Ideal and Tornqvist-Theil Divisia indices are a class of superlative index.

The Fisher Ideal index which was proposed by Fisher (1922) is given as

$$QF_t = QF_{t-1} \{ [(\sum_{i=1}^{N} p_{it}m_{it})(\sum_{i=1}^{N} p_{it-1}/m_{it})] / [(\sum_{i=1}^{N} p_{it}m_{it})(\sum_{i=1}^{N} p_{it-1}/m_{it})] \}^{1/2} \quad (3.10)$$

where m_i represent components of monetary asset i, and p_i is the i-th asset's 'rental' price. On the other hand, the Divisia index due to Tornqvist (1936) and Theil (1967) is given as

$$QD_t = QD_{t-1} \prod_{i=1}^{N} (m_{it}/m_{it-1})^{1/2(s_{it} + s_{it-1})} \tag{3.11}$$

where $s_{it} = p_{it}m_{it}/\sum_{k=1}^{N} p_{kt}m_{kt}$ is the expenditure share of monetary asset i.

According to the index number approach, there are two weighting methods proposed in the literature to derive the weighted monetary aggregates, and these are the user cost and turnover rate methods which proxy for the rental price (p) of the monetary assets. The former was derived by Barnett (1980) and the latter was proposed by Spindt (1985). As commonly known in computing the index number, information on both prices and quantities are required. The weighting method proposed by Barnett is the user cost of a financial asset evaluated as the expenditure shares of each of the components included in the aggregates. The user cost of a financial asset is the price imputed to the service flow of that asset during a given holding period. In its simplest form, the user cost of a financial asset is equal to the difference between the rate of return of that asset and the maximum expected holding period yield available in the economy.

On the other hand, according to the weighting method proposed by Spindt (1985), in computing the index, the user cost is replaced by the monetary turnover rate. Based on the Fisher Ideal index, Spindt arrives at the following new monetary aggregate which corresponds closely to the monetary aggregate contemplated in the equation of exchange, MV=PT,

$$QS_t = QS_{t-1} [\sum_{i=1}^{N} s_{it-1}(m_{it}/m_{it-1}) \cdot \sum_{i=1}^{N} s_{it}(m_{it-1}/m_{it})]^{1/2} \tag{3.12}$$

where $s_{it} = v_{it}m_{it}/\sum_{k=1}^{N} v_{kt}m_{kt}$, and v_i is the turnover rate of monetary asset i.

However, more recently, Rotemberg (1991) and Rotemberg et al. (1995) proposed an alternative weighted monetary aggregate which is closely related to Divisia aggregate. They called this aggregate the Currency-equivalent (CE) aggregate which is interpreted as the stock of currency that yields the same transactions services as provided by all monetary assets. The index is a time-varying weighted average of the stock of different monetary assets with weights given by the ratio of each asset's user cost to a benchmark rate.

The CE aggregate index is given as follows

$$CE_t = M_t + \Sigma[(R-r_i)/R]m_{it} \qquad (3.13)$$

The CE aggregate has the property that assets that do not pay interest such as M (includes currency, demand deposits and travellers' cheques) are added together with weights of unity. Other assets are added with weight between 0 and 1. Assets with higher rate of return receive a smaller weight because their marginal liquidity services are lower. Comparing between Divisia and CE aggregate, the former is a weighted average of growth rates of monetary assets, while the later is a weighted average of the levels of monetary assets.

Among the four statistical indices above, Barnett (1980, 1982) prefers the Divisia index. Barnett (1980) has shown that between Divisia and Fisher Ideal indices, the differences between the two are of little empirical importance since both are in the same class of superlative index, they will move very closely together. But, the Divisia index is potentially the most useful to policymakers because it has the most easily understood form of any of the index numbers in Diewert's (1976) superlative class. In fact, Ishida (1984) argues that 'Divisia index is the "best" statistical index'.

Further, Barnett (1990) and Barnett *et al.* (1992) pointed that Spindt's (1985) monetary aggregate is inconsistent both with existing aggregation and index number theories. Barnett (1990) strongly argued that Spindt's (1985) approach is entirely arbitrary and using that formulation in practice 'is a hazardous venture'. On the other hand, as for the CE aggregate, Barnett (1991) clearly states that while Divisia monetary aggregate measure the service flow, the CE aggregate measure the economic stock of money. Therefore, the CE aggregate is not suitable to represent the flow of monetary services of a nation.

The Construction of a Divisia Monetary Aggregate

According to Barnett (1980), a Divisia monetary aggregate is constructed in the following manner: Let q_{it} and p_{it} represent the quantities and user costs of each asset to be included in the aggregate at time t. The expenditure share on the services of monetary asset i in period t is:

$$s_{it} = p_{it}q_{it}/\Sigma_j p_{jt}q_{jt}. \qquad (3.14)$$

The user cost (see Barnett, 1978) of each asset is measured as:

$$p_{it} = (R_t - r_{i,j})/(1 + R_t) \qquad (3.15)$$

where R_t is the benchmark rate, the maximum $[r_j, r_i; i=1,2,...,n)$. $j=1,2,..k$. $i \neq j]$. The growth rate of a Divisia aggregate then can be written as

$$G(Q_t) = \sum_{I=1}^{N} s_{it}^* G(q_{it}) \qquad (3.16)$$

where $s_{it}^* = 0.5(s_{it}+s_{it-1})$ and n is the number of assets in the aggregate. Single period changes, beginning with a base period can be cumulated to determine the level of the Divisia aggregate in each succeeding period.[7]

However, before we can construct a Divisia monetary aggregate, we have to consider two important questions, that is, 1) the selection of an admissible aggregate and 2) the choice of the benchmark asset.

Selection of an Admissible Aggregate

The main question here is: Which components of the various monetary assets are to be included in the Divisia monetary aggregate? According to Barnett (1982), an admissible aggregate is where the selected assets included in the aggregate satisfy the weak separability condition. Weak separability implies that the marginal rate of substitution between any two assets in a group, say A, is independent of the quantity of any assets not in A. This will ensure that changes in the quantity of an asset not in the group will not affect the marginal utilities derived from consuming assets within the group. Barnett (1982) argues that weak separability is needed to ensure the existence of behaviourally stable aggregates. In the absence of separability, changes in the price of its components will result in different levels of demand for the aggregate as a whole.

However, in the majority of studies conducted on the developed countries, most researchers have ignored the separability issue. Fisher *et al.* (1993: p. 13) argue that 'separability does not, however, provide an objective criterion for deciding what is money and what is not. The restrictions imposed are entirely subjective and separability is simply a technical issue regarding the consistency of such restrictions with aggregation theory. For example, the chosen separable group of "monetary assets" may itself be a subset of a larger separable group; there is no reason for the smaller aggregate to be "money" and the larger not. Indeed, the Divisia approach does not impose a definition of "money"; it is the monetary services provided that are important'.

Barnett (1982) also notes that the issue of separability is less serious compared to one using Simple-sum in aggregating monetary assets. If the Divisia index formula had been used, there is a great possibility that the component groupings that were selected would have satisfied the weak separability condition by chance.

Furthermore, as pointed by Barnett et al. (1992), the existing method of conducting the separability test is not a very effective tool. The parametric approach of testing for separability by specifying certain functional forms suffers from the restrictive nature of their implicit assumptions about the underlying preference structure of the consumer. While the non-parametric procedure has undesirable features of being nonstatistical and thus, not appropriate for dynamic models (see also Fisher et al., 1993). Consequently, it has been a common practice to compute the Divisia index under the maintained hypothesis that the assets that compose the aggregate satisfy this condition and the issue of an admissible aggregate be treated separately (Thornton and Yue, 1992).

Choice of the Benchmark Asset

In computing a monetary aggregate using the Divisia index approach, information on both prices and quantities are required. In economic aggregation theory, monetary assets are treated as commodities and their prices are defined similarly to the rental price or user cost of a durable goods. The user cost represents the opportunity costs of foregone interest associated with holding funds in different types of monetary assets. Barnett (1978) and Donovan (1978) have independently derived the user cost of a monetary asset. The opportunity cost of a monetary asset is obtained by comparing the asset's rate of return to that on a benchmark asset with the highest rate of return. If the user costs of the monetary assets can be correctly defined and accurately measured, the Divisia aggregate can be used to measure the monetary service flows provided by various monetary assets in the economy.

Thus, the computation of a user cost depends on the choice of the benchmark asset. As Goldfeld (1982) points out, the benchmark asset is not easily defined or may not even exist. As a result, the value and quality of the Divisia monetary aggregate is influenced by the chosen benchmark asset. According to Barnett and Spindt (1982), the benchmark asset is the one that is held only for accumulating and transferring wealth across time and its rate of return should be the highest in the economy. The benchmark asset is a non-monetary asset and thus, provides no transaction services. Although Barnett and Spindt (1982) suggest that human capital is the 'best' to represent the benchmark asset, its data availability is the major constraint. Nevertheless, the majority of studies of Divisia aggregates utilised the highest available rate of return on a given set of monetary assets. Barnett *et al.* (1992: p. 2105) agree on this point and further note that 'the role of the benchmark asset is to establish a nonmonetary alternative. It is acceptable for this to be a different asset in each period, since the maximization is repeated each period. In theory, any measurement of R_t could be viewed as a proxy for the unknown rate of return on human capital'. In practice, however, the benchmark rate is defined in such a way that the user costs for the monetary assets are positive and this method of selecting the benchmark rate will avoid the problem of negative user cost. Therefore, it is for this reason that the benchmark rate is made to dominate all rate of return of monetary asset components.

In this study, we compute the Divisia monetary aggregates for the Asian countries, using the method proposed by Barnett (1980). For computation, we used the narrow money M1 and broader money M2 for all countries in the Asian region.[8] Details of the monetary components and their respective user costs are presented in Table 3.1. The computed Divisia aggregates and its counterpart Simple-sum aggregates are presented in Table 3.2. From Table 3.1, we can observe that the rate of return on currency is assumed to be zero since it is a perfectly liquid asset. On the other hand, although the explicit rate of return on demand deposits is also zero, Offenbacher (1980) and Barnett *et al.* (1981) strongly argued that an implicit rate of return must be imputed to demand deposits, if the substitutability between currency and demand deposits is to be estimable. Barnett (1982: p. 699) proposes that 'in some cases implicit rates of return must be used in computing the interest rates in the formula p_i, especially when the own rate of return on an asset is subject to govenrmental rate regulation. An implicit imputation is also used in the measurement of R. The Divisia quantity index has been found to be robust to those imputations within the plausible ranges of error in the imputation'.

However, the proper implicit rate imputation to demand deposits remains an open issue. Following Offenbacher (1980), the approach taken in this study is to compute an implicit rate using Klein's (1974) methodology. The formula used for constructing the implicit rate on demand deposits (DDr) is given as follows

$$DDr = r_L [1 - (BR/DD)] \qquad (3.17)$$

where r_L is the rate of return on bank's earning assets and BR is bank reserves. For arriving at the rate of return on foreign currency deposits (FCDr), we follow Musi (1989) using the following formula

$$FCDr = Dr.e \qquad (3.18)$$

where Dr is the rate of return on saving or time deposits and e is the expected rate of devaluation.

As for the benchmark asset, as shown in Table 3.1, it varies between countries. Nonetheless, using the envelope approach, a series of benchmark rates is formed by selecting that benchmark rate which is higher than the rate of return of each monetary components. This will ensure that $p_i \geq 0$ (see Mullineux, 1996). Furthermore, Binner (1990) proposes adding 0.10 points to the benchmark rate to ensure that this rate will be non-zero.

Information Content of Monetary Aggregates: Some Preliminary Results

Monetary aggregates are widely used as indicators of unobservable economic activity. This is because monetary aggregates, in some way, convey information about the current state of the economy. Thus, one potentially useful characteristic of a monetary aggregate is that it contains information relevant to certain key macroeconomic variables, say for example, current nominal income. Most information content studies adopt a methodology which originated in information theory introduced by Shannon (1948) and later developed by Theil (1967), but it was Tinsley *et al.* (1980) who applied this method in monetary aggregation literature. In its simplest form, the approach tries to measure the contemporaneous information in money M, with respect to income Y, defined as

$$I(Y|M) = -1/2 \ln(1 - R^2) \qquad (3.19)$$

where R^2 is the coefficient of determination from the following linear regression

$$Y_t = \alpha + \beta M_t + \varepsilon_t \qquad (3.20)$$

This procedure measures the value of using contemporaneous information only. The measure of information is based on the behaviour of ε_t. Equation (3.20) assume that ε_t has constant variance, zero serial correlation and zero non-contemporaneous correlation between Y and M. As for time series data, these assumptions are rather restricted. To avoid these strong assumptions and to be more consistent with economic theory, equation (3.20) can be generalised to a dynamic framework in defining information content of M relative to Y as follows

$$I(Y|M) = -1/2 \ln(SSR_2/SSR_1) \qquad (3.21)$$

where SSR_1 and SSR_2 are sum of squared residuals from the following equations (3.22) and (3.23) respectively,

$$Y_t = \alpha + \sum_{i=1}^{K} \beta_i Y_{t-i} + \varepsilon_{1t} \qquad (3.22)$$

$$Y_t = \alpha + \sum_{i=1}^{K} \beta_i Y_{t-i} + \sum_{i=1}^{N} \theta_i M_{t-i} + \varepsilon_{2t} \qquad (3.23)$$

Equation (3.21) measures whether M is informative about Y in addition to what Y is to itself. In other words, in the regression framework, this is to test whether equation (3.23) gives a better fit compared to equation (3.22). This will involve testing the statistical significance of the θ's in equation (3.23).

As pointed by Sims (1972), the information content analysis is closely related to the Granger causality test in the voluminous literature on money-income relationship. In the notion of Granger causality testing, money is said to *Granger cause* (or be informative about) income if the θ's are statistically significant in equation (3.23). Schwert (1979) notes that Granger causality test of incremental information content have an important bearing on the usefulness of monetary aggregates as indicators.

Granger's (1969) definition of causality is based on the predictability of a time series. Formally, the above proposition can be stated as follows: if $\sigma^2(Y|Y,M)<\sigma^2(Y|Y)$, then M is said to *Granger cause* Y. The term $\sigma^2(Y|Y,M)$ is the prediction error variance of Y derived from the information set that includes past values of Y and M. The term $\sigma^2(Y|Y)$ is the variance of the prediction error of Y based on information contained only in the past values of Y. If, however, $\sigma^2(M|M,Y)<\sigma^2(M|M)$ then Y is said to *Granger cause* M. Bidirectional causality is said to occur when the above outcomes occur simultaneously. Finally, if $\sigma^2(Y|Y)<\sigma^2(Y|Y,M)$ and $\sigma^2(M|M)<\sigma^2(M|M,Y)$, then the two series are temporally unrelated over time and therefore are independent of each other.

The usual *F*-statistics can be used to test for the joint statistical significance of θ's=0. The test of the null hypothesis that M does not *Granger cause* Y based on equations (3.22) and (3.23) can be carried out with the following *F*-statistic,

$$F = [(SSR_1-SSR_2)/T]/[SSR_2/(T-K-N-1)] \qquad (3.24)$$

Here SSR_1 and SSR_2 refer to the sum of squared residuals from ordinary least squares regressions on equations (3.22) and (3.23) respectively. T is the number of observations and K and N are the chosen lag length for Y and M respectively. Under the null hypothesis, *F* is distributed as F with (N, T-K-N-1) degrees of freedom. For a suitably large value of *F*, we reject the hypothesis that M does not *Granger cause* Y. In other words, in this case, M is not informative about income Y. However, despite using the Granger causality test, the aim is not to establish a causal link between money and income, but simply to describe a statistical relationship between the two to measure informativeness.

In estimating equations (3.22) and (3.23), all variables are required to be stationary. To ensure the use of stationary time series data, the sequential scheme of multiple unit root tests suggested by Dickey and Pantula (1987) were used. Dickey and Pantula (1987) suggest using sequential tests that first check for three unit roots, then two unit roots, and finally, a single unit root; these tests consist of regressing $\Delta^3 X_t$ on $\Delta^2 X_{t-1}$, then on $\Delta^2 X_{t-1}$ and ΔX_{t-1}, and finally, on $\Delta^2 X_{t-1}$, ΔX_{t-1} and X_{t-1}. One proceeds with this sequence until the coefficient on the most recently added variable is insignificantly different from zero. Our result suggests that the null hypothesis of the presence of three unit roots can be rejected for all five series for all countries, while one cannot reject the hypothesis of two unit roots in some of the series investigated. In particular, for the money series two unit roots can be rejected for Myanmar, the Philippines and South Korea. In most cases real output variable has a single unit root for all Asian countries, except for South Korea where real output has two unit roots.[9]

After transforming all the series in their stationary form, we conduct the Granger causality test from money to income. As for the lag length K and N, there are several options that can be used to determine the K and N of the series. Diebold and Nerlove (1990) 'rule-of-thumb' consists in setting K or N = int($T^{1/4}$) where 'int' denotes the integer portion of the term in brackets. Other procedure which is often employed is the one proposed by Said and Dickey (1984) with K or N = int($T^{1/3}$), and Schwert (1987) proposes two range of K or N = int$[4(T/100)^{1/4}]$ or int$[12(T/100)^{1/4}]$. However, when quarterly data are used, as in this study, it is common practice to used a range of lag length - four, eight and twelve lags. The results of the Granger causality tests are presented in Table 3.3. The main entries in Table 3.3 are values of the *F*-statistic as described above, comparing the sums of squares between the unrestricted and the restricted regressions. Then, in parentheses, are the *p*-values (probabilities) associated with these *F*-statistics. Reading across the table for the lags length- 4, 8 and 12 lags, the results clearly show that except for South Korea, monetary aggregates *Granger cause* income in the Asian region. For Myanmar, the Philippines and Sri Lanka, all measurements of monetary aggregates used are informative of national income (output). Both Simple-sum and Divisia M1 and M2 *Granger cause* income at shorter lags length. On one hand, the Simple-sum aggregates dominate the Divisia money aggregates in Indonesia, on the other, in Thailand, Divisia money dominate the Simple-sum aggregates. As for Malaysia and Singapore, both narrow money - Simple-sum and Divisia M1 are informative about income. However, for Nepal and Taiwan, broad money *Granger cause* national income.

In summary, we note that monetary aggregate can be a useful indicator for monetary policy purposes in the majority of the countries under study. More interesting, the Divisia monetary aggregate shows potential roles as intermediate indicators for policy purposes of Malaysia, Myanmar, the Philippines, Singapore, Sri Lanka and Thailand.

Conclusions

In this paper we attempt to construct and compute Divisia monetary aggregates for selected Asian countries, namely; Indonesia, Malaysia, Myanmar, Nepal, Philippines, Singapore, South Korea, Sri Lanka, Taiwan and Thailand. Except for Myanmar, all these countries have experienced financial liberalisation during the mid-1970s and in the 1980s. As suggested by Judd and Scading (1982), in countries where financial deregulation, in particular where interest rate liberalisation has been the main key financial reform, there is a role for Divisia monetary aggregates act as monetary indicators for policy purposes. Since it has been recognised that Simple sum measurements of money are distorted, there is impetus to find alternative measurements of money that will appropriately measure the monetary services of a nation.

In this study we have computed both narrow Divisia M1 and broad Divisia M2 and together with their counterpart Simple sum M1 and M2 we test for information content of each monetary aggregate about national income using the standard Granger causality analysis. The results suggest that monetary aggregates are informative about national income in most of the Asian countries analysed. Except for South Korea, Indonesia, Nepal and Taiwan, the results indicate that there a potential role for Divisia monetary aggregates in the Asian developing countries to act as monetary indicators for monetary policy purposes.

As for future research, it would be interesting to extend the present analysis to test the robustness of Divisia monetary aggregates in these countries by subjecting these aggregates to the standard tests proposed in Barnett *et al.* (1984) and Chrystal and MacDonald (1994). These test results would be of considerable importance because they will allow us to directly evaluate the usefulness of Divisia aggregates as alternative measure of money that is useful for the monetary authorities for policy purposes.

Notes

1. For a detail discussion on the theoretical background of Divisia aggregates, see Barnett (1980, 1990).
2. Barnett (1990) surveys and provides critical criticisms of these approaches.

3. Except for Germany where her main monetary target is M3.
4. Except studies by Huang *et al.* (1992) for Taiwan, and Subrahmanyam and Swami (1991) for India.
5. For example, see Thornton and Yue (1992) and Issing *et al.* (1993).
6. For further discussions on the various financial innovations and deregulation in the Asian countries, see World Bank (1989, 1993), Tseng and Corker (1991, 1993), Talib (1993), Adhikary (1989a) and Cho and Khatkhate (1989b).
7. Recently, several modification has been made in the construction of Divisia aggregate. Hermann *et al.* (1994) propose monetary measure with 'constant' and 'smooth' weights along with the usual 'current' weights as in equation (3.14) above. On the other hand, Ford *et al.* (1992) propose a modified Divisia aggregate by taking into account the effect of technological innovation by modifying the calculation of user costs.
8. In various Asian countries, the official Simple sum monetary aggregates range from M1, M2 and M3. Apart from Indonesia, Myanmar, Nepal, South Korea, Taiwan and Thailand, other countries like Malaysia, the Philippines, Singapore and Sri Lanka, the broadest definition of money supply M3 is used as one of the monetary indicators. However, published data on most of the components of M3 and their respective rate of returns are not available.
9. See Table 4.2 for further details on the Dickey-Pantula unit root tests for the Divisia money series. In this study, since nominal income (GDP) for other Asian developing countries apart from Singapore, South Korea and Taiwan is available in annual form, a corresponding quarterly series was created by using the technique proposed by Chow and Lin (1976). See also Huang (1995), Bahmani-Oskooee (1986) and Hataiseree (1993) for similar application of this approach. Further descriptions and sources of data are provided in Data Appendix.

Data Appendix

This study is based on quarterly time series data for the period 1981:1 to 1994:4. Sources of data for each countries are as follows.

1. Monetary Asset Components, Bank Reserves, Exchange Rates (Domestic Currency/US$)

    For all countries, The SEACEN Centre, *SEACEN Financial Statistics*.

2. Rates of Return on Financial Assets, Bank Lending Rate

    Indonesia: Bank of Indonesia, *Indonesian Financial Statistics, Weekly Report and Report for the Financial Year.*

    Malaysia: Bank Negara Malaysia, *Monthly Statistical Bulletin and Quarterly Bulletin.*

    Myanmar: The SEACEN Centre, *SEACEN Financial Statsitics.*

    Nepal: Nepal Rastra Bank, *Quarterly Economic Bulletin and Main Economic Indicator-Monthly Report.*

    Philippines: The Central Bank of Philippines, *Philippines Financial Statistics, Annual Report and CB Review.*

    Singapore: The Monetary Authority of Singapore, *Monthly Statistical Bulletin.*

    South Korea: Bank of Korea, *Monthly Statistical Bulletin and Annual Report.*

    Sri Lanka: Central Bank of Ceylon, *Bulletin and Annual Report.*

    Taiwan: The SEACEN Centre, *SEACEN Financial Statistics.*

    Thailand: Bank of Thailand, *Quarterly Bulletin, Monthly Bulletin and Key Economic Indicator.*

3. Gross Domestic Product (GDP)

    Singapore: Department of Singapore, *Monthly Digest of Statistics.*

    South Korea: Bank of Korea, *Monthly Statistical Bulletin.*

    Taiwan: Central Bank of China, *Financial Statistics Monthly.*

For other Asian countries, since nominal income (GDP) are only available in annual form, a corresponding quarterly series was created by using the technique proposed by Chow and Lin (1976). See also Huang (1995), Bahmani-Oskooee (1986) and Hataiseree (1993) for similar application of this approach. Following this method, we have interpolated quarterly data for GDP from annual observations according to the pattern of quarterly movements in certain macroeconomic variables. In this study we interpolated quarterly GDP from annual observations according to the pattern of quarterly movement in government expenditure and exports.

For Indonesia, Malaysia, Nepal, Philippines, Sri Lanka and Thailand, quarterly data for GDP were interpolated from annual data using the pattern of quarterly movements in government expenditure and exports.

For Myanmar, quarterly data for GDP were interpolated from annual data using the pattern of quarterly movements in exports only.

To compute quarterly GDP, we follow the following steps;

Step 1. Regress annual gross domestic product (GDP_a) on annual government expenditure (G_a) and exports (X_a). For example, the following estimated regression is illustrated,

$$GDP_{at}\!{}^{\wedge} = \alpha + \beta G_{at}\!{}^{\wedge} + \theta X_{at}\!{}^{\wedge} + \varepsilon_t\!{}^{\wedge}$$

The estimated coefficients β and θ are used in step two.

Step 2. Compute quarterly GDP_i (i=1,2,3,4) as follows,

$$GNP_{qit} = GNP_a\{[(\beta/(\beta+\theta))(G_i/\Sigma_i G_i)]+[(\theta/(\beta+\theta))(X_i/\Sigma_i X_i)]\}$$

Table 3.1
Information used to construct Divisia aggregates

Country	Money	Asset components	Rates of return
Indonesia	DM1	Currency in circulation	Zero
		Demand deposits	Implicit rate of return. Using Klein's (1974) method. The basic formula for computing Demand deposit rate of return (DDr) is as follows; DDr = r_L*(1-RRDD), where r_L is commercial bank's lending rate for working capital loans (percent p.a.), and RRDD is reserve requirement on demand deposits.
		Foreign currency demand deposits	Implicit rate of return. Using Musi's (1989) method. The basic formula for computing Foreign currency demand deposits rate (FCDDr) is as follows; FCDDr = DDr*e, where e is expected rate of devaluation. e is computed as e=E_{t-1}/E_{t-2}, where E is the actual exchange rate (Rupiah/US$).
	DM2	Saving deposits	Saving deposit rate (Sdr). Proxied with the SBI (State Bank of Indonesia) 30 days discount rate (percent p.a.).
		Time deposits	Time deposit rate (TDr). TDr = max {(r_{ij})}, where i=state, National private and Foreign banks. j=1, 3, 6, 12 and 24 months maturity (percent p.a.).
		Foreign currency time deposits	Foreign currency time deposit rate (FCTDr). FCTDr = max {(r_{ij})}, where i=state, National private and Foreign banks. j=1, 3, 6, 12 and 24 months maturity (percent p.a.).
		Benchmark asset	*Maximum available rate. Max = {(DDr, FCDDr, SDr, TDr, FCTDr, r_i] + 0.1}, where i= certificate of deposits, Bank Indonesia certificates and Jakarta interbank call money (weighted average).*
Malaysia	DM1	Currency in circulation	Zero
		Demand deposits	Implicit rate of return. Using Klein's (1974) method. The basic formula for computing Demand deposit rate of return (DDr) is as follows; DDr = r_L*(1-RRDD), where r_L is commercial bank's base lending rate (percent p.a.), and RRDD is reserve requirement on demand deposits.
	DM2	Saving deposits	Savings deposit rate (SDr) in percent p.a.
		Fixed deposits	Fixed deposit rate (FDr). FDR= max {(r_i)}, where i=1, 3, 6, 9 & 12 months maturity (percent p.a.).
		Negotiable Certificate of Deposits	Rate on NCDs (NCDr). Proxied with the Interbank rates, r. NCDr= max {(r_i)}, where i=overnight, 7-days, 1 month & 3-months call money (percent p.a.).
		Repurchase agreement (Repos)	Repo rate (REPOr). Proxied with the call money rate at discount houses, r. REPOr= max {(r_i)}, where i=3, 6 & 12-months maturity (percent p.a.).
		Benchmark asset	*Maximum available rate. Max = {(DDr, SDr, TDr, NCDr, REPOr, r_j] + 0.1}, where i=rates at commercial banks and Finance companies; j= Treasury bill rates (3, 6 & 12-months) and yield on Goverment securities (5 & 20 years).*

Table 3.1 (continued)

Country	Money	Asset components	Rates of return
Myanmar	DM1	Currency in circulation Demand deposits	Zero Implicit rate of return. Using Klein's (1974) method. The basic formula for computing Demand deposit rate of return (DDr) is as follows: $DDr = r_L*(1-RRDD)$, where r_L is commercial bank's lending rate for working capital loans (percent p.a.), and RRDD is reserve requirement on demand deposits.
	DM2	Saving deposits Fixed deposits	Saving deposit rate (SDr) in percent p.a. Fixed deposit rate (FDr). FDr= max [(r_i)], where i=3, 6 & 9-months maturity (percent p.a.).
		Benchmark asset	*Maximum available rate. Max = {[DDr, SDr, FDr, r_i] + 0.1}, where i=3 months Treasury bills, 3 & 5-years Treasury bonds (percent p.a.).*
Nepal	DM1	Currency in circulation Demand deposits	Zero Implicit rate of return. Using Klein's (1974) method. The basic formula for computing Demand deposit rate of return (DDr) is as follows: $DDr = r_L*(1-RRDD)$, where r_L is commercial bank's lending rate on Industry loans (percent p.a.), and RRDD is reserve requirement on demand deposits.
	DM2	Saving deposits Fixed deposits Margin deposits	Saving deposit rate (SDr) in percent p.a. Fixed deposit rate (FDr). FDr= max [(r_i)], where i=3, 6, 12, 24 months maturity (percent p.a.). Margin deposit rate (MDr). Proxied with - Mdr = Export bill rate less saving deposit rate
		Benchmark asset	*Maximum available rate. Max = {[DDr, SDr, FDr, MDr, r_i] + 0.1}, where i=Treasury bills, National savings certificate, Development bonds and Nepal Rastra Bank Bonds.*
Philippines	DM1	Currency in circulation Demand deposits	Zero Implicit rate of return. Using Klein's (1974) method. The basic formula for computing Demand deposit rate of return (DDr) is as follows: $DDr = r_L*(1-RRDD)$, where r_L is commercial bank's secured loans (over 2 years) rate (percent p.a.), and RRDD is reserve requirement on demand deposits.
	DM2	Saving deposits Time deposits	Saving deposit rate (SDr) in percent p.a. Time deposit rate (TDr). TDr = max [(r_i)], where i=1, 2, 3, 6, 12 & 24-months maturity (percent p.a.).
		Benchmark asset	*Maximum available rate. Max = {[DDr, SDr, TDr, r_i] + 0.1}, where i=interbank call, Treasury bills, Promissory notes, Repurchase agreement (private), Certificate of assignment, Repurchase agreement (government) and Commercial paper (non-financial).*

Table 3.1 (continued)

Country	Money	Asset components	Rates of return
Singapore	DM1	Currency in circulation	Zero
		Demand deposits	Implicit rate of return. Using Klein's (1974) method. The basic formula for computing Demand deposit rate of return (DDr) is as follows: $DDr = r_L*(1-RRDD)$, where r_L is commercial bank's lending rate on loans and advances (percent p.a.), and RRDD is reserve requirement on demand deposits.
	DM2	Saving deposits	Saving deposit rate (SDr) in percent p.a.
		Fixed deposits	Fixed deposit rate (FDr). $FDr = \max\{(r_i)\}$, where i=3, 6 & 12-months maturity (percent p.a.).
		Negotiable Certificate of Deposits	NCD rate (NCDr). $NCDr = \max\{(r_i)\}$, where i=3 & 6-months Singapore dollar NCDs (percent p.a.).
		Benchmark asset	*Maximum available rate. $Max = \{[DDr, SDr, FDr, NCDr, r_k] + 0.1\}$, where i=commercial banks, Finance companies & Post Office savings bank; j=commercial banks & Finance companies; k=3-month Treasury bills, interbank (overnight, 1 & 3-months), commercial bills, 3-month SIBOR and 5-years Yield on Government securities.*
South Korea	DM1	Currency in circulation	Zero
		Demand deposits	Demand deposit rate (DDr) in percent p.a.
	DM2	Saving deposits	Saving deposit rate (SDr) in percent p.a.
		Time deposits	Time deposit rate (TDr). $TDr = \max\{(r_i)\}$, where i=3, 12 and 24 months maturity (percent p.a.)
		Foreign currency deposit	Implicit rate of return. Using Musi's (1989) method. The basic formula for computing Foreign currency deposits rate (FCDr) is as follows; $FCDr = SDr*e$, where e is expected rate of devaluation. e is computed as $e = E_{t-1}/E_{t-2}$, where E is the actual exchange rate (Won/US$).
		Benchmark asset	*Maximum available rate. $Max = \{[DDr, SDr, TDr, FCDr, r_i] + 0.1\}$, where i=yield on Government public bonds and yield on corporate bonds.*

Table 3.1 (continued)

Country	Money	Asset components	Rates of return
Sri Lanka	DM1	Currency in circulation	Zero
		Demand deposits	Implicit rate of return. Using Klein's (1974) method. The basic formula for computing Demand deposit rate of return (DDr) is as follows; DDr = r_L*(1-RRDD), where r_L is commercial bank's lending rate on loans and overdrafts (percent p.a.), and RRDD is reserve requirement on demand deposits.
	DM2	Saving deposits	Saving deposit rate (SDr) in percent p.a.
		Fixed deposits	Fixed deposit rate (FDr). FDr= max [(r_i)], where i=3, 6 & 24-months maturity (percent p.a.).
		Benchmark asset	*Maximum available rate.* Max = {[DDr, SDr, FDr, r_i] + 0.1}, where i=interbank rates, Government securities, Treasury bills and Fixed deposit rates (6, 12, 18 & 24 months) at National Savings bank.
Taiwan	DM1	Currency in circulation	Zero
		Checking accounts	Implicit rate of return. Using Klein's (1974) method. The basic formula for computing Checking account rate of return (CAr) is as follows; CAr = r_L*(1-RRCA), where r_L is commercial bank's prime lending rate (percent p.a.), and RRCA is reserve requirement on checking accounts.
		Passbook deposits	Passbook deposit rate (PDr) in percent p.a.
		Passbook savings deposits	Passbook savings deposit rate (PSDr) in percent p.a.
	DM2	Saving deposits	Saving deposit rate (SDr) in percent p.a.
		Postal savings redeposits	Postal saving redeposit rate (PSRr). Proxied with the savings deposit rate.
		Time deposits	Time deposit rate (TDr). TDr = max [(r_i)], where i=3 & 12-months maturity (percent p.a.).
		Foreign currency time deposits	Implicit rate of return. Using Musi's (1989) method. The basic formula for computing Foreign currency time deposits rate (FCTDr) is as follows; FCTDr = TDr*e, where e is expected rate of devaluation. e is computed as e=E_{t-1}/E_{t-2}, where E is the actual exchange rate (new Taiwan dollars/US$).
		Benchmark asset	*Maximum available rate.* Max = {[CAr, PDr, PSDr, SDr, TDr, FCTDr, r_i] + 0.1}, where i=*Government bonds and Money market rates.*

Table 3.1 (continued)

Country	Money	Asset components	Rates of return
Thailand	DM1	Currency in circulation	Zero
		Demand deposits	Implicit rate of return. Using Klein's (1974) method. The basic formula for computing Demand deposit rate of return (DDr) is as follows; $DDr = r_L*(1-RRDD)$, where r_L is commercial bank's lending rate on loans and overdrafts (percent p.a.), and RRDD is reserve requirement on demand deposits.
	DM2	Saving deposits	Saving deposit rate (SDr) in percent p.a.
		Time deposits	Time deposit rate (TDr). $TDr = \max [(r_i)]$, where i=3, 6, 12 & 24 months maturity (percent p.a.).
	Benchmark asset		*Maximum available rate. $Max = \{[DDr, SDr, TDr, r_i] + 0.1\}$, where i=Government bonds, Treasury bills (30, 60, 120 & 183 days) and Interbank rates.*

Table 3.2
Simple-sum and Divisia monetary aggregates for the Asian developing countries

Year	Simple-sum M1	Divisia M1	Simple-sum M2	Divisia M2
	Indonesia (in billion rupiah)			
1981:1	6711.00	6711.00	8808.00	8808.00
1981:2	6925.00	7026.83	9243.00	9234.95
1981:3	7518.00	7491.44	10007.00	9863.32
1981:4	7937.00	7876.48	10567.00	10406.68
1982:1	8049.00	7930.78	10801.00	10525.21
1982:2	8424.00	8285.79	11432.00	11063.95
1982:3	8555.00	8567.74	11760.00	11513.30
1982:4	8330.00	8559.79	11802.00	11693.00
1983:1	8914.00	9070.65	13190.00	13053.89
1983:2	9224.00	9563.04	13917.00	13529.03
1983:3	9501.00	9786.55	14966.00	13873.56
1983:4	9364.00	9699.64	15730.00	14012.16
1984:1	9904.00	10278.33	16891.00	14872.42
1984:2	10291.00	10915.09	17866.00	15734.60
1984:3	10441.00	10863.67	18346.00	15931.97
1984:4	10677.00	11111.29	19210.00	16332.75
1985:1	10973.00	11397.91	20473.00	17283.28
1985:2	10921.00	12240.47	21742.00	18971.48
1985:3	11048.00	12291.59	22944.00	19091.84
1985:4	11867.00	12974.72	24614.00	20240.74
1986:1	12085.00	14132.83	25887.00	22708.37
1986:2	11783.00	13624.59	25688.00	21122.27
1986:3	13952.00	16824.92	29616.00	26232.23
1986:4	13495.00	15210.25	28849.00	24168.95
1987:1	13235.00	15762.84	29733.00	25085.74
1987:2	13724.00	15912.95	30733.00	25594.38
1987:3	13818.00	15956.17	33142.00	26434.47
1987:4	14578.00	16626.54	35113.00	27733.54
1988:1	14354.00	16629.96	36843.00	28887.45
1988:2	15224.00	17332.51	39563.00	30488.67
1988:3	15252.00	17359.46	41715.00	31291.30
1988:4	16596.00	18290.59	43756.00	33383.30
1989:1	17102.00	19101.09	46062.00	35164.13
1989:2	18250.00	19525.77	49714.00	36616.55
1989:3	19428.00	20347.65	54207.00	39418.63
1989:4	22576.00	22272.89	61801.00	44686.61
1990:1	23758.00	23355.79	66972.00	49851.94
1990:2	27400.00	25011.65	75228.00	55531.94
1990:3	27921.00	26900.05	85125.00	64532.59
1990:4	28348.00	27379.26	92248.00	71164.21

Table 3.2 (continued)

Year	Simple-sum M1	Divisia M1	Simple-sum M2	Divisia M2
	Indonesia (in billion rupiah)			
1991:1	26975.00	26861.53	86537.00	71223.40
1991:2	29051.00	26697.17	93265.00	70893.50
1991:3	29282.00	27333.24	98914.00	76372.61
1991:4	31359.00	28338.75	104464.0	80050.73
1992:1	32453.00	33106.23	106736.0	88587.63
1992:2	32819.00	30179.16	112736.0	88462.91
1992:3	34133.00	31679.18	119864.0	94280.73
1992:4	35240.00	34767.94	126328.0	103367.9
1993:1	37401.00	37282.44	129960.0	111181.7
1993:2	40369.00	37917.33	135615.0	114416.1
1993:3	45512.00	40446.67	148934.0	122894.1
1993:4	46753.00	44258.85	156378.0	130907.5
1994:1	47427.00	47734.31	159422.0	140765.6
1994:2	50218.00	48417.39	163352.0	141803.0
1994:3	53657.00	53472.90	174641.0	151905.2
1994:4	57667.00	56914.38	187584.0	158995.3
	Malaysia (in million ringgit)			
1981:1	10172.00	10172.00	29199.00	29199.00
1981:2	10507.00	10211.68	30168.00	29642.70
1981:3	10166.00	10152.79	30917.00	29944.19
1981:4	11015.00	10795.71	32773.00	31044.66
1982:1	11103.00	11046.19	33370.00	31553.93
1982:2	11547.00	11267.04	34495.00	33272.35
1982:3	11501.00	11495.08	35185.00	33556.80
1982:4	12477.00	12152.76	37900.00	35188.81
1983:1	12433.00	12331.25	39509.00	36697.11
1983:2	12575.00	12294.16	39423.00	36659.66
1983:3	12827.00	12334.60	40555.00	38203.36
1983:4	13432.00	12891.03	42263.00	40303.76
1984:1	13429.00	12949.81	43336.00	40875.30
1984:2	13702.00	13315.28	44875.00	42106.09
1984:3	13177.00	12584.76	45479.00	40864.69
1984:4	13356.00	12786.74	47733.00	42356.22

Table 3.2 (continued)

Year	Simple-sum M1	Divisia M1	Simple-sum M2	Divisia M2
	Malaysia (in million ringgit)			
1985:1	13331.00	13013.42	48430.00	42752.32
1985:2	12955.00	12611.09	48838.00	42324.07
1985:3	12989.00	12609.28	48858.00	42541.86
1985:4	13579.00	13136.86	50413.00	45746.54
1986:1	13173.00	13323.59	51590.00	47141.92
1986:2	13021.00	12975.30	51965.00	46847.61
1986:3	13065.00	13448.29	54282.00	48195.63
1986:4	13956.00	13816.12	56095.00	50414.93
1987:1	14101.00	14233.68	56857.00	51011.38
1987:2	14463.00	14183.96	57620.00	54420.66
1987:3	14969.00	14642.89	58374.00	55547.55
1987:4	15768.00	15454.95	59772.00	57476.67
1988:1	15889.00	15868.96	59662.00	57735.69
1988:2	16069.00	15747.42	60797.00	60296.18
1988:3	16452.00	16164.21	61359.00	60695.59
1988:4	17840.00	17592.62	64072.00	64192.26
1989:1	18156.00	17775.03	66614.00	66254.77
1989:2	18784.00	17726.88	66756.00	66355.59
1989:3	19459.00	18182.28	69517.00	68598.70
1989:4	21249.00	19403.07	74393.00	72071.20
1990:1	22240.00	19972.81	78160.00	76029.86
1990:2	22458.00	20415.08	78700.00	76452.80
1990:3	22980.00	20925.47	80397.00	77771.02
1990:4	24240.00	21594.22	83902.00	79830.37
1991:1	24980.00	22716.75	88345.00	83411.43
1991:2	25074.00	22542.84	88311.00	82730.66
1991:3	25772.00	23002.46	91104.00	83895.70
1991:4	26902.00	23859.27	96091.00	86780.15
1992:1	27850.00	24940.22	100114.0	89331.47
1992:2	27398.00	24328.75	104774.0	90025.24
1992:3	28399.00	24980.82	110161.0	92365.48
1992:4	30395.00	26643.99	114480.0	98256.98
1993:1	31583.00	27576.61	117541.0	100639.3
1993:2	33241.00	27785.00	122878.0	103540.1
1993:3	35170.00	29174.93	128313.0	108759.5
1993:4	41792.00	31226.49	139800.0	117551.4
1994:1	42762.00	33301.60	154480.0	128940.4
1994:2	43794.00	33134.38	151018.0	126990.3
1994:3	46153.00	34423.40	155861.0	131592.3
1994:4	46472.00	35862.61	160367.0	137743.5

Table 3.2 (continued)

Year	Simple-sum M1	Divisia M1	Simple-sum M2	Divisia M2
	Myanmar (in million kyats)			
1981:1	8946.00	8946.00	11213.00	11213.00
1981:2	8781.00	8762.47	11259.00	11203.88
1981:3	9291.00	9265.28	12021.00	11936.21
1981:4	9157.00	9092.85	12010.00	11855.04
1982:1	9985.00	9907.10	13135.00	12957.37
1982:2	9822.00	9763.06	13146.00	12946.37
1982:3	9927.00	9865.79	13508.00	13269.99
1982:4	9844.00	9779.35	13565.00	13291.81
1983:1	10751.00	10576.66	14797.00	14407.46
1983:2	10606.00	10508.60	14831.00	14477.97
1983:3	10952.00	10854.56	15446.00	15062.04
1983:4	11128.00	10991.33	15702.00	15257.79
1984:1	12242.00	12161.42	17187.00	16805.88
1984:2	12263.00	12206.50	17655.00	17249.64
1984:3	12553.00	12501.57	18156.00	17726.46
1984:4	12830.00	12723.97	18469.00	17969.51
1985:1	13732.00	13592.57	19715.00	19184.49
1985:2	13669.00	13603.48	19825.00	19340.56
1985:3	14064.00	13954.38	20475.00	19925.82
1985:4	11612.00	11360.79	18145.00	17432.30
1986:1	13344.00	13234.75	20125.00	19642.62
1986:2	14468.00	14458.38	21480.00	21130.37
1986:3	15734.00	15727.61	23148.00	22826.69
1986:4	16404.00	16452.33	23819.00	23573.45
1987:1	18480.00	18418.37	26226.00	25955.06
1987:2	18510.00	18411.31	26390.00	26061.13
1987:3	9057.00	8232.52	17574.00	17741.54
1987:4	9713.00	8989.77	18126.00	18512.96
1988:1	11041.00	10331.38	19454.00	20115.54
1988:2	11217.00	10463.99	20021.00	20693.45
1988:3	13211.00	12418.74	21784.00	22814.76
1988:4	15937.00	15865.52	23521.00	26166.79
1989:1	18097.00	18277.53	25757.00	29123.66
1989:2	18896.00	19099.85	27130.00	30733.04
1989:3	20089.00	20164.70	29637.00	33248.36
1989:4	21536.00	21564.39	30942.00	35098.75
1990:1	25300.00	25128.72	35021.00	40236.87
1990:2	26372.00	26142.15	36289.00	41751.63
1990:3	30066.00	29503.10	40965.00	46984.21
1990:4	32333.00	31618.99	43739.00	50208.45

Table 3.2 (continued)

Year	Simple-sum M1	Divisia M1	Simple-sum M2	Divisia M2
	Myanmar (in million kyats)			
1991:1	38918.00	38036.91	51006.00	59495.46
1991:2	29323.00	27552.96	42074.00	45929.67
1991:3	40882.00	39749.48	55084.00	64013.38
1991:4	43737.00	42533.84	57346.00	67576.45
1992:1	52307.00	50434.68	66791.00	79152.81
1992:2	53139.00	51810.13	68387.00	81572.98
1992:3	56999.00	55811.86	74232.00	88445.26
1992:4	60200.00	58922.20	77773.00	92951.45
1993:1	70428.00	69142.18	89542.00	108134.8
1993:2	71210.00	70583.92	91770.00	111112.9
1993:3	72221.00	71220.86	95706.00	114107.0
1993:4	74979.00	74325.04	98615.00	118490.2
1994:1	84380.00	83082.10	109927.0	131940.2
1994:2	85594.00	84272.91	113550.0	135006.5
1994:3	-	-	-	-
1994:4	-	-	-	-
	Nepal (in million rupees)			
1981:1	3225.00	3225.00	6026.00	6026.00
1981:2	3297.00	3304.46	6327.00	6299.60
1981:3	2997.00	3012.77	6242.00	5857.46
1981:4	3205.00	3256.06	6599.00	6312.15
1982:1	3533.00	3611.38	7074.00	6937.10
1982:2	3592.00	3661.34	7406.00	7139.59
1982:3	3487.00	3515.55	7601.00	7006.03
1982:4	3695.00	3736.41	7995.00	7464.24
1983:1	4088.00	4121.71	8505.00	8083.22
1983:2	4157.00	4214.99	8965.00	8506.91
1983:3	3896.00	3924.55	9035.00	8155.78
1983:4	4366.00	4380.41	9631.00	8893.29
1984:1	4809.00	4910.57	10104.00	9778.48
1984:2	4968.00	5057.61	10537.00	10155.90
1984:3	4647.00	4759.50	10320.00	9636.43
1984:4	4944.00	5059.49	10884.00	10209.26

Table 3.2 (continued)

Year	Simple-sum M1	Divisia M1	Simple-sum M2	Divisia M2
	Nepal (in million rupees)			
1985:1	5419.00	5646.21	11699.00	11459.36
1985:2	5601.00	5770.22	12472.00	12042.36
1985:3	5097.00	5242.26	12153.00	10978.89
1985:4	5616.00	5786.44	13082.00	12144.73
1986:1	6571.00	6921.07	14350.00	14210.83
1986:2	7021.00	7337.77	15232.00	15109.13
1986:3	6360.00	6616.51	14724.00	13704.78
1986:4	6951.00	7190.70	15624.00	14844.96
1987:1	7698.00	8122.49	16494.00	16674.44
1987:2	8047.00	8474.37	17448.00	17614.05
1987:3	7972.00	8158.90	17829.00	17038.69
1987:4	8681.00	8782.29	19126.00	18452.97
1988:1	9340.00	9640.07	20171.00	19980.31
1988:2	9638.00	9769.05	21422.00	20772.90
1988:3	9042.00	8954.18	21613.00	19512.49
1988:4	9826.00	10009.22	23363.00	22097.18
1989:1	10696.00	11026.89	24963.00	24175.26
1989:2	11698.00	11945.53	26540.00	25717.04
1989:3	10791.00	10930.93	26699.00	24027.07
1989:4	11721.00	11927.77	28312.00	26210.43
1990:1	12570.00	13150.03	29377.00	28323.84
1990:2	13849.00	14564.01	31155.00	30849.10
1990:3	14107.00	14555.48	32764.00	31522.81
1990:4	14205.00	14773.98	33566.00	32183.55
1991:1	15075.00	16102.55	35308.00	34777.04
1991:2	16067.00	17030.45	37466.00	36675.95
1991:3	15389.00	16260.83	37975.00	36155.03
1991:4	17547.00	18541.31	41366.00	40252.26
1992:1	19165.00	20099.88	44165.00	43381.13
1992:2	19661.00	20596.07	45785.00	44731.23
1992:3	19775.00	20308.77	48027.00	45623.48
1992:4	20836.00	22012.17	50473.00	48831.34
1993:1	22482.00	23876.31	53949.00	52720.43
1993:2	23005.00	24351.55	57126.00	54766.93
1993:3	22919.00	24019.96	59896.00	55953.82
1993:4	25320.00	26526.04	63479.00	60728.04
1994:1	27745.00	28953.94	66901.00	64747.97
1994:2	29437.00	30750.42	70220.00	68333.17
1994:3	29003.00	29944.20	71829.00	69076.66
1994:4	30661.00	32162.37	74895.00	72966.39

Table 3.2 (continued)

Year	Simple-sum M1	Divisia M1	Simple-sum M2	Divisia M2
Philippines (in million pesos)				
1981:1	21712.00	21712.00	56912.00	56912.00
1981:2	22098.00	22402.81	58611.00	60573.66
1981:3	20468.00	21486.56	58503.00	60090.57
1981:4	23524.00	26515.68	65639.00	70541.05
1982:1	22330.00	23838.83	67117.00	68369.27
1982:2	22471.00	23395.13	70054.00	69267.51
1982:3	20963.00	22928.01	71576.00	69164.26
1982:4	23495.00	28865.81	78703.00	81607.55
1983:1	22165.00	27373.26	78329.00	83290.11
1983:2	23050.00	26125.56	83853.00	82757.23
1983:3	23504.00	28087.18	85286.00	84673.41
1983:4	32571.00	42618.40	97105.00	107733.6
1984:1	30176.00	38918.85	98826.00	107921.2
1984:2	31500.00	41139.33	97004.00	106716.1
1984:3	31528.00	42607.32	97097.00	106821.6
1984:4	33737.00	45707.53	111156.0	122262.5
1985:1	29632.00	40907.59	110314.0	116920.7
1985:2	29068.00	39235.52	111799.0	117966.5
1985:3	28999.00	38375.73	113966.0	118710.1
1985:4	35893.00	50558.19	125531.0	143250.8
1986:1	38164.00	54147.70	124272.0	147917.8
1986:2	33978.00	46643.46	121883.0	138898.9
1986:3	33508.00	45773.27	123921.0	141878.7
1986:4	42694.00	62246.83	139474.0	181815.6
1987:1	40997.00	56987.27	138303.0	178087.8
1987:2	42158.00	58707.67	139045.0	179361.8
1987:3	43708.00	60259.25	142746.0	184685.2
1987:4	52416.00	74869.13	158271.0	208690.8
1988:1	51818.00	71595.28	163162.0	210382.8
1988:2	50140.00	68032.34	169025.0	215989.6
1988:3	49423.00	69133.50	173868.0	224390.5
1988:4	59718.00	86796.16	195921.0	262039.4
1989:1	58411.00	81724.56	207879.0	273591.0
1989:2	59983.00	83134.91	210652.0	274206.0
1989:3	58971.00	82969.04	212578.0	277289.8
1989:4	78530.00	112768.7	251091.0	340255.1
1990:1	70774.00	100284.2	244952.0	334338.6
1990:2	69771.00	97158.65	260696.0	354209.1
1990:3	71633.00	101293.2	271819.0	376737.4
1990:4	89012.00	131177.0	297307.0	433990.5

Table 3.2 (continued)

Year	Simple-sum M1	Divisia M1	Simple-sum M2	Divisia M2
	Philippines (in million pesos)			
1991:1	82154.00	120864.8	296202.0	425474.7
1991:2	83225.00	116897.1	317175.0	445092.6
1991:3	83868.00	115583.0	307988.0	430960.2
1991:4	101374.0	148109.8	344057.0	501291.3
1992:1	95126.00	132808.3	340067.0	483430.0
1992:2	100539.0	137643.3	354771.0	503019.7
1992:3	93504.00	128718.0	346646.0	492062.3
1992:4	112092.0	161203.5	381873.0	569308.2
1993:1	105445.0	142922.9	370316.0	531380.4
1993:2	108320.0	145029.1	383118.0	545751.8
1993:3	110609.0	146017.0	396500.0	562374.0
1993:4	133877.0	183453.4	475716.0	691559.6
1994:1	123371.0	168793.4	448640.0	652736.3
1994:2	128163.0	168755.5	475009.0	684611.5
1994:3	130297.0	171695.8	514455.0	741192.0
1994:4	151952.0	213460.8	602004.0	894780.2
	Singapore (in million S$)			
1981:1	6294.00	6294.00	17304.00	17304.00
1981:2	6629.00	6502.41	17564.00	17639.73
1981:3	6450.00	6408.59	17720.00	17735.12
1981:4	7242.00	7107.72	19671.00	19665.33
1982:1	7148.00	7081.75	19488.00	19574.32
1982:2	7411.00	7312.25	19527.00	19715.45
1982:3	7563.00	7512.55	20970.00	21028.46
1982:4	8157.00	8149.63	22804.00	22900.42
1983:1	8306.00	8301.83	23229.00	23397.51
1983:2	8240.00	8255.18	23723.00	23721.20
1983:3	8091.00	8236.23	23729.00	23827.93
1983:4	8607.00	8698.31	25525.00	25461.37
1984:1	8227.00	8516.76	25615.00	25559.62
1984:2	8432.00	8687.82	25794.00	25807.55
1984:3	8207.00	8506.13	25644.00	25620.87
1984:4	8866.00	9081.43	27120.00	27125.26

Table 3.2 (continued)

Year	Simple-sum M1	Divisia M1	Simple-sum M2	Divisia M2
	Singapore (in million S$)			
1985:1	8662.00	8988.55	26373.00	26657.38
1985:2	8673.00	9034.60	26545.00	26857.40
1985:3	8293.00	8693.45	26904.00	26973.96
1985:4	8785.00	9145.29	28148.00	28199.67
1986:1	8786.00	9178.29	27970.00	28110.64
1986:2	8894.00	9206.06	28588.00	28529.72
1986:3	9124.00	9348.99	29514.00	29419.57
1986:4	9821.00	10005.06	30954.00	31181.76
1987:1	9996.00	10187.54	31474.00	31741.63
1987:2	10631.00	10599.98	33631.00	33593.31
1987:3	10322.00	10423.52	34806.00	34712.20
1987:4	11031.00	11083.55	37089.00	36943.52
1988:1	11702.00	11601.18	36728.00	36747.22
1988:2	11182.00	11278.75	37534.00	37577.78
1988:3	11046.00	11219.99	38733.00	38678.80
1988:4	11958.00	12099.64	42088.00	41917.38
1989:1	12013.00	12178.21	43927.00	43615.02
1989:2	12537.00	12631.25	46719.00	46123.22
1989:3	12839.00	12914.44	49087.00	48227.03
1989:4	13745.00	13793.46	51546.00	50717.30
1990:1	13690.00	13762.20	53866.00	52565.61
1990:2	13688.00	13738.87	55999.00	53895.77
1990:3	13694.00	13824.34	58819.00	55937.01
1990:4	15260.00	15147.46	61844.00	59192.35
1991:1	14937.00	15020.63	62951.00	60233.93
1991:2	14633.00	14784.75	65033.00	61082.74
1991:3	14721.00	14760.18	67222.00	61876.06
1991:4	16430.00	16121.77	69542.00	65933.42
1992:1	16694.00	16366.02	71621.00	67629.23
1992:2	17033.00	16607.24	73073.00	68809.16
1992:3	17905.00	17030.36	74675.00	70392.44
1992:4	18515.00	17962.79	75727.00	72814.56
1993:1	18769.00	18075.89	75737.00	73244.63
1993:2	19219.00	18290.69	76482.00	74207.66
1993:3	19978.00	18553.96	78535.00	76097.69
1993:4	22882.00	20207.60	82130.00	82492.74
1994:1	22491.00	20208.02	82313.00	81615.77
1994:2	22397.00	20107.88	85710.00	83581.47
1994:3	23139.00	20587.22	89990.00	87131.38
1994:4	23411.00	21053.26	93980.00	90560.91

Table 3.2 (continued)

Year	Simple-sum M1	Divisia M1	Simple-sum M2	Divisia M2
	South Korea (in billion won)			
1981:1	3825.00	3825.00	13013.00	13013.00
1981:2	3711.00	3709.57	13398.00	13265.25
1981:3	3286.00	3357.52	14265.00	13769.80
1981:4	3982.00	4067.08	15671.00	15519.72
1982:1	3942.00	4025.34	16269.00	15926.25
1982:2	4213.00	4297.54	17288.00	16977.96
1982:3	5552.00	5689.91	19012.00	19510.45
1982:4	5800.00	5935.96	19905.00	20410.14
1983:1	5625.00	5751.05	20181.00	20530.56
1983:2	5690.00	5807.15	20972.00	21209.93
1983:3	6288.00	6444.59	21979.00	22553.11
1983:4	6783.00	6982.44	22938.00	23766.38
1984:1	6610.00	6803.94	23020.00	23708.01
1984:2	6142.00	6328.32	22908.00	23371.58
1984:3	6631.00	6838.73	23761.00	24561.11
1984:4	6820.00	7110.04	24705.00	25529.98
1985:1	6527.00	6811.43	24895.00	25638.21
1985:2	6017.00	6289.79	25718.00	26248.71
1985:3	6894.00	7229.75	27496.00	28730.98
1985:4	7557.00	7919.49	28564.00	30391.01
1986:1	7143.00	7489.03	29143.00	30734.12
1986:2	6893.00	7230.11	30456.00	31612.04
1986:3	7576.00	7951.26	31890.00	33857.93
1986:4	8809.00	9261.95	33833.00	36973.46
1987:1	7712.00	8104.25	33409.00	36090.99
1987:2	8283.00	8698.57	35999.00	38623.04
1987:3	9632.00	10108.87	38036.00	42041.04
1987:4	10108.00	10774.01	40280.00	44900.65
1988:1	8542.00	9107.29	39812.00	43122.37
1988:2	9248.00	9860.12	42079.00	45533.48
1988:3	10372.00	11116.79	45113.00	49266.15
1988:4	12151.00	13016.25	48938.00	54124.99
1989:1	10029.00	10762.96	47739.00	51095.43
1989:2	10750.00	11532.91	49292.00	52659.52
1989:3	11881.00	12752.57	52455.00	56203.89
1989:4	14329.00	15394.76	58638.00	63715.15
1990:1	13347.00	14338.36	58454.00	63687.56
1990:2	12812.00	13777.36	60470.00	65209.70
1990:3	14786.00	16476.10	64553.00	71429.91
1990:4	15905.00	17893.15	68707.00	76333.43

Table 3.2 (continued)

Year	Simple-sum M1	Divisia M1	Simple-sum M2	Divisia M2
	South Korea (in billion won)			
1991:1	15328.00	17247.43	70168.00	77536.27
1991:2	15060.00	16953.49	72213.00	79923.65
1991:3	16178.00	18240.91	76170.00	84662.70
1991:4	21752.00	24685.68	83746.00	96443.63
1992:1	19702.00	22351.64	83804.00	95571.06
1992:2	21496.00	24430.76	86184.00	99654.19
1992:3	22084.00	25144.00	89346.00	103927.4
1992:4	24587.00	28069.31	96259.00	113305.1
1993:1	23735.00	27179.64	97500.00	113592.6
1993:2	24170.00	27655.61	100760.0	117442.8
1993:3	30644.00	36000.18	111388.0	134470.4
1993:4	29041.00	34106.34	112219.0	134757.5
1994:1	26392.00	30969.60	112212.0	132924.7
1994:2	28344.00	33232.93	117849.0	139580.5
1994:3	28819.00	33892.32	122747.0	144875.5
1994:4	32510.00	38225.79	133178.0	156371.5
	Sri Lanka (in million rupees)			
1981:1	10124.00	10124.00	21983.00	21983.00
1981:2	9033.00	9628.29	21681.00	21821.38
1981:3	9444.00	9935.50	23459.00	22927.63
1981:4	10024.00	10474.63	24446.00	24202.52
1982:1	11671.00	11921.02	28240.00	27234.62
1982:2	10815.00	11405.66	28739.00	27443.46
1982:3	11171.00	12178.00	29781.00	29390.49
1982:4	11760.00	12999.52	30510.00	31315.04
1983:1	12986.00	14996.34	32874.00	34891.13
1983:2	12589.00	14165.81	32798.00	34455.35
1983:3	13322.00	15154.40	34620.00	36591.87
1983:4	14748.00	15970.78	37257.00	38931.89
1984:1	15440.00	16985.17	39763.00	41378.82
1984:2	14768.00	16555.09	39690.00	41226.43
1984:3	15549.00	17516.42	40809.00	42904.73
1984:4	16824.00	18591.71	43428.00	46412.85

Table 3.2 (continued)

Year	Simple-sum M1	Divisia M1	Simple-sum M2	Divisia M2
	Sri Lanka (in million rupees)			
1985:1	17236.00	20818.84	45230.00	50631.01
1985:2	17340.00	20114.98	46234.00	50538.39
1985:3	17461.00	20353.07	47918.00	52117.48
1985:4	18760.00	21312.80	48408.00	53588.94
1986:1	20453.00	24016.67	49410.00	56582.59
1986:2	19949.00	23609.27	48960.00	56131.18
1986:3	20398.00	23992.49	49429.00	56688.25
1986:4	21179.00	25115.41	50860.00	58944.64
1987:1	22556.00	27286.39	53855.00	62990.57
1987:2	22075.00	26648.71	53942.00	62984.60
1987:3	22973.00	27578.73	55927.00	65135.01
1987:4	25047.00	29218.54	58299.00	67436.99
1988:1	26640.00	33312.54	61081.00	72892.52
1988:2	27791.00	33744.32	63117.00	74555.77
1988:3	28453.00	34607.79	63932.00	76094.72
1988:4	32379.00	40120.38	69945.00	82737.46
1989:1	32609.00	40771.30	69835.00	85139.98
1989:2	32037.00	39858.96	69717.00	84897.84
1989:3	34527.00	42578.34	72965.00	89208.84
1989:4	35368.00	42716.33	76464.00	93442.06
1990:1	37401.00	46634.13	81168.00	100297.0
1990:2	36386.00	44622.66	81407.00	99480.22
1990:3	37429.00	45428.68	85057.00	102870.6
1990:4	37429.00	45428.68	88568.00	107329.2
1991:1	41941.00	51298.72	93880.00	114861.2
1991:2	41624.00	49754.81	96477.00	115832.2
1991:3	43274.00	51676.65	101896.0	121474.1
1991:4	47054.00	53973.87	112097.0	131249.1
1992:1	48311.00	57230.22	116192.0	137590.9
1992:2	47006.00	54621.32	117626.0	137796.8
1992:3	47285.00	55783.82	120446.0	142365.8
1992:4	50490.00	59282.96	130701.0	153569.1
1993:1	53868.00	64507.82	140061.0	165934.8
1993:2	52465.00	62749.61	139509.0	166597.8
1993:3	55148.00	66680.24	146286.0	176762.5
1993:4	60104.00	69631.68	161362.0	190539.2
1994:1	63764.00	73852.02	167443.0	198565.3
1994:2	63082.00	73151.44	172529.0	203534.8
1994:3	66866.00	78962.06	179287.0	214943.0
1994:4	71520.00	84307.73	192990.0	231583.8

Table 3.2 (continued)

Year	Simple-sum M1	Divisia M1	Simple-sum M2	Divisia M2
	Taiwan (in billion new Taiwan dollars)			
1981:1	381.00	381.00	963.00	963.00
1981:2	409.00	406.59	1024.00	1024.39
1981:3	397.00	396.40	1032.00	1017.79
1981:4	450.00	450.86	1130.00	1140.61
1982:1	435.00	432.05	1160.00	1117.10
1982:2	465.00	458.70	1247.00	1189.84
1982:3	479.00	473.71	1305.00	1235.04
1982:4	521.00	511.82	1410.00	1333.31
1983:1	525.00	513.99	1482.00	1351.84
1983:2	557.00	541.32	1584.00	1425.45
1983:3	566.00	550.86	1657.00	1452.82
1983:4	616.00	600.35	1781.00	1582.10
1984:1	603.00	587.53	1842.00	1553.36
1984:2	634.00	607.91	1947.00	1608.63
1984:3	635.00	607.03	2026.00	1609.81
1984:4	669.00	643.35	2134.00	1705.89
1985:1	665.00	638.49	2236.00	1712.40
1985:2	682.00	651.29	2355.00	1768.53
1985:3	686.00	660.31	2475.00	1830.48
1985:4	752.00	720.21	2634.00	1970.20
1986:1	790.00	753.11	2739.00	2053.81
1986:2	881.00	833.19	2868.00	2198.03
1986:3	966.00	911.29	3026.00	2372.48
1986:4	1138.00	1075.31	3299.00	2784.51
1987:1	1199.00	1128.69	3466.00	2922.54
1987:2	1318.00	1226.97	3694.00	3171.88
1987:3	1375.00	1280.30	3807.00	3310.11
1987:4	1568.00	1466.21	4175.00	3781.04
1988:1	1578.00	1472.32	4274.00	3802.12
1988:2	1719.00	1589.82	4509.00	4101.12
1988:3	1778.00	1659.62	4642.00	4278.86
1988:4	1951.00	1824.24	4921.00	4692.59
1989:1	2056.00	1924.17	5090.00	4943.57
1989:2	1847.00	1759.30	5272.00	4644.80
1989:3	1899.00	1814.93	5350.00	4776.19
1989:4	2068.00	1984.29	5671.00	5206.04
1990:1	1878.00	1821.12	5734.00	4929.75
1990:2	1821.00	1761.45	5767.00	4830.22
1990:3	1756.00	1694.95	5938.00	4716.20
1990:4	1931.00	1859.07	6230.00	5136.92

Table 3.2 (continued)

Year	Simple-sum M1	Divisia M1	Simple-sum M2	Divisia M2
	Taiwan (in billion new Taiwan dollars)			
1991:1	1962.00	1900.87	6504.00	5266.75
1991:2	2069.00	1981.06	6777.00	5490.66
1991:3	1972.00	1890.10	6967.00	5331.67
1991:4	2165.00	2076.57	7396.00	5787.53
1992:1	2265.00	2165.77	7574.00	5991.23
1992:2	2366.00	2249.09	8082.00	6273.34
1992:3	2263.00	2153.10	8416.00	6187.36
1992:4	2434.00	2331.40	8864.00	6622.65
1993:1	2429.00	2328.98	9091.00	6694.21
1993:2	2531.00	2410.86	9429.00	6936.24
1993:3	2499.00	2375.82	9727.00	6886.44
1993:4	2805.00	2701.48	10204.00	7750.46
1994:1	2774.00	2670.60	10481.00	7698.34
1994:2	2979.00	2852.69	10875.00	8203.09
1994:3	2939.00	2810.16	11076.00	8145.66
1994:4	3148.00	3022.97	11638.00	8679.42
	Thailand (in million baht)			
1981:1	76976.00	76976.00	265127.0	265127.0
1981:2	69989.00	70541.82	269730.0	263006.8
1981:3	67062.00	68139.28	272000.0	261634.0
1981:4	73922.00	75866.85	292904.0	292435.0
1982:1	78190.00	79432.37	310318.0	307867.0
1982:2	71486.00	74331.85	320275.0	312286.7
1982:3	72293.00	74888.68	332590.0	320109.8
1982:4	78946.00	85170.84	363820.0	370411.1
1983:1	86617.00	88350.45	391084.0	390329.4
1983:2	78891.00	84144.49	404960.0	398014.3
1983:3	76665.00	85625.58	417051.0	412446.3
1983:4	83015.00	93780.72	450500.0	451950.8
1984:1	86283.00	97002.51	464098.0	461818.1
1984:2	80170.00	89994.67	484927.0	458339.6
1984:3	78368.00	88404.50	496836.0	446426.2
1984:4	88769.00	100013.6	537885.0	503526.4

Table 3.2 (continued)

Year	Simple-sum M1	Divisia M1	Simple-sum M2	Divisia M2
	Thailand (in million baht)			
1985:1	88756.00	100014.0	549632.0	502988.4
1985:2	78452.00	90924.17	563645.0	493345.1
1985:3	81084.00	91948.71	574193.0	499848.0
1985:4	85864.00	99064.09	593494.0	527023.3
1986:1	95950.00	105237.2	613414.0	545857.6
1986:2	88975.00	99987.77	627621.0	547630.2
1986:3	92737.00	101509.8	641025.0	561319.7
1986:4	103427.0	114427.6	672773.0	621847.4
1987:1	115991.0	120498.9	703900.0	656364.4
1987:2	112229.0	114864.4	726501.0	683791.1
1987:3	110322.0	116308.9	749076.0	723790.3
1987:4	132396.0	138598.5	808585.0	782188.6
1988:1	141169.0	141408.8	833929.0	796512.3
1988:2	135470.0	138725.6	865919.0	826653.4
1988:3	130349.0	141676.4	887638.0	858848.5
1988:4	148493.0	158537.0	956126.0	934713.6
1989:1	165743.0	169416.4	1004309.	969404.6
1989:2	160760.0	163926.9	1060147.	998540.4
1989:3	164202.0	163794.2	1113678.	1019274.
1989:4	174701.0	189635.5	1207097.	1163022.
1990:1	200868.0	204172.6	1302562.	1233764.
1990:2	181952.0	193666.0	1376634.	1268216.
1990:3	186696.0	198627.6	1447788.	1307437.
1990:4	195414.0	214392.1	1529115.	1363561.
1991:1	201216.0	217220.3	1589796.	1376800.
1991:2	186813.0	205553.9	1641779.	1381330.
1991:3	188281.0	204434.0	1718510.	1345336.
1991:4	222401.0	238670.5	1832378.	1529380.
1992:1	238807.0	247840.7	1911473.	1622774.
1992:2	223922.0	240935.6	1948691.	1645976.
1992:3	225054.0	242146.1	2005013.	1660196.
1992:4	249708.0	280578.1	2117786.	1808940.
1993:1	249540.0	275936.2	2165879.	1825243.
1993:2	243736.0	270594.4	2256536.	1871408.
1993:3	251943.0	277159.5	2350802.	1936424.
1993:4	296156.0	328777.6	2507100.	2141196.
1994:1	307351.0	334078.0	2473519.	2116262.
1994:2	290715.0	324694.0	2539545.	2161086.
1994:3	315095.0	345504.2	2648337.	2235820.
1994:4	346441.0	385994.4	2829384.	2437659.

Table 3.3
Tests of Granger causality from money to output (real income)

Money series	4 lags	8 lags	12 lags	4 lags	8 lags	12 lags
	Indonesia			**Singapore**		
Simple sum M1	2.718	2.463	2.067	0.713	1.844	2.073
	[0.042]**	[0.035]**	[0.083]*	[0.587]	[0.108]	[0.082]*
Divisia M1	0.972	0.789	1.090	1.543	1.505	2.194
	[0.432]	[0.615]	[0.424]	[0.207]	[0.198]	[0.067]*
Simple sum M2	2.467	2.316	1.283	1.133	0.355	0.317
	[0.059]*	[0.046]**	[0.310]	[0.354]	[0.935]	[0.975]
Divisia M2	1.369	1.024	0.759	2.003	0.978	0.747
	[0.261]	[0.440]	[0.681]	[0.111]	[0.472]	[0.691]
	Malaysia			**South Korea**		
Simple sum M1	0.567	1.968	2.229	0.304	0.896	0.557
	[0.687]	[0.087]*	[0.063]*	[0.873]	[0.532]	[0.846]
Divisia M1	2.871	1.766	5.065	0.280	0.839	0.512
	[0.034]**	[0.125]	[0.001]**	[0.889]	[0.576]	[0.878]
Simple sum M2	1.621	1.356	0.794	0.039	0.380	0.388
	[0.187]	[0.256]	[0.651]	[0.996]	[0.922]	[0.949]
Divisia M2	0.837	0.673	0.894	0.078	0.570	0.387
	[0.509]	[0.710]	[0.568]	[0.988]	[0.793]	[0.949]
	Myanmar			**Sri Lanka**		
Simple sum M1	4.634	1.242	0.713	3.967	1.487	0.542
	[0.003]**	[0.312]	[0.719]	[0.008]**	[0.203]	[0.858]
Divisia M1	4.499	1.249	0.729	2.656	2.199	1.210
	[0.004]**	[0.308]	[0.706]	[0.046]**	[0.057]*	[0.349]
Simple sum M2	3.676	1.041	0.611	2.415	1.226	0.980
	[0.012]**	[0.430]	[0.803]	[0.064]*	[0.318]	[0.501]
Divisia M2	3.565	1.000	0.558	4.044	2.320	1.671
	[0.014]**	[0.457]	[0.844]	[0.007]**	[0.046]**	[0.161]
	Nepal			**Taiwan**		
Simple sum M1	1.638	1.358	1.382	1.683	1.471	1.326
	[0.182]	[0.255]	[0.263]	[0.172]	[0.210]	[0.289]
Divisia M1	1.590	1.349	0.986	1.758	1.459	1.302
	[0.194]	[0.259]	[0.497]	[0.155]	[0.214]	[0.301]
Simple sum M2	2.095	1.413	0.998	1.353	2.012	2.944
	[0.098]*	[0.232]	[0.488]	[0.266]	[0.080]*	[0.020]**
Divisia M2	1.876	1.937	0.978	1.836	1.789	1.358
	[0.133]	[0.092]*	[0.503]	[0.140]	[0.120]	[0.274]
	Philippines			**Thailand**		
Simple sum M1	2.995	2.356	1.205	1.833	1.680	1.201
	[0.029]**	[0.042]**	[0.349]	[0.140]	[0.145]	[0.355]
Divisia M1	3.973	3.431	1.061	0.783	1.936	2.701
	[0.008]**	[0.006]**	[0.441]	[0.542]	[0.092]*	[0.030]**
Simple sum M2	4.210	2.177	2.202	0.738	2.934	1.388
	[0.005]**	[0.058]*	[0.063]*	[0.571]	[0.015]**	[0.261]
Divisia M2	5.131	3.296	2.090	0.503	2.188	2.042
	[0.001]**	[0.008]**	[0.076]*	[0.733]	[0.058]*	[0.086]*

Notes: The numbers in square brackets are p-values. Asterisks (**), (*) denote statistically significant at 5 percent and 10 percent level respectively.

4 The P-Star Model Approach: Linking Divisia Money and Prices in the Asian Countries

Introduction

If money is to have a useful role in the Central Bank's policy process, at least two fundamental questions must be answered. First, how close is the relationship between money and the general price level in the economy? If money growth is to be a good predictor of inflation, there must be a stable relationship between the monetary aggregates and the general level of prices. Without such a close relationship, the Central Bank cannot determine the level of growth in monetary aggregates that is consistent with sustainable, non-inflationary economic growth. Second, insofar as money remains a useful predictor of inflation, which measure of money should receive the most attention? The issue of the measurement of money to be used as policy guide has not only been centered on narrow versus broad money but also between other 'weighted' monetary aggregates as potential intermediate or information variables.[1]

In the 1980s changing financial markets had disrupted the historical relationships between monetary aggregates and income and prices. The reliability of monetary aggregates as intermediate variables for monetary policy purposes has been questioned and subjected to various empirical testing.[2] Studies have concluded that the experience in the industrialised countries such as Australia, Canada, France, Italy, Japan, the United Kingdom and the United States, suggest that as a result of financial deregulation and innovations, the relationships between money and economic activities have been distorted. As a consequence, monetary aggregates, notably the narrow money M1 in those countries were dropped, and the emphasis shifted to broader monetary aggregates for policy purposes.

The experience in the United States provides a good example of the importance of financial deregulation in destabilising a particular monetary aggregate, one which had previously been the most stable. Friedman (1988: p. 440), for example, claims 'money growth has simply been irrelevant to any outcome that matters for monetary policy'. Friedman and Kuttner (1996) found that the growth of M1 has been unable to explain the price behaviour in the United States in the early 1980s. Friedman and Kuttner (1996: p. 120) conclude that 'the evidence drawn from this more structural analysis of the four-variable autoregression system suggests that increasing instability of money demand is the most consistent explanation for the fact that, sometime during the mid- to late 1980s, fluctuations in money growth ceased to anticipate subsequent fluctuations in either output or prices'.

Despite the voluminous literature that has cast doubt on the role of money in predicting output or prices, studies using the simple quantity theory were able to explain the long-run relationship between money and inflation. For example, Vogel (1974) finds that there is a proportional relationship between the rate of growth of the money supply and the rate of inflation with a lagged period of two years. Using cross-country data, Duck (1993), Dwyer and Hafer (1988) and McCandles and Weber (1995) conclude that the quantity theory was able to establish the long-run behaviour between money and the price level. Further, Dwyer and Hafer point out that countries which experience high rates of inflation also have high rates of money growth. According to McCandles and Weber (1995) and Bullard (1994) the above conclusion is robust to using different measures of money.[3]

More recently, Hallman *et al.* (1989, 1991) at the Federal Reseve Board of the United Sates have ingeniously proposed a simple 'new' model that links money and prices in the so-called P-Star approach based on the quantity theory.[4] The P-Star model approach in linking money and prices advocated by Hallman *et al.* has resulted in widespread empirical applications in other developed countries.[5] Generally, results of multi-country studies by Hoeller and Poret (1991) and Kool and Tatom (1994) indicate that the data are supportive of the P-Star model and are able to track inflation movements successfully.[6]

To date, the P-Star model approach has only been widely tested in the developed countries.[7] The empirical results obtained for the majority of the developed countries are supportive of the P-Star approach. This implies that in the long-run, some monetary aggregates (either narrow or broad or both measures) are closely linked to the price level and the rate of inflation. Clearly, the quantity theory and the equation of exchange has provided a proven and useful framework to empirically analyse the relevance of money in an economy. However, one neglected aspect of this area of research is the applicability of the P-Star approach in linking money and the price level in the developing countries. Therefore, the purpose of this chapter is to assess its usefulness for ten Asian countries, namely; Indonesia, Malaysia, Myanmar, Nepal, Philippines, Singapore, South Korea, Sri Lanka, Taiwan and Thailand.

In the estimation of the relationship of prices to monetary aggregates, the P-Star approach is preferred because in the standard reduced-form approach, the inflation equation is sensitive to the specification of its determinants such as on long distributed lags of past growth rates of money and on other factors such as supply shocks, price control or expectation variables (see Tatom, 1990). On the other hand, to determine inflation, the P-Star model depends on the level of the money stock in the previous level and the equilibrium price level (p*).

The P-Star (P*) Model: The Quantity Theory Approach

In a standard reduced-form model, the determinants of inflation range from money supply, wages, productivity, import prices, exchange rates, etc. Modelling inflation becomes more complicated when expectations are incorporated in the model and long lags of each independent variables are allowed.[8] However, more recently Hallman et al. (1989) have proposed a more simplistic modelling of inflation. In the Hallman et al. model, the discrepancy between actual price level and the equilibrium price level is the key determinant of inflation. The equilibrium price level or the so-called P-Star (P*) is determined by the level of money stock, the equilibrium velocity (V*) and the potential output (Q*). Using quarterly data covering the period 1870 to 1988 for the United States, Hallman et al. (1989, 1991) found out that 'P* ties together the level of money and prices' very well, and seem to support the contention that 'inflation is a monetary phenomenon'. Hallman et al. (1991: p. 857) conclude that, 'P* through its dependence on long-run values of velocity and output can be used to indicate long-term price developments'.

The P* approach is based on the equation of exchange. According to the equation of exchange

$$PQ = MV \qquad (4.1)$$

where the product of the price level (P) and real GNP (Q) equals the stock of money (M), multiplied by its velocity (V). Taking logarithms (lowercase notation) for equation (4.1) gives

$$p + q = m + v \qquad (4.2)$$

From equation (4.2), the price level can be expressed as

$$p = m + v - q \qquad (4.3)$$

According to Hallman *et al.* (1991), the equilibrium price level (p*) is written as follows

$$p^* = m + v^* - q^* \qquad (4.4)$$

where v^* is the equilibrium level of velocity and q^* is the real potential output. Equation (4.4) says that the equilibrium price level, p^*, is defined as money stock per unit of real potential output and the long-run equilibrium level of the velocity of money. Subtracting equations (4.4) from (4.3) we have the following P-Star model derived by Hallman *et al.* (1989, 1991),

$$p - p^* = (v - v^*) + (q^* - q) \qquad (4.5)$$

According to equation (4.5), the gap between the actual and equilibrium prices, $p - p^*$, is determined by a velocity gap, $v - v^*$, and an output gap, $q^* - q$. The P-Star model indicates inflationary pressure if there is a monetary overhang, that is when current velocity is below its long-run equilibrium level and/or when current output is above its potential level.

Hallman *et al.* (1991) hypothesize that in the long-run, the discrepancy between actual and equilibrium prices, $p - p^*$, becomes zero as p adjusts to p*. Assuming the long-run relationship between p and p*, the short-run dynamic model of inflation is therefore given by the following model,

$$\Delta \pi_t = \phi + \alpha(p_{t-1} - p^*_{t-1}) + \sum_{i=1}^{k} \beta_i \Delta \pi_{t-i} + \varepsilon_t \qquad (4.6)$$

where π is the inflation rate, and α is the speed of adjustment of actual prices to p* and should be negative. Hallman *et al.* (1991) also propose estimating an alternative inflation model based on its components. Substituting equations (4.5) into (4.6) we have the unrestricted inflation model of the following form

$$\Delta \pi_t = \phi + \gamma_1(v_{t-1} - v^*_{t-1}) + \gamma_2(q^*_{t-1} - q_{t-1})$$
$$+ \sum_{i=1}^{k} \beta_i \Delta \pi_{t-i} + \varepsilon_t \qquad (4.7)$$

Hallman *et al.* (1991) constrained the velocity gap, $v_{t-1} - v^*_{t-1}$, and the output gap, $q^*_{t-1} - q_{t-1}$, in equation (4.7) to have equal weights, that is $\gamma_1 = \gamma_2$. Equation (4.7) presents two competing view of how the rate of inflation adjusts from a disequilibrium position. The Phillips curve view or the output gap model of inflation is the special case of equation (4.7) in which $\gamma_1 = 0$. In this case, the inflation rate adjusts to the output gap. On the other hand, the monetarist model of inflation is when $\gamma_2 = 0$, in which the inflation rate adjusts to monetary disequilibrium.

A central issue in empirical testing of the P-Star modelling approach is how to measure potential output (q*) and equilibrium velocity (v*) since these two series are unobservable. In implementing the P-Star approach, Hoeller and Poret (1991) and Kool and Tatom (1994) apply the HP-filter to compute potential output and equilibrium velocity. Hoeller and Poret (1991) and Razzak and Dennis (1996) have pointed out that the HP-filter is easy to implement (compared to the more complicated Kalman filter) and the trends it produces usually appear 'plausible'. However, the HP-filter has been criticised on several grounds, which among others are (a) the computation of the trend component is sensitive to the choice of λ, (b) the filter can alter the properties of the series, (c) the filter can lead to spurious cyclical behaviour and (d) the filter can generate business cycle dynamics even if none are present in the original series. See for example King and Rebelo (1993), Jaeger (1994) and Cogley and Nason (1995).

Nevertheless, other approaches to calculating equilibrium velocity are provided by Corker and Haas (1991), Atta-Mensah (1996), Kole and Leahy (1991) and Todter and Reimers (1994). Corker and Haas (1991) have estimated a velocity function in testing the usefulness of the P-Star model for the South Korea. The relationship between income velocity and interest rate was tested for cointegration and the residuals from the cointegrating regression was used as the velocity gap, $v - v^*$, in the calculation of the price gap, $p - p^*$ (see equation (4.5)).

On the other hand, Kole and Leahy (1991), Todter and Reimers (1994) and Atta-Mensah (1996) have estimated a long-run money demand function to compute equilibrium velocity, v^*. Let the long-run money demand be of the following form

$$m_t - p_t = \theta_0 + \theta_1 q_t + \theta_2 r_t + \varepsilon_t \qquad (4.8)$$

where m, p, q and r are respectively money, the price level, output and the nominal interest rate. The long-run equilibrium price level, p^*, that will correspond to the current level of money, potential output and equilibrium interest rate can be expressed as

$$p^*_t = m_t - \theta_0 - \theta_1 q^*_t - \theta_2 r^*_t \qquad (4.9)$$

From equations (4.8) and (4.9) the implied price gap is

$$p_t - p^*_t = \theta_1(q^*_t - q_t) + \theta_2(r^*_t - r_t) - \varepsilon_t \qquad (4.10)$$

where the price gap is defined as the sum of the output gap, the interest rate gap and the money gap (ε_t). Substituting equations (4.8) into (4.10) we have the following equation

$$p_t - p^*_t = \theta_1(q^*_t - q_t) + \theta_2(r^*_t - r_t) - [(m_t - p_t) \\ - (\hat{\theta}_0 + \hat{\theta}_1 q_t + \hat{\theta}_2 r_t)] \qquad (4.11)$$

In their empirical analysis, Todter and Reimers (1994) have estimated equation (4.9) to arrive at the estimates of parameter θ's.[9] The time series of p^* was then calculated from the fitted values of this regression. Atta-Mensah (1996), on the other hand, has estimated the following P-Star equation which was derived from substituting equations (4.10) into (4.6),

$$\pi_t = \Theta_0 + \Theta_1(q^*_t - q_t) + \Theta\Theta_2(r^*_t - r_t) - \Theta_3[(m_t - p_t)$$
$$- (\hat{\theta}_0 + \hat{\theta}_1 q_t + \hat{\theta}_2 r_t)] + \sum_{i=1}^{k} \beta_i \pi_{t-i} + \eta_t \qquad (4.12)$$

In estimating equation (4.12), equilibrium output (q^*) and interest rate (r^*) need to be defined and estimated.

To construct an equilibrium velocity, Kole and Leahy define the equilibrium velocity, v^*, as follows. From equation (4.4) we expressed v^* as

$$v^* = p^* - m + q^* \qquad (4.13)$$

Substituting equations (4.9) into (4.13) we have

$$v^* = q^* - (\theta_0 + \theta_1 q^*_t + \theta_2 r^*_t)] \qquad (4.14)$$

and finally,

$$v^* = - [\theta_0 + (1-\theta_1)q^*_t + \theta_2 r^*_t] \qquad (4.15)$$

The next step in determining v^* in equation (4.15) is to obtain the long-run equilibrium values for q^* and r^*. In their study on Japan and Germany, Kole and Leahy (1991) have included wealth as an additional regressor as determinant for money demand. The v^* obtained is then used to compute p^* as defined by equation (4.4).

Cointegration and the P-Star Approach

The theory of cointegration suggests that if the P-Star approach is to qualify as a valid empirical model, p and p^* must be cointegrated. In other words, there must be a long-run relationship between the two, and the difference between p and p^* must be stationary. To illustrate this point, we express v, as

$$v = p - m + q \qquad (4.16)$$

Now we define a model for v (say, nominal interest rate, r, as the only determinant) as follows

$$v = \varphi_0 + \varphi_1 r_t + \mu_t \qquad (4.17)$$

where r_t is the nominal interest rate, φ's are parameters to be estimated and μ is the error term. We then can define v* as the long-run equation given below

$$v^* = \hat{\varphi}_0 + \hat{\varphi}_1 r_t \qquad (4.18)$$

Using equations (4.16) and (4.18), we can also express v* as follows

$$v^* = p - m + q - \mu_t \qquad (4.19)$$

For illustrative purposes we define p* as follows[10]

$$p^* = m + v^* - q \qquad (4.20)$$

Now, the cointegration theory says that, if p and p* is cointegrated then p - p* must be stationary. Thus

$$p - p^* = v_t \qquad (4.21)$$

where v_t is stationary. Now by substituting equations (4.20) into (4.21) we have the following

$$p - m - v^* + q = v_t \qquad (4.22)$$

Substitute equations (4.19) into (4.22) we have

$$p - m - p + m - q + \mu_t + q = v_t \qquad (4.23)$$

or equivalently

$$\mu_t = v_t \qquad (4.24)$$

Equation (4.24) imply that for v_t (i.e. p - p*) to be stationary we require that μ_t is stationary. For μ_t to be stationary we will require that r (or any set of relevant determinants of velocity) and v or r (or any set of relevant determinants of velocity), p, q and m form a cointegrating set of variables.

On the other hand, following Bordes *et al.* (1993), one can also arrive at the P-Star model as follows. Let specify the standard velocity function as

$$v_t = \alpha_0 + \alpha_1 q_t + \alpha_2 r_t + \varepsilon_t \qquad (4.25)$$

Substituting equations (4.25) into (4.3), we have the following reduced form equation,

$$p_t = \alpha_0 - (1 - \alpha_1)q_t + \alpha_2 r_t + m_t + \varepsilon_t \qquad (4.26)$$

In the long-run the price level, p, should be cointegrated with its determinants - q, r and m. According to the Granger Representation Theorem, not only does cointegration imply the existence of an error-correction model but also the converse is true, that is the existence of an error-correction model implies cointegration of the variables (Engle and Granger, 1987). Therefore it follows that the P-Star model can be represented by the following error-correction representation

$$\Delta p_t = \beta_0 + \beta_1 \varepsilon_{t-1} + \sum_{i=1}^{K} \beta_i \Delta p_{t-i} + \varpi_t \qquad (4.27)$$

where ε_{t-1} is the lagged residuals (i.e. $p_{t-1} - p^*_{t-1}$) saved from running the static cointegrating equation (4.26). The hypothesis that p_t is not cointegrated with m_t, q_t and r_t can be rejected if the coefficient on the error-correction term, β_1 is significant, regardless of the joint significance of the β_i coefficients. Thus, our point of interest is that $\beta_1<0$ and significantly different from zero implies that p and p* are cointegrated.

Our main concern is regarding the appropriate specification of the velocity function. It has been shown that the standard velocity function (or money demand) as specified in equation (4.25) is inadequate to represent a long-run velocity function. Studies in the 1980s in the majority of the developed countries have indicated that income velocity has been variable. In other words the movement of monetary aggregates cannot be used to predict the movements in income. The breakdown in the historical relationship between monetary aggregates and income to a greater extent reflects structural changes and financial innovations in the financial system. This has led reseachers to re-specify the money demand or velocity function to take into account 'new' variables that could better explain the recent behaviour in money and velocity.

Friedman (1984) argues that the decline in velocity during the 1980s in the United States is due to the significant volatility of money growth. An increase in uncertainty about the future course of monetary growth leads individuals to hold more money, thus reducing velocity. Following Friedman, others have incorporated other measures of financial uncertainty into the velocity function. On the one hand, Payne (1995) includes interest rate variability, and on the other, Caruso (1996) includes among others, a measure of risk and the uncertainty in stock prices in the velocity function. In refining the work of Friedman (1984), Serletis (1990) proposes that monetary variability should be decomposed into anticipated and unanticipated components. Serletis points out that since uncertainty about the future leads to a change in behaviour about velocity, uncertainty is more properly captured by unanticipated movements in the money supply. For the United States, Serletis (1990: p. 782) concludes that 'expanding the velocity growth information set to include unanticipated monetary growth data increases the predictability of velocity growth'.

Attempts at explaining why conventional models have failed to accurately predict the behaviour of velocity has led Bordo and Jonung (1987) to propose institutional and financial factors as determinants in a velocity function. According to the so-called institutional approach, velocity is influenced by two sets of institutional factors, namely; the monetisation and financial development variables. In the former, Bordo and Jonung propose using two sets of proxies, that is the share of the labor force in non-agricultural pursuits and currency-money ratio. For the latter, Bordo and Jonung have used the ratio of total non-bank financial assets to total financial assets. Apart from these variables, Bordo and Jonung also propose including a proxy for economic stability in the velocity function. Bordo and Jonung (1990) explain that the process of monetisation accounts for the downward trend in velocity. With the spread of banking (reflected by the currency-money ratio) and growing urbanisation (measured by the share of labor force in non-agricultural pursuit), velocity falls at first because of the growing dependence on money for conducting transactions (monetisation of the economy). In a later stage of development, velocity will rise as a result of financial sophistication and improved economic stability. Financial sophistication refers both to the emergence of close substitutes for money and to the development of methods of economising on cash balances. Economic stability will reduce the precautionary demand for money and thus raises velocity. Bordo and Jonung (1990: p. 167) stress that 'these institutional explanatory variables are additional to or supercede the standard determinants of velocity, including real income and interest rates'. Studies by Siklos (1993) and Raj (1995) have supported the institutional hypothesis of the velocity of money and they conclude that these institutional factors are necessary to maintain a long-run relationship.

In another development, Hoggarth and Pill (1992) have proposed incorporating a direct measure of financial innovation in a velocity function. Following the work of Hall *et al.* (1990), a cumulative interest rate was used to capture the effect of transaction technology - interest-bearing current accounts, liquid savings accounts and Automated Teller Machines (ATMs) for the United Kingdom. Yet in another study, Melvin and Shiau (1990) propose a velocity model that incorporates 'political instability' as one of its determinants. According to Melvin and Shiau, in a developing country, the effect of a shift in the expected loss of private non-monetary assets due to political instability is substantial. If such assets are subject to loss while money is not, we would expect a greater demand for liquidity as property rights become less certain. Thus, due to changes in political regime and as the probability of losing such assets increases, we would expect individuals to seek to sell assets in an attempt to hold more liquid assets, like money. Using a cross-sectional data on 63 developing countries, Melvin and Shiau found that the threat of loss due to political instability (proxied by the number of political crisis events) has a significant negative effect on velocity.

The Empirical Results

The Model Used

In this study, we specify the following velocity function

$$v_t = f(q_t, r_t, cm_t) \quad (4.28)$$

It follows that, the price equation can then be specified as follows

$$p_t = g(q_t, r_t, m_t, cm_t) \quad (4.29)$$

where p and q are respectively price level and real output. Variable r is the interest rate to proxy for opportunity cost, m_t is Divisia money and cm refers to monetisation variable proxy by currency-money ratio. In estimating the cointegration relation (4.29) we have transformed all variables into logarithm except for the interest rate.

Data Used in the Analysis

In the analysis, we use quarterly time series data for the period 1981:1 to 1994:4.[11] For the purpose of this study, we have used the consumer price index as a measure of the price level for all ten Asian countries. Since there is no *a priori* evidence as to which measure of money should be used - narrow or broad money, we examined both Divisia monetary aggregates M1 and M2 in the construction of P-Star.[12] Empirical studies have shown that different monetary aggregates used to construct P-Star have different implications for the performance of the P-Star approach. For example, in the United States, Hallman *et al.* (1991) have indicated that M2 can be a good anchor for the price level, but Tatom (1990) on the other hand, suggests that money and the price level are linked when M1 is used to construct P-Star. For France, Bordes *et al.* (1993) use monetary aggregates M1, M2 and M3 to calculate P-Star, and found that a long-run relationship between money and the price level was established using M1 and M2. On the contrary, Todter and Reimers (1994) found that between the three monetary aggregates (M1, M2 and M3), 'the best results were obtained when M3 is used to estimate the equilibrium price'.

For output, we have used gross domestic product (GDP) deflated by the consumer price index for Singapore, South Korea and Taiwan. Since GDP for other Asian countries are only available in annual form, we have used total exports as a proxy for nominal income for these countries. The rationale of using exports as proxy for income in the Asian countries has been supported by numerous empirical studies, for example by Tyler (1981), Feder (1983), Kavoussi (1984), Ram (1987), Moschos (1989) and Odedokun (1991). Furthermore, Dutt and Ghosh (1994, 1996) found that exports and economic growth are cointegrated in the majority of the developing countries. These studies have empirically detected positive and significant effects of export expansion on economic growth.[13] Data on the consumer price index, gross domestic product, total exports, monetary aggregates and their components were compiled from various issues of the *SEACEN Financial Statistics-Money and Banking* published by the SEACEN Centre, and *International Financial Statistics* published by the International Monetary Fund.

Statistical Properties of the Series

The first stage of the procedure consists in examining the statistical properties of the different time series used. Unit root tests were conducted to determine whether the series are stationary processes. Both the standard Dickey-Fuller (DF) and augmented Dickey-Fuller (ADF) tests are based on the assumption of at most one unit root. However, Dickey and Pantula (1987) suggest using sequential tests that check for three unit roots, then two unit roots and finally a single unit root. The Dickey-Pantula sequential 'testing-down' procedure comprises the following three steps.

Step I:

$$HO_3: y_t \sim I(3); \qquad HA: y_t \sim I(2)$$

Compute *t*-statistic of α_3 from the following auxiliary regression:

$$\Delta^3 y_t = \alpha_0 + \alpha_3 \Delta^2 y_{t-1} + \sum_{i=1}^{k} \Delta^3 y_{t-i} + \varepsilon_t \qquad (4.30)$$

If HO_3 is rejected (compare *t*-statistic associated with estimated α_3 against critical value from τ_μ Tables of Fuller (1976)), go to step II.

Step II:

$$HO_2: y_t \sim I(2); \qquad HA: y_t \sim I(1)$$

Compute *t*-statistic for α_2 from the following equation

$$\Delta^3 y_t = \alpha_0 + \alpha_2 \Delta y_{t-1} + \alpha_3 \Delta^2 y_{t-1} + \sum_{i=1}^{k} \Delta^3 y_{t-i} + \varepsilon_t \qquad (4.31)$$

If HO_2 is rejected, go to step III.

Step III:

$$HO_1: y_t \sim I(1); \qquad HA: y_t \sim I(0)$$

Compute t-statistic for α_1 from the regression

$$\Delta^3 y_t = \alpha_0 + \alpha_1 y_{t-1} + \alpha_2 \Delta y_{t-1} + \alpha_3 \Delta^2 y_{t-1}$$
$$+ \sum_{i=1}^{k} \Delta^3 y_{t-i} + \varepsilon_t \qquad (4.32)$$

The presence of lagged dependent variables is to ensure the error terms are white noise. The results of the Dickey-Pantula unit root tests on all seven series for each country are presented in Table 4.1.

It follows from Table 4.1 that the null hypothesis of the presence of three unit roots can be rejected for all seven series for all Asian countries, while one cannot reject the hypothesis of two unit roots in some of the series investigated. In particular, for the price level, two unit roots cannot be rejected for all Asian countries, while for the money series two unit roots can be rejected for Myanmar, the Philippines and South Korea. In most cases real output, interest rate and monetisation variables have a single unit root. Nevertheless, the order of integration of each series for each country is shown in Table 4.2. For example, in the case of Malaysia, the price, money and real output series are stationary after second differencing and the interest rate and monetisation series are stationary after first differencing. Hence, we may write: $p_t \sim I(2)$, $m_t \sim I(2)$, $q_t \sim I(2)$, $cm_t \sim I(1)$, $r_t \sim I(1)$, $\Delta p_t \sim I(1)$, $\Delta m_t \sim I(1)$, $\Delta q_t \sim I(1)$, $\Delta cm_t \sim I(0)$, $\Delta r_t \sim I(0)$, $\Delta^2 p_t \sim I(0)$, $\Delta^2 m_t \sim I(0)$, $\Delta^2 q_t \sim I(0)$. The presence of two unit roots for the price level implies that the inflation rate (π) for Malaysia has a unit root, that is $\pi \sim I(1)$.

Cointegration Analysis

After determining the order of integration among the series involved, we will determine the long-run equilibrium for the p* described by relation (4.29). To test this proposition we run the cointegrating regressions with all I(1) variables and the results are presented in Table 4.3. The null hypothesis of no cointegration can be inferred from the CRDW and ADF statistics. In the case of Indonesia, in both cases, we observe that the CRDW statistics are significantly different from zero and thus implies the existence of a cointegration relationship. The ADF statistics for both money series used to construct p* are significantly different from zero. These test results suggest that the residuals from (4.29) are I(0) and hence lend evidence supporting cointegration and also implying a long-run equilibrium relationships between p_t and m_t, q_t, r_t and cm_t.

As shown in Table 4.3, similar results showing the presence of a long-run equilibrium for the p* are also supported for Malaysia, Myanmar, the Philippines, Singapore, Sri Lanka, Taiwan and Thailand. For South Korea, only in the case of Divisia M1 that cointegration can be rejected. Despite these results, we run the error-correction models for all countries. In doing so, we allow for the possibility of any relationship between p_t and m_t, r_t, q_t and cm_t by specifying a restricted error-correction model (equation 4.27), thus permitting a direct test for cointegration. Kremers *et al.* (1992) show that the statistical significance of the error-correction term (ε_{t-1}) can be interpreted as evidence of cointegration.

P-Star and the Error-Correction Models

The estimated error-correction model described the P-Star model equation where the rate of inflation - measured by the quarterly variation in p, depends on its own lagged values and on the gap between the actual value of the price level and its value corresponding to the long-term equilibrium of the economy ($p_t - p^*_t = \varepsilon_t$). In Tables 4.4 through 4.6 we present the estimates of the error-correction models. Interestingly, our results show that the error-correction regressions for both Divisia monetary aggregates used to form p* performed satisfactorily for all countries. In all cases the coefficients of the error-correction terms are significantly different from zero and show correctly negative signs. Furthermore, none of the diagnostic test statistics are significant at the 5 percent level suggesting no evidence of misspecification or of autocorrelated, heteroscedastic, or non-normal errors.[14] Thus, all estimated error-correction equations appear as a data admissible simplication of the general model.

For example, for South Korea, in particular in the case of Divisia M1, the error-correction terms are highly significantly different from zero at the five percent level for both models implying the existence of cointegration between p_t and its determinants. This is contrary to the results obtained from the Engle-Granger cointegration tests. These contradictory results clearly show the low power of the Engle-Granger two-step test for cointegration demonstrated by Banerjee *et al.* (1986) and Kremers *et al.* (1992).

To summarise the results presented above it appears that; (i) it most cases the price level and Divisia money series are I(2) variables and thus need second differencing to achieve stationarity, (ii) the model that comprises of money supply, real output, interest rate, and a monetisation variable as regressors does constitute a cointegration vector - as determinant in the price equation, (iii) although the estimates of the Engle-Granger two-step method are inferior to those derived from the error-correction, the results suggest that most cases, exhibit cointegration between p_t and q_t, r_t, m_t and cm_t, (iv) the satisfactory results of the error-correction models clearly suggest that the monetary data of the Asian countries support the P-Star approach of modelling inflation, and (v) comparing the estimated price equations between the two monetary aggregates used to construct p*, our results indicate that both monetary aggregates performed equally well, in that the P-Star significantly influences the price development in all the countries investigated.

Further Results: Model Forecasts Evaluation

The above results clearly suggest that both monetary aggregates can be used as an anchor for the price level in all ten Asian developing countries investigated. Our question is: Can we discriminate between the two competing P-Star models? Since one of the criteria of a 'good' model is its forecasting ability, then do one of the models perform better than the other in terms of forecasts? In their study, Hallman et al. (1991) suggested using the method proposed by Chong and Hendry (1986) in order to discriminate between models by comparing competing forecasts. Using this approach, we determine whether forecast error from a given model can be explained ('encompassed') by the forecasts of another model. For example, let f_{it} and f_{jt} denote the forecasts made by models i and j, and let the model-i forecast error be denoted by e_{it}. Define $t(i,f)$ as the statistic for β in the following regression

$$e_{it} = \beta(f_{jt} - f_{it}) + \eta_t \qquad (4.33)$$

Model i is said to forecast-encompass model j if $t(i,j)$ is not significantly different from zero but $t(j,i)$ is. Table 4.7 show the $t(j,i)$ and $t(i,j)$ from running between the two competing monetary aggregates - Divisia M1 and Divisia M2, and to determine whether Divisia M1 'forecast-encompassed' Divisia M2 or otherwise. In Table 4.7 we have run each of the P-Star models defined by each of the monetary aggregates - Divisia M1 against Divisia M2 for each of the Asian countries.

Results in Table 4.7 suggest that for Indonesia and Sri Lanka, narrow Divisia money forecast-encompassed the broad Divisia money. In the cases of Malaysia, Myanmar, Singapore, South Korea and Thailand Divisia M2 used to construct P-Star seem to be the forecast-encompassed model. On the other hand, for the remainder of the Asian countries (Nepal, the Philippines and Taiwan), our results suggest that both narrow and broad Divisia monies are equally useful in linking money and the price level in these countries.

Conclusions

The growth rate of the money supply has been a major instrument of central banks, targeted either directly or indirectly through the reserve money, interest rate or exchange rate of a country. In the 1970s the United States, United Kingdom, Canada, Germany, France and Australia were among the developed countries adopting monetary aggregate targeting. However, by late 1980s most of these countries except for Germany had de-emphasised monetary targeting. Money has been 'downgraded' from 'intermediate target' to merely an 'information variable' (see Friedman, 1997).

All in all, economists are sceptical about the role of money in predicting key economic activities. Mayer (1993) points out that as a result of financial innovations, monetarism has been weakened. On the other hand, Dewald (1988) believes that monetarism is 'dead'. Dewald argues that monetarism, which was interpreted as providing an alternative to short-run Keynesian model forecasts, has failed miserably in the 1980s. But, he points out that the quantity theory with its focus on the long-run has survived.

In recent years, there has been increasing interest among researchers to investigate the long-run relationship between money and inflation using the simple Fisher-quantity equation. Studies conducted on cross-section of countries found that the growth rates of the money supply and the rate of inflation were highly correlated with a correlation of close to one. Apart from the cross-country data, evidence on the United States using time series data has also supported the quantity theory.

The primary aim of this chapter is to investigate the long-run relationship between Divisia money and the price level of ten Asian countries. Using quarterly time series data for the period 1981:1 to 1994:4, we have employed the P-Star approach (based on the quantity theory) in linking Divisia money and the price level. Since different central banks choose different definitions of money, in this study we used both Divisia M1 and M2 as alternative monetary aggregates used to construct p*.

Generally, the results presented in this study are supportive of a long-run relationship between money (via p*) and the price level in all the Asian countries investigated. The results indicate that both narrow Divisia money M1 and broad Divisia money M2 can be an anchor to the price level in each country. The results further imply that the Divisia money (both M1 and M2) can be useful intermediate indicators for monetary policy purpose in these countries. Thus, the evidence here supports the view that inflation in the Asian countries under study is a monetary phenomenon.

The above results suggest that an indicator of inflationary pressures based on p* can be successfully constructed for the Asian developing countries under study. However, the construction of p* depends crucially on the long-run stability of the income velocity of money. Our results also suggest that an equilibrium velocity for the Asian countries are best accomplished by estimating a long-run income velocity of money that incorporates the effects of financial development indicator as an additional variable to income and the interest rate.

Comparing the results from the forecast-encompassing tests between the two competing monetary aggregates used for the construction of p*, our results indicate that for Indonesia and Sri Lanka, the p* model using Divisia M1 contains useful information beyond that contained in the forecasts from the broad Divisia money. For Malaysia, Myanmar, Singapore, South Korea and Thailand, the p* model with Divisia M2 forecast-encompassed the other competing p* model - Divisia M1. This means that the p* model constructed using Divisia M2 can better track inflation in these five countries. However, for the three remaining Asian countries, i.e. Nepal, the Philippines, and Taiwan the forecast-encompassing tests failed to discriminate between the two monetary aggregates used to compute p*. In other words, there is a stable link between any of the two monetary aggregates - Divisia M1 and M2, and the price level. Therefore, it implies that any potential risks of price instability can be curtailed by monitoring the growth of either Divisia M1 or Divisia M2 for these three Asian countries.

The above results are consistent with similar studies in linking money and the price level conducted in the developed countries. In fact, our results for the Asian developing countries conform to Laidler's (1997: p. 67) remarks that 'policymakers have finally digested that inflation is a monetary phenomenon'. However, an important implication of these results is that the evidence of this study further suggests that Divisia monetary aggregates have potential roles as intermediate targets and/or indicators in the 'deregulated' Asian economies. Although empirical testing for the superiority of Divisia aggregate against its counterpart Simple-sum aggregate is beyond the scope of this study, Barnett and his associates have again and again warned against using the Simple-sum money measures. More recently, Barnett (1997: p. 1183-1184) stresses again that 'it is worth repeating that the basic principle that distinguishes the high road (referring to Divisia aggregate) from the low road (referring to Simple-sum aggregate) is that the high road uses the relevant theory and insists upon internal coherence and consistency between the theory that produced the model, the inference methods used to estimate the model, and the theory implied by the data construction procedures. The basic principles of aggregation and index number theory are relevant to the objectives of the high road, and violations of those basic principles are the basis for what Chrystal and MacDonald (1994) have called the "Barnett critique" in monetary economic. The high road is a difficult road to travel, but it is the right road'.

Notes

1. The more popular 'weighted' monetary aggregate is the one proposed by Barnett (1980).
2. For a broad general survey of these issues from an international perspective, see Akhtar (1983) and Argy *et al.* (1989).
3. In studying the United States data, McCandles and Weber (1995) use M0, M1 and M2, while Bullard (1994) uses M1, M2, M3 and L and their Divisia counterparts.
4. See Humphrey (1989) for a review of the precursors of this approach.
5. See Bordes *et al.* (1993) for a brief survey on the empirical applications of the P-Star model in the developed countries.

6. Hoeller and Poret (1991) investigate the OECD countries, while Kool and Tatom (1994) investigate on five European countries-Austria, Belgium, Denmark, the Netherlands and Switzerland.
7. Except for South Korea. See Corker and Haas (1991).
8. Hagger (1977) and Frisch (1976) provide a survey and empirical modelling of the inflationary process in the developed countries.
9. In their study, Todter and Reimers (1994) exclude interest rate variable.
10. Potential output is ignored for ease of exposition. See Allen and Hall (1991) and Funke and Hall (1994) on this point.
11. Except for Myanmar which ended 1994:2.
12. Barnett (1980) stresses that Divisia monetary aggregates is an appropriate measure of monetary services. Barnett and Spindt (1982) have provided a 'Divisia Cookbook' index for the computation of a Divisia aggregate. For the ten Asian countries investigated in this study, we provide a brief discussions on Divisia aggregate and their computations in Chapter 3.
13. Furthermore, the use of export will minimise any spurious results that will arise when using income that had been generated using some interpolation technique. Nevertheless, one has to be cautious when interpreting the results.
14. The diagnostic tests presented in Table 4.4 are broadly defined as follows. LM(4) is the lagrange multiplier test for residual serial correlation of the fourth-order process based on Breusch (1978) and Godfrey (1978). Arch (4) is the fourth-order autoregressive conditional heteroscedasticity test of Engle (1982). Norm (2) is a test for the normality of the residuals based on Jarque and Bera (1980). Reset (2) is based on Ramsey (1969), is used to test whether the coefficients of powers of predicted dependent variables (Y^2, Y^3) are jointly zero. This test may also be regarded as tests of heteroscedasticity but usually regarded as general tests for detection of missing explanatory variables or incorrect functional form.

Table 4.1
Dickey-Pantula integration tests results

Country & Series	Step 1 Test for three unit roots			Step 2 Test for two unit roots			Step 3 Test for single unit root		
	α_3	Lag	LM(4)	α_2	Lag	LM(4)	α_1	Lag	LM(4)
Indonesia									
p	-3.47**	8	2.14	-2.60	5	6.81	-		
dm1	-6.96**	3	1.80	-2.53	4	1.21	-		
dm2	-9.91**	1	4.15	-2.38	6	3.02	-		
cdm1	-6.50**	5	5.14	-6.54**	1	6.90	-1.79	0	8.14
cdm2	-9.29**	2	1.42	-1.65	2	1.24	-		
q	-4.18**	7	4.23	-3.95**	6	7.16	-0.38	6	7.36
r	-6.70**	4	8.97	-6.29**	3	1.71	-1.69	3	0.83
Malaysia									
p	-7.18**	2	6.23	-2.15	10	2.24	-		
dm1	-13.62**	2	2.44	-1.64	2	3.57	-		
dm2	-3.37**	10	3.52	-2.78	2	3.69	-		
cdm1	-9.34**	2	4.48	-3.18**	6	2.40	-0.31	6	3.88
cdm2	-4.76**	5	4.52	-3.03**	2	5.72	-2.10	6	1.70
q	-3.92**	7	5.29	-2.48	2	5.08	-		
r	-6.02**	4	2.28	-4.79**	0	0.62	-2.30	3	6.85
Myanmar									
p	-5.60**	7	4.19	-1.03	7	4.02	-		
dm1	-5.10**	6	3.33	-5.31**	0	0.24	0.45	0	0.56
dm2	-4.87**	6	3.44	-4.99**	0	2.53	1.16	0	2.47
cdm1	-4.72**	5	4.65	-4.16**	3	2.72	-1.34	3	2.26
cdm2	-5.43**	5	3.71	-5.76**	0	3.53	-2.18	0	1.07
q	-6.13**	6	2.14	-7.91**	1	3.33	-1.43	9	5.06
r	-6.70**	2	4.90	-5.04**	0	0.09	-0.79	0	0.12
Nepal									
p	-3.73**	9	5.57	-2.45	6	7.95	-		
dm1	-4.06**	10	2.77	-1.79	10	1.58	-		
dm2	-8.23**	6	3.22	-1.97	6	2.12	-		
cdm1	-3.81**	9	2.37	-7.38**	1	1.05	-1.30	1	2.23
cdm2	-5.05**	6	3.80	-3.90**	4	7.74	-1.67	2	6.48
q	-4.00**	6	4.97	-4.78**	5	2.99	-1.03	5	2.63
r	-5.43**	5	4.81	-3.99**	12	5.11	1.06	12	4.23

Notes: The variables are defined as follows: p = price level, dm1 = Divisia M1, dm2 = Divisia M2, cdm1 = currency-Divisia M1 ratio, cdm2 = currency-Divisia M2 ratio, q = real output and r = interest rate. Critical values are from Fuller (1976); for T=50 at 5 percent level, τ_μ = 2.93.

Table 4.1 (continued)

Country & Series	Step 1 Test for three unit roots			Step 2 Test for two unit roots			Step 3 Test for single unit root		
	α_3	Lag	LM(4)	α_2	Lag	LM(4)	α_1	Lag	LM(4)
Philippines									
p	-4.05**	4	2.57	-2.64	1	8.64	-		
dm1	-5.16**	10	5.51	-4.40**	9	3.85	-1.26	10	4.51
dm2	-3.38**	10	2.19	-3.93**	5	7.72	-0.38	5	7.56
cdm1	-9.11**	3	3.37	-2.20	5	2.30	-		
cdm2	-5.34**	6	6.87	-3.92**	5	8.62	1.08	5	8.73
q	-9.01**	2	3.55	-7.28**	0	0.94	-0.93	0	2.04
r	-6.39**	3	4.05	-4.44**	2	4.35	-2.55	0	8.05
Singapore									
p	-6.11**	4	3.91	-1.47	4	2.76	-		
dm1	-3.47**	10	2.17	-2.53	6	6.74	-		
dm2	-4.89**	6	3.49	-2.11	7	5.13	-		
cdm1	-3.96**	10	2.04	-5.66**	0	3.66	0.00	0	3.77
cdm2	-4.61**	6	1.81	-2.48	2	4.96	-		
q	-3.71**	6	2.69	-3.29**	4	5.27	0.64	4	5.50
r	-5.16**	5	5.98	-6.27**	0	6.96	-1.49	4	3.80
South Korea									
p	-9.00**	2	3.11	-1.63	11	1.27	-		
dm1	-5.31**	6	1.46	-7.85**	1	3.16	0.14	1	3.19
dm2	-4.40**	6	2.29	-3.53**	9	4.98	1.50	9	6.10
cdm1	-4.10**	6	4.82	-4.29**	5	2.58	-1.46	5	0.35
cdm2	-4.75**	10	3.67	-4.22**	9	6.51	-1.81	9	5.43
q	-5.56**	6	1.96	-1.99	6	3.15	-		
r	-11.51**	2	1.04	-3.66**	3	3.62	-2.13	5	3.22
Sri Lanka									
p	-5.31**	6	6.87	-1.35	6	8.24	-		
dm1	-4.61**	6	4.26	-2.69	9	3.35	-		
dm2	-5.45**	6	5.67	-2.06	6	6.23	-		
cdm1	-6.23**	4	7.99	-6.49**	1	4.72	-1.29	12	5.07
cdm2	-4.55**	6	2.52	-0.46	6	2.99	-		
q	-4.46**	12	1.63	-4.94**	6	4.26	1.36	6	5.49
r	-4.82**	8	3.18	-6.35**	0	1.25	-1.77	8	3.62

Notes: The variables are defined as follows: p = price level, dm1 = Divisia M1, dm2 = Divisia M2, cdm1 = currency-Divisia M1 ratio, cdm2 = currency-Divisia M2 ratio, q = real output and r = interest rate. Critical values are from Fuller (1976); for T=50 at 5 percent level, $\tau_\mu = 2.93$.

Table 4.1 (continued)

Country & Series	Step 1 Test for three unit roots			Step 2 Test for two unit roots			Step 3 Test for single unit root		
	α_3	Lag	LM(4)	α_2	Lag	LM(4)	α_1	Lag	LM(4)
Taiwan									
p	-5.83**	5	1.38	-1.35	5	0.63	-		
dm1	-3.11**	6	3.81	-2.09	9	4.72	-		
dm2	-11.30**	2	6.37	-2.87	5	2.97	-		
cdm1	-4.37**	8	3.70	-1.89	9	1.35	-		
cdm2	-3.50**	10	4.22	-2.01	9	5.11	-		
q	-4.37**	11	1.43	-6.50**	1	2.87	-0.80	1	2.80
r	-7.84**	2	2.29	-3.26**	1	2.55	-2.85	1	1.15
Thailand									
p	-7.29**	2	2.57	-1.55	9	1.76	-		
dm1	-4.81**	7	9.29	-1.57	8	4.70	-		
dm2	-5.63**	6	4.85	-2.70	7	3.13	-		
cdm1	-5.98**	4	5.48	-4.70**	1	5.68	-2.44	10	6.17
cdm2	-6.58**	6	3.28	-1.45	6	3.53	-		
q	-4.40**	8	5.68	-4.05**	7	4.42	-1.40	8	1.90
r	-5.30**	6	1.92	-7.06**	0	2.46	-2.43	0	1.00

Notes: The variables are defined as follows: p = price level, dm1 = Divisia M1, dm2 = Divisia M2, cdm1 = currency-Divisia M1 ratio, cdm2 = currency-Divisia M2 ratio, q = real output and r = interest rate. Critical values are from Fuller (1976); for T=50 at 5 percent level, τ_μ = 2.93.

Table 4.2
Summary of the order of integration

Series	Indonesia	Malaysia	Myanmar	Nepal	Philippines
p	I(2)	I(2)	I(2)	I(2)	I(2)
dm1	I(2)	I(2)	I(1)	I(2)	I(1)
dm2	I(2)	I(2)	I(1)	I(2)	I(1)
cdm1	I(1)	I(1)	I(1)	I(1)	I(2)
cdm2	I(2)	I(1)	I(1)	I(1)	I(1)
q	I(1)	I(2)	I(1)	I(1)	I(1)
r	I(1)	I(1)	I(1)	I(1)	I(1)

Series	Singapore	South Korea	Sri Lanka	Taiwan	Thailand
p	I(2)	I(2)	I(2)	I(2)	I(2)
dm1	I(2)	I(1)	I(2)	I(2)	I(2)
dm2	I(2)	I(1)	I(2)	I(2)	I(2)
cdm1	I(1)	I(1)	I(1)	I(2)	I(1)
cdm2	I(2)	I(1)	I(2)	I(2)	I(2)
q	I(1)	I(2)	I(1)	I(1)	I(1)
r	I(1)	I(1)	I(1)	I(1)	I(1)

Notes: The variables are defined as follows: p = price level, dm1 = Divisia M1, dm2 = Divisia M2, cdm1 = currency-Divisia M1 ratio, cdm2 = currency-Divisia M2 ratio, q = real output and r = interest rate

Table 4.3
Results of cointegration tests

Money series used to construct p*	Relevant statistics on cointegrating regressions		Unit root test on residuals of cointegrating regressions		
	R^2	CRDW	ADF	Lag	LM(4)
Indonesia					
dm1	0.01	2.30**	-8.48**	0	5.73
dm2	0.01	2.31**	-8.51**	0	5.31
Malaysia					
dm1	0.14	1.16**	-7.78**	0	2.32
dm2	0.16	1.30**	-7.96**	0	4.14
Myanmar					
dm1	0.42	1.91**	-6.83**	0	2.07
dm2	0.46	2.05**	-7.33**	0	2.72
Nepal					
dm1	0.56	1.81**	-6.63**	0	2.47
dm2	0.46	1.76**	-6.44**	0	6.87
Philippines					
dm1	0.29	1.53**	-5.78**	0	6.73
dm2	0.30	1.58**	-5.94**	0	7.34
Singapore					
dm1	0.38	1.42**	-7.22**	2	1.87
dm2	0.30	1.33**	-7.22**	2	1.06
South Korea					
dm1	0.27	1.70**	-4.06	2	5.60
dm2	0.29	1.59**	-6.58**	0	7.90
Sri Lanka					
dm1	0.10	1.32**	-5.21**	0	0.83
dm2	0.08	1.31**	-5.18**	0	0.42
Taiwan					
dm1	0.22	2.13**	-8.81**	1	6.97
dm2	0.22	2.11**	-8.79**	1	7.44
Thailand					
dm1	0.22	2.16**	-9.37**	0	2.54
dm2	0.24	1.93**	-8.43**	0	0.46

Notes: Critical value for CRDW for T=50 at 5 percent level is 0.78 (see Engle and Yoo, 1987). Critical value for ADF for T=50 at 5 percent level for n=4 is –4.32 (see MacKinnon, 1991).

Table 4.4
The P-Star models from the error-correction mechanisms

Variables	Indonesia		Malaysia		Myanmar	
	Divisia M1	Divisia M2	Divisia M1	Divisia M2	Divisia M1	Divisia M2
Constant	-0.0007	-0.0008	-0.0011	-0.0011	0.0070	0.0072
	(0.4465)	(0.4682)	(1.3323)	(1.3353)	(1.4936)	(1.5246)
ecm_{t-1}	-0.9378	-0.9342	-0.5288	-0.4874	-0.9956	-0.9436
	(2.7748)**	(2.8637)**	(2.9900)**	(2.5020)**	(6.2434)**	(5.8330)**
dum84:1			0.0234	0.0208		
			(3.7602)**	(3.3313)**		
dum87:3,4					-0.0733	-0.0701
					(3.2474)**	(3.0612)**
dum89:1					-0.1385	-0.1451
					(4.4514)**	(4.5855)**
dum93:1	0.0424	0.0422				
	(3.4239)**	(3.4236)**				
$\Delta^2 p_{t-1}$	-0.1389	-0.1500	-0.4977	-0.5109		
	(0.5035)	(0.5665)	(3.8917)**	(3.0265)**		
$\Delta^2 p_{t-2}$	-0.2696	-0.2751	-0.1620	-0.2248		
	(1.3081)	(1.3760)	(1.6145)	(1.4852)		
$\Delta^2 p_{t-3}$	0.2700	-0.2754		-0.1285		
	(2.1157)**	(2.2090)**		(1.2030)		
$\Delta^2 p_{t-6}$	0.0993	0.0919			-0.2296	-0.1904
	(1.1752)	(1.0907)			(2.3510)**	(1.9380)
$\Delta^2 p_{t-7}$					-0.1203	
					(1.2384)	
R-squared	0.701	0.704	0.597	0.590	0.682	0.653
SER	0.011	0.011	0.006	0.006	0.030	0.031
D.W.	1.766	1.741	1.773	1.648	1.593	1.685
LM χ^2 (4)	6.344	6.517	7.271	6.699	4.078	3.545
	[0.175]	[0.163]	[0.122]	[0.153]	[0.395]	[0.471]
Arch χ^2 (4)	3.720	4.763	3.735	0.840	1.845	1.209
	[0.445]	[0.312]	[0.443]	[0.933]	[0.764]	[0.876]
Norm χ^2 (2)	1.606	1.595	0.873	0.808	1.426	2.187
	[0.447]	[0.450]	[0.646]	[0.667]	[0.489]	[0.335]
Reset χ^2 (2)	0.079	0.021	2.462	4.715	3.726	4.480
	[0.961]	[0.989]	[0.292]	[0.095]	[0.155]	[0.106]

Notes: ecm denotes error correction term, i.e. the residuals from running the cointegrating regression. SER and DW denote standard error of regression and Durbin-Watson statistic respectively. Numbers in parentheses (.) are *t*-statistics and numbers in the square brackets [.] are *p*-values. Asterisks (**) denote statistically significant at 5 percent level. For Indonesia, dum93:1: 1 in 1993:1; 0 otherwise: This dummy accounts for a large outlier in the price equation. For Malaysia, dum84:1: 1 in 1984:1; 0 otherwise: This dummy accounts for the effect of a new system of interest rate regime. At the end of 1983, all borrowing rates was anchored to the commercial banks declared base lending rate (BLR). The new interest rate system was imposed as the Central Bank found that lending rates were rigid downwards with falling interest rates. For Myanmar, dum87:3,4: 1 in 1987:3 and 1987:4; 0 otherwise: This dummy accounts for the effect of a major demonetisation in September 1987 in which notes of higher denomination were declared illegal tender. dum98:1: 1 in 1989:1; 0 otherwise: This dummy captures the effects of a drastic change in the economy, that is from one of socialist to market-oriented economy.

Table 4.5
The P-Star models from the error-correction mechanisms

Variables	Nepal		Philippines		Singapore	
	Divisia M1	Divisia M2	Divisia M1	Divisia M2	Divisia M1	Divisia M2
Constant	-0.0000	0.0004	-0.0059	-0.0059	0.0001	-0.0001
	(0.0000)	(0.1386)	(2.7224)**	(2.6711)**	(0.4022)	(0.2565)
ecm_{t-1}	-0.5308	-0.4713	-0.7827	-0.7787	-0.8166	-0.6842
	(3.7710)**	(3.7155)**	(9.6255)**	(9.3466)**	(6.8508)**	(5.6941)**
dum83:4			0.0549	0.0577		
			(3.6568)**	(3.7591)**		
dum84:1,2					0.0151	0.0168
					(6.1537)**	(6.4097)**
dum84:1,3			0.0959	0.0930		
			(7.8138)**	(7.4470)**		
dum90:2			0.0562	0.0545		
			(3.6381)**	(3.4510)**		
$\Delta^2 p_{t-2}$			0.2645	0.2486	0.2973	0.3688
			(3.1238)**	(2.8860)**	(3.5749)**	(4.3213)**
$\Delta^2 p_{t-3}$			0.1435	0.1318		
			(1.6605)	(1.5020)		
$\Delta^2 p_{t-4}$	0.3643	0.3518				
	(3.3081)**	(3.1833)**				
$\Delta^2 p_{t-6}$					0.1265	
					(1.6596)	
$\Delta^2 p_{t-8}$	0.4922	0.4957			-0.1348	-0.1280
	(4.3911)**	(4.4062)**			(1.9479)	(1.7118)
R-squared	0.796	0.795	0.825	0.818	0.778	0.727
SER	0.021	0.021	0.014	0.015	0.003	0.003
D.W.	2.399	2.387	1.544	1.419	2.051	1.982
LM χ^2 (4)	7.825	7.016	3.943	6.702	8.534	2.730
	[0.098]	[0.135]	[0.414]	[0.152]	[0.074]	[0.604]
Arch χ^2 (4)	2.302	2.158	5.541	6.153	2.722	1.572
	[0.680]	[0.707]	[0.236]	[0.188]	[0.605]	[0.814]
Norm χ^2 (2)	3.085	2.174	0.953	1.931	0.527	0.613
	[0.213]	[0.337]	[0.621]	[0.381]	[0.768]	[0.735]
Reset χ^2 (2)	0.547	0.653	3.358	4.528	0.205	2.075
	[0.760]	[0.721]	[0.187]	[0.104]	[0.902]	[0.354]

Notes: ecm denotes error correction term, i.e. the residuals from running the cointegrating regression. SER and DW denote standard error of regression and Durbin-Watson statistic respectively. Numbers in parentheses (.) are t-statistics and numbers in the square brackets [.] are p-values. Asterisks (**) denote statistically significant at 5 percent level. For the Philippines, dum83:4, and dum84:1,3: 1 in 1983:4; 1984:1 and 1984:3; 0 otherwise: These dummies account for the effects of the depreciation of the pesos against the dollar, with cumulative depreciation of 117.9 percent for the period 1983-85. It also accounts for the political and economic crises with the assasination of Senator Benigno Aquino in August 1983. dum90:2: 1 in 1990:1; 0 otherwise: This dummy accounts for the effect the fourth major depreciation of the peso by 25 percent. For Singapore, dum84:1,2: 1 in 1984:1 and -1 in 1984:2; 0 otherwise: This dummy accounts for the effect of the wage cost increases between 1980 to 1984. The government had a 'high wage policy' in 1979-1981 with the objective of shifting the economy towards more capital and skill-intensive activities. Although the high wage policy ended in 1981, wage costs continued to increase rapidly, caused mainly by increased rates of CPF contribution, keen competition for workers in a tight labour market and optimistic growth expectations. However, productivity increases failed to match wage cost increases and unit labour cost rose, averaging 10 percent from 1980 to 1984.

Table 4.6
The P-Star models from the error-correction mechanisms

Variables	South Korea		Sri Lanka		Taiwan		Thailand	
	Divisia M1	Divisia M2	Divisia M1	Divisia M2	Divisia M1	Divisia M2	Divisia M1	Divisia M2
Constant	0.0000	-0.0000	-0.0005	-0.0002	0.0000	0.0000	-0.0006	-0.0004
	(0.0469)	(0.0232)	(0.1824)	(0.0934)	(0.0709)	(0.0554)	(0.5888)	(0.4268)
ecm_{t-1}	-0.7808	-0.7020	-0.6700	-0.6743	-0.9850	-0.9704	-1.0671	-0.8907
	(3.8451)**	(3.3654)**	(4.5938)**	(4.6504)**	(6.7865)**	(6.6702)**	(5.2637)**	(4.5059)**
$\Delta^2 p_{t-1}$	-0.2351	-0.2690					-0.1372	-0.2363
	(1.8873)	(2.1163)**					(0.8762)	(2.0408)**
$\Delta^2 p_{t-2}$					-0.0901	-0.0891	-0.0386	
					(0.9167)	(0.8984)	(0.3453)	
$\Delta^2 p_{t-4}$	0.3649	0.3676						
	(3.7681)**	(3.6874)**						
$\Delta^2 p_{t-6}$			-0.2959	-0.2956	-0.2069	-0.2135		
			(1.9785)	(1.9846)	(2.1779)**	(2.2309)**		
$\Delta^2 p_{t-7}$			-0.3372	-0.3386				
			(2.1359)**	(2.1534)**				
R-squared	0.532	0.503	0.401	0.405	0.608	0.601	0.593	0.526
SER	0.009	0.009	0.019	0.019	0.009	0.009	0.007	0.007
D.W.	2.201	2.098	1.892	1.973	2.018	2.013	1.865	2.077
LM χ^2 (4)	3.157	2.974	0.698	0.283	4.509	4.668	4.174	1.894
	[0.531]	[0.562]	[0.951]	[0.990]	[0.341]	[0.323]	[0.383]	[0.755]
Arch χ^2 (4)	2.792	3.375	5.873	4.875	2.456	2.849	8.678	5.471
	[0.593]	[0.496]	[0.209]	[0.300]	[0.652]	[0.583]	[0.070]	[0.242]
Norm χ^2 (2)	0.632	1.491	1.013	1.198	1.835	1.788	1.460	2.250
	[0.728]	[0.474]	[0.602]	[0.549]	[0.399]	[0.409]	[0.482]	[0.324]
Reset χ^2 (2)	0.813	2.176	1.386	1.778	0.016	0.002	3.328	1.082
	[0.665]	[0.336]	[0.499]	[0.411]	[0.991]	[0.999]	[0.189]	[0.582]

Notes: ecm denotes error correction term, i.e. the residuals from running the cointegrating regression. Numbers in parentheses (.) are t-statistics and numbers in the square brackets [.] are p-values. Asterisks (**) denote statistically significant at 5 percent level.

Table 4.7
Results of forecast-encompassing tests for narrow versus broad Divisia money

Countries	Money series	$t(f_j - f_i)$	$t(f_i - f_j)$
Indonesia	Divisia M1 (e_i) vs	-2.23**	-
	Divisia M2 (e_j)	-	0.48
Malaysia	Divisia M1 (e_i) vs	-0.42	-
	Divisia M2 (e_j)	-	-1.76*
Myanmar	Divisia M1 (e_i) vs	-0.18	-
	Divisia M2 (e_j)	-	-1.79*
Nepal	Divisia M1 (e_i) vs	0.13	-
	Divisia M2 (e_j)	-	-1.54
Philippines	Divisia M1 (e_i) vs	-0.26	-
	Divisia M2 (e_j)	-	-0.48
Singapore	Divisia M1 (e_i) vs	-0.41	-
	Divisia M2 (e_j)	-	-2.05**
South Korea	Divisia M1 (e_i) vs	0.38	-
	Divisia M2 (e_j)	-	-1.77*
Sri Lanka	Divisia M1 (e_i) vs	-2.87**	-
	Divisia M2 (e_j)	-	1.48
Taiwan	Divisia M1 (e_i) vs	-1.43	-
	Divisia M2 (e_j)	-	-0.30
Thailand	Divisia M1 (e_i) vs	0.05	-
	Divisia M2 (e_j)	-	-2.89**

Notes: Asterisks (**), (*) denote statistically significant at 5 percent and 10 percent level respectively.

5 Divisia Money and Income in the Asian Countries

Introduction

Financial innovation is a worldwide phenomenon. In the United States, it started in the 1960s (Hester, 1981). Most literature suggests that financial innovations in the United States[1] were largely a response to legislation and regulation, taxes and the profit motive of financial institutions (see Minsky, 1957; Ben-Horim and Silber, 1977; Miller, 1986). For example, the emergence of CDs, the development of the Eurodollar market and the introduction of bank related commercial paper are all credited to interest rate ceilings under Regulation Q. As a result of taxes, the Eurobond market was established. The profit-motivated financial institutions, on the other hand, are responsible for the development of electronic money transfer systems, the spread of new types of mortgage instruments, the growth of an active future market in financial instruments and the widening adoption of interest-bearing payments accounts.

Akhtar (1983) notes that the important implication of financial innovations in the United States and other developed economies[2] is that, apart from lowering financial transaction costs through the development of new means of payment system such as credit cards and automatic fund transfer, they also promote the emergence of new interest-bearing financial assets that have higher liquidity and profitability, thereby decreasing the risk burden associated with financial investments. However, the emergence of various new interest-bearing financial assets at both the commercial banks and non-bank financial intermediaries has consequently increased the substitutability among those assets.

Substitution among the various interest-bearing financial assets and changes in their rates of return had rendered it even more untenable for the Central Bank to pursue an appropriate monetary policy that was aimed at a monetary aggregate, chosen as a proxy for an intermediate target, before the advent of these financial innovations.

More important, these structural changes and financial innovations in the financial system have significant implications for public portfolio behaviour and consequently, for the conduct of monetary policy. According to Laumas and Porter-Hudak (1986), the success of monetary policy depends on the extent to which the demand for money function can be estimated, and on the stability of the money demand function. Judd and Scadding (1982) further point out that the stability of the money demand function depends on financial and monetary developments which include financial innovations in the financial markets. These innovations will alter public behaviour in the holding of real money balances. With financial and monetary development, the role of the non-bank financial intermediaries becomes apparent, offering a spectrum of interest-bearing financial instruments of various maturity dates. A shift out of money (currency and demand deposits) to these interest-bearing financial assets will subsequently affect the stability of money demand function.

The purpose of this chapter is to investigate the long-run relationship between Divisia money and nominal income in ten Asian countries with respect to two important issues. First, is the question of whether measurement of money matters in the relationship between money and income. In other words, is there a long-run relationship between Divisia money and income in the Asian countries? And secondly, how stable is the Divisia money-income relationship in an economy with a structurally changing financial system? For a monetary aggregate to be useful as a monetary policy indicator, there must be a stable long-run relationship between money and nominal income.

Financial Liberalisation and the Effectiveness of Monetary Policy

Experience of the Asian Countries

Not surprisingly, the aftermath of recent financial liberalisation has created new problems for the monetary authorities of the developing countries. The relationship between monetary aggregates, in particular, narrow money M1 and national income has been questioned recently. There is evidence that there has been a breakdown in the link between M1 and income in the developing countries. This has led the monetary authorities to focus on broader monetary aggregates as monetary indicators for policy action. Tseng and Corker (1991, 1993) have concluded from their study of nine Asian countries[3] that, as a consequence of the changing financial system, the relationships between money, income and interest rates in those countries have been altered. Tseng and Corker pointed out that financial liberalisation leads to one time or more gradual shifts in the level of money holdings, as well as to changes in the measured income and interest elasticity of money demand. Earlier, Gurley and Shaw (1960) have pointed out that the increased availability of interest-bearing financial assets as a result of an expanding financial sector, can raise the sensitivity of money holdings to changes in interest rates. The implications of the growth of these money substitutes are important for monetary policy since with a high interest elasticity of money demand, monetary policy becomes less effective.

On the other hand, Adhikary (1989b) points out that as a result of financial innovations, most of the countries in the Asian region have emphasised the use of broader definitions of money as intermediate targets. For example, M2 has been the major monetary target in Indonesia, Nepal, Sri Lanka and Thailand. In Malaysia, Philippines, Singapore and South Korea, both M2 and M3 have assumed increasing importance for monetary policy actions as they have a more stable and predictable relationship with underlying economic activity. For example, in Malaysia, the Governor of the Central Bank (Bank Negara Malaysia, 1985: p. 122) reports that 'the task of monetary policy has been complicated by structural changes in the demand for money. Traditionally, monetary management by the Central Bank was centered on narrow money or M1, that is, currency holdings and demand deposits of the non-bank private sector. However, the behaviour of M1 in 1984 and 1985 was affected significantly by growing sophistication in the financial system and increasing sensitivity to interest rates, which caused large shifts out of currency holdings and demand deposits into interest-bearing deposits not only with the commercial banks, but also the finance companies, merchant banks, and other financial instituitons. As a result, the broader definitions of money, M2 and M3, have become increasingly important in terms of a more stable and predictable relationship with underlying economic activity'.

South Korea faces the same problem. Shin (1986: p. 28) notes that 'the demand for a narrower monetary aggregate, M1, in particular, tended to decline relatively during the past five years, which indicates that interest earning assets occupied a larger share of the total financial assets available in financial markets. Also, M1 fluctuated more than M2 or M3, due to partly to the weakening role of M1 as a means of payment, and partly to higher substitutability between M1 and other financial assets. With such structural changes, the relationship between M1 and economic activity has become less clear while that between M2 or M3 and economic activity has become more evident'. In Thailand, Hataiseree (1991: p. 38) points out that 'the effect of financial development impair the value of M1 (money as a medium of exchange) as an indicator in the control of money supply, since the traditional distinction between demand deposits and saving deposits can hardly be established. As part of the response to these new developments, the Bank has in recent years placed more emphasis on the broader money (M2) as a monetary policy indicator when periodically reviewing the developments of monetary situations. This is because the broader monetary aggregates like M2 were considered broad enough to internalise the portfolio shifts if any, thus stabilizing the growth rate of M2 relative to M1'.

In summary, the rapid transformation of the financial system in the Asian countries in recent years has resulted in depth and sophistication of the banking system.[4] However, the more market-oriented structure along with deregulation and financial innovation have complicated the task of monetary management. The structural changes in the financial system had resulted in volatile movements in the velocity of M1, which consequently led to the breakdown in the relationship between M1 and income. As a result, the broader definitions of monetary aggregates, M2 and M3, have assumed greater significance in terms of a more stable and predictable relationship with the underlying economic activity. Therefore, increasing emphasis has been placed on M2 and M3 as the intermediate targets for monetary management in those countries.[5]

Experience of the Developed Countries

As a result of financial innovations, in the United States, narrow money M1 has been de-emphasised as an intermediate target variable in conducting monetary policy, and instead broad money M2 was chosen as the best monetary aggregate for policy action. Belongia and Chalfant

(1990) point out that the breakdown in the relationships between M1 growth and both the rate of inflation and the growth rate of nominal GNP was mainly due to financial innovations and deregulation. Uncertainty about the effects of financial innovations on M1, in addition to velocity growth, weakened M1's informational content in predicting future income or price movements. Thornton (1983: p. 10) observes that 'financial innovations can produce velocity changes. In general, innovations that reduce the implicit or explicit cost, or both, of transferring funds from non-transaction to transaction forms (perhaps by giving transaction characteristics to assets not included in M1) tend to increase the velocity of M1. In contrast, innovations that lower the cost of holding M1 relative to non-M1 assets tend to reduce the velocity of M1'.

According to Thornton, innovations such as money market deposit accounts and money market mutual funds would increase the velocity of M1 to the extent that they lower these costs. On the other hand, automatic transfer of savings, negotiable order of withdrawal (NOW), and Super-NOW accounts may produce a temporary decline in velocity that lasts only until individuals realign their portfolios.

In Japan, as a result of financial innovation, the Central Bank of Japan has focussed on broader monetary aggregates as intermediate targets. The use of monetary indicators has shifted from M1 to M2, and then to M2+CD.[6] In Germany, the Bundesbank has taken M3 as the intermediate target for monetary policy because it was found that M3 has a stable relationship with actual economic activities. In the United Kingdom, the Bank of England targeted the growth rate of Sterling M3 in the 1970s, and changed to narrow monetary aggregate M0 in 1982. But, currently the Bank of England prefers M4, a broader definition of monetary aggregate for policy action.

On the other hand, financial innovation in Canada which was the consequence of competition, technological innovation and high interest rates, has resulted in the shift in the demand for M1, while broader money M2 and M3 has remained relatively constant. In France and Italy, Dooley and Spinelli (1989) reported that financial innovation and deregulation have played an important part in explaining the downward shift in money demand. For both France and Italy, the processes of financial innovation and deregulation were initiated as a result of the issuance of securities by the government in order to finance large budget deficits. As a consequence of this action, the new government securities provided an attractive base for new types of financial instruments issued by both existing and other financial intermediaries in order to defend their market shares. In Australia, Swamy and Tavlas (1989) conclude that financial deregulation has distorted the relationship between the monetary aggregates, on the one hand, and real economic activity and nominal interest rates, on the other. The conventional money demand models have severely underpredicted the surge in the targeted aggregate, M3, which led to the abandonment of the practice of announcing conditional projections of M3 in 1985.

Thus, as the result of financial innovations and deregulation, the major Central Banks of the world have broadened the concept of money and have tended to put more emphasis on broader monetary aggregates as monetary indicators for monetary management. Financial innovations have presented a number of difficulties for the interpretation of the monetary aggregates and for the conduct of monetary policy. Judd and Trehan (1988) suggest monitoring two broad monetary aggregates, M2 and M3 in the United States as M2 and M3 are not as susceptible as M1 to being disturbed by portfolio shifts because they are broad enough to internalize most of those shifts. However, other researchers have suggested different steps in dealing with financial innovations, that is, by changing the definitions of the monetary aggregates. Freedman (1983) suggests redefining the Canadian monetary aggregate in such a way as to internalise the shifts that are occuring, by incorporating nonpersonal chequable and nonchequable deposits and daily interest chequing accounts in M1 in Canada. In the United States, Simpson (1979) proposes a new M1 which contains newly introduced transactions deposits such as NOW and ATS accounts.

On the other hand, other researchers have re-estimated the money demand function by incorporating proxies for financial innovation in the model. Enzler *et al.* (1976), Goldfeld (1976), and Simpson and Porter (1980) have included ratchet variables in money demand models. Kimball (1980) and Lieberman (1979) include the number of wire transfers and a time trend respectively as proxies for financial innovation in their model. In a more recent study, Bordo and Jonung (1987) conclude that institutional factors such as 'monetisation' and 'financial development' proxy variables are important in explaining the velocity behaviour of five advanced countries.[7] According to Bordo and Jonung, the institutional variables can explain well the rise and fall of velocities in those countries.

Divisia Money as Plausible Explanation for a Stable Money-Income Relationship

Nevertheless, there are other persuasive explanations for the breakdown in the seemingly stable relationships between money and income in the developed economies. Barnett and his colleagues[8] have argued that the recent instability between money and income was the result of measurement error in measuring the nation's monetary aggregate. Barnett (1980) proposes the use of the Divisia aggregate for measuring monetary services. Instead of adding together all the asset components and treating each component with equal weights to form an aggregate, the Divisia aggregate uses the basic monetary components' user costs to calculate their contributions to the consistent monetary aggregates. These user costs measure the marginal money services yielded by each asset component. The share of each component's user cost in total user cost is used to weight that component's growth rate, and the sum of these weighted growth rates equals the change in the total Divisia aggregate.

More recently, Chrystal and MacDonald (1994) investigate the role of Divisia aggregates for the United States, United Kingdom, Australia, Germany, Switzerland, Canada and Japan. They find support for the Divisia aggregate as opposed to the Simple sum aggregate in these developed countries, even during the financial innovation era. They questioned the conclusion derived from previous influential studies that financial innovation causes the breakdown of the relationship between money and income. Instead they pointed to inappropriate measurement of money as being the main reason for instability in the link between money and income. This point has been stressed by Chrystal and MacDonald (1994: p. 74) that 'there has been a major measurement error in virtually all of the previous literature on money. Instability in empirical relationships has been primarily due to the fact that Simple sum measures of money are not admissible aggregates on index-theoretic grounds. This error has been especially important in a period when characteristics of components which are added together have been changing'.

Chrystal and MacDonald (1994: p. 76) further conclude that 'the problems with tests of money in the economy in recent years may be more due to bad measurement theory rather than to an instability in the link between the true money and the economy. Rather than a problem associated with the Lucas Critique, it could instead be a problem stemming from the Barnett Critique'.

As a matter of fact, recent studies discovered that using Divisia as opposed to Simple sum aggregate, alters significantly the conclusions reached by previous influential studies.[9] As a result, Belongia (1996) asserts that many of the monetary puzzles of the 1980s would have been resolved if Divisia monetary aggregates had been used. Belongia (1996: p. 1082) argues that 'the basic inferences about the direction, magnitude, and significance of money growth on economic activity can depend crucially on the chosen measure. Because simple-sum indexes violate basic theoretical principles, the sensitivity of empirical results illustrated here offers practical evidence against further use of the reported simple-sum monetary aggregates'.

Since the asset components of a monetary aggregate are not perfect substitutes, imposing equal weights violates the basic aggregation principles. For example, in determining the services of the transportation sector, it is illogical to add the physical units of trains, buses, taxis to come up with an aggregate flow of transportation services. This is inconsistent with economic theory. As a matter of fact, the voluminous studies existing in the literature have indicated that each monetary asset has a certain degree of 'moneyness' associated with it. Therefore, according to the proponents of the Divisia approach, it is not which assets are to be included in the measure of money stock which is important, but rather how much of each monetary asset is to be included. This argues that each component should be given a different weight when adding the various components of financial assets to arrive at the official monetary aggregates.[10]

Testing for Long-Run Relationship between Divisia Money and Income: The Seasonal Error-Correction Model Approach

Recent advances in time series analysis have yielded new procedures for estimating long-run and short-run econometric relationships between non-stationary variables. One such procedure which has become widespread in the economic literature is the use of dynamic specification with an error correction mechanism (ECM) in single-equation and multi-equation macroeconomic forecasting models. However, the ECM model is not of recent origin as it was introduced by Phillips (1954) and first used in economics by Sargan (1964). But, the ECM models have only gained recognition amongst the economists and econometricians since the published work of Davidson *et al.* (1978). In Davidson *et al.* (1978), the ECM models which include the dynamics of both short-run (changes) and long-run (levels) adjustment process was used to specify U.K.'s consumption function. The favourable performance of the ECM model relative to the traditional model has inspired other researchers to use the ECM approach in economic modelling. Although the work of Hendry (1979, 1983) and associates on aggregate consumption and money demand has been very influential, it was Granger (1981, 1986) who linked the time series properties of economic time series, in particular, to the concept of cointegration and the ECM modelling approach.

According to Granger (1988), if two non-stationary variables, say X and Y are integrated of the same order and are found to be cointegrated, a usual conventional model which includes only dependent and independent variables in their stationary form is subject to mis-specification error. However, a conventional model is said to be well specified with the inclusion of the lagged residuals from the cointegrating regression between X and Y in their level form. Furthermore, with new development in the behaviour of the properties of time series, previous influential studies, particularly on causality in the economic literature has to be revalidated. In his words, Granger (1988: p. 204) concludes that 'without z_t being explicitly used, the model will be mis-specified and the possible value of lagged y_t in forecasting x_t will be missed. Thus, many of the papers discussing causality tests based on the traditional time-series modelling techniques could have missed some of the forecastability and hence reached incorrect conclusions about non-causality in mean. It does seem that many of the causality tests that have been conducted should be re-considered'.

And more recently, Granger (1994) comments on the so-called the voluminous 'cointegration-syndrome' studies exists in the literature. Granger points out that an empirical exercise should never just test for cointegration but should always be followed with estimation of a full error-correction model of some form, as the extra gain in interpretation can be very worthwhile.

However, recent attention has been directed to the testing of integration and cointegration for the presence of seasonality in economic time series. Previous studies that used high frequency (monthly and quarterly) data have either ignored the seasonal components or used seasonal adjusted data in their analysis. Osborn *et al.* (1988) and Hylleberg *et al.* (1990) have pointed out that high frequency economic time series might also have seasonal unit roots besides the unit root at zero frequency. Despite this warning most researchers avoided the issue of seasonality in economic time series. Kunst (1994) gives three reasons for disregarding the role of seasonality in economic study. Firstly, researchers assumed that the dummy-style determination system can appropriately eliminate seasonal variations in economic time series. Secondly, researchers regard seasonal phenomena as a nuisance and as such seasonal adjustment procedure are used to eliminate them. Thirdly, the usefulness of findings for seasonal integration and cointegration for empirical tests and application has yet to be established.

Nevertheless, the important role of seasonality in economic time series has been given serious attention in recent years. Among the most recent studies includes Osborn (1990), Engle et al. (1993), McDougall (1994, 1995), Hurn (1993) and Hylleberg et al. (1993). The finding of the studies on seasonality in macroeconomic time series by Osborn (1990) for the United Kingdom, Otto and Wirjanto (1990) for Canada, Ghysels et al. (1994) for the United States, McDougall (1995) for New Zealand and Hylleberg et al. (1993) for several developed countries suggest that many macroeconomic time series exhibit significant seasonality. Osborn (1990) concludes that the finding for seasonal integration in those economic time series have important implications for seasonal cointegration.[11]

Despite the increasing interest in testing for seasonality in macroeconomic series among the researchers, most of the existing studies are mainly confined to the testing of seasonal unit roots on key macroeconomic variables. However, only McDougall (1994) and Hurn (1993) have tested for a long-run relationship between income and money in the seasonal framework. McDougall (1994) investigates the long-run relationship between money and income for New Zealand by testing for seasonal unit root in money income velocity series and also conducted seasonal cointegration tests between money supply and nominal income. He finds a non-seasonal long-run relationship between money and income for the New Zealand economy.

On the other hand, Hurn (1993) prefers estimating the seasonal error-correction models and examining the significance of the error-correction terms due to the low power of the seasonal cointegration tests.[12] In his study, Hurn finds support for the existence of seasonal cointegration in the South African monetary data. Hurn further notes that the inclusion of seasonal components improves the overall performance of the final error-correction models.

The presence of seasonal unit roots in income and money supply have also been noted by Lee and Siklos (1991) and Mills and Mills (1992). They point out that the presence of seasonal unit roots in GDP and the money supply series suggests that these series may be cointegrated at some of the seasonal frequencies. Failure to take into account of the seasonal structure of the variables will pose important problems, in particular, the correct specification of the model on which certain policy action may be based. In a more recent study, Moosa (1995) clearly indicates the importance of the order of (seasonal) integration of time series variables. Moosa (1995: p. 275) concludes from his study on Australian consumption function that 'the failure of these equations is due to the use of inappropriate filters (by overlooking the time series properties of the variables) and faulty error-correction terms (by only allowing for cointegration at the zero frequency or the long run and not at other frequencies). A finding of this study is that Australian non-durable consumption and disposable income are cointegrated at the frequency 1/4 (annual cycle), implying that the consumption-income relationship should be modelled as a seasonal error-correction model'.

Testing For Seasonal Unit Roots

The importance of seasonality in economic time series has been recognised and has been given proper treatment in economic literature. The work of Box and Jenkins (1970) implicitly assume that there are seasonal unit roots in the series by using the seasonal differencing filter. Other researchers prefer using seasonally adjusted data in the analysis. However, these approaches have been criticised by Miron (1992) and Ghysels (1988, 1990, 1992). They pointed out that seasonal adjustment might lead to wrong inference about economic relationships between the series under study. The seasonal adjustment biases the outcome toward accepting the null hypothesis that a unit root exists. Olekalns (1994) warns that tests of the unit root hypothesis should not be carried out with seasonally adjusted data.

When comparing the performance of a series between seasonally adjusted and seasonally unadjusted data, Ghysels (1990, 1992) found that the nature of unit root between the seasonally adjusted and seasonally unadjusted series gave contradictory results. Ghysels concludes that the seasonal adjustment procedure might alter the outcome of the conventional test and therefore gave substantially different results. On the other hand, Miron (1992) points out that seasonal fluctuations are not a nuisance, instead seasonality has economic importance in economic analysis and acts as a source of information in understanding economic relationships.

Thus, the problems associated with seasonal adjustment have led to the examination of seasonal unit roots and hence tests to determine orders of seasonal integration for economic time series. The essence of seasonality is that not only must each of the series be integrated of the same order but they must be seasonally integrated of the same order, otherwise the estimates of the cointegrating equations will be inconsistent. In other words, the estimates result in a spurious regression problem (see Hylleberg *et al*. 1990).

For a seasonally unadjusted economic time series, the concept of integration will include the possibility of seasonal unit roots. A seasonal economic time series, X_t, is said to be integrated of order (d, D), that is $X_t \sim I(d, D)$ if the series is stationary after first period differencing d times (unit root) and seasonal differencing D times (seasonal unit root) (see Osborn *et al*., 1988). According to Hylleberg *et al*. (1990) and Engle *et al*. (1993), for quarterly data, the seasonal difference operator $(1-B^4)$ can be decomposed into four possible roots in the generating process as follows

$$(1-B^4) = (1-B)(1+B)(1-iB)(1+iB) \qquad (5.1)$$

In equation (5.1), the roots are 1, -1, i and -i. These roots correspond to different cycles of a series in the time domain. The root 1 has a single period cycle and this corresponds to zero frequency in the frequency domain. The root -1 has two period cycles and corresponds to one-half (1/2) cycle per quarter or two cycles per year in quarterly data. The complex root i has one fourth (1/4) period cycle corresponding to one-quarter cycle per quarter or one cycle per year in quarterly data. However, the last root , -i, is indistinguishable from the one at i with quarterly data and therefore it is treated as the annual cycle.

The testing procedure for seasonal unit roots has been provided by Hasza and Fuller (1982), Dickey *et al*. (1984), Osborn *et al*. (1988), Osborn (1990), Hylleberg *et al*. (1990) and Engle *et al*. (1993). The latter two seasonal unit root testing procedures are the most popular among researchers. Furthermore, Ghysels *et al*. (1994) found out that Hylleberg *et al*. (1990) (thereafter HEGY) procedure compares favourably with other alternative procedure, in particular, with Dickey *et al*. (1984) tests.

Furthermore, Hurn (1993) points out that HEGY test has an advantage over other testing procedures in that it enable one to test for unit roots at all the seasonal cycles.

The HEGY (1990) approach consists in estimating the following regression

$$\Delta_4 x_t = \pi_1 y_{1t-1} + \pi_2 y_{2t-1} + \pi_3 y_{3t-2} + \pi_4 y_{3t-1} + \sum_{i=1}^{p} \Delta_4 x_{t-i} + \varepsilon_t \qquad (5.2)$$

where $y_{1t} = (1+B+B^2+B^3)x_t$, $y_{2t} = -(1-B+B^2-B^3)x_t$ and $y_{3t} = -(1-B^2)x_t$. For quarterly time series data, deterministic components are added in equation (5.2). The test regression now becomes

$$\Delta_4 x_t = \alpha_0 + \alpha_1 SD_{1t} + \alpha_2 SD_{2t} + \alpha_3 SD_{3t} + \theta t \\ + \pi_1 y_{1t-1} + \pi_2 y_{2t-1} + \pi_3 y_{3t-2} + \pi_4 y_{3t-1} \\ + \sum_{i=1}^{p} \Delta_4 x_{t-i} + \varepsilon_t \qquad (5.3)$$

where α_0 is a constant, t is a linear time trend and SD_{it}'s are quarterly seasonal dummy variables. The test for seasonal unit roots is by running ordinary least square (OLS) on equation (5.3) and the test statistics on π's can be used for inference. According to a simulation study by Ghysels *et al.* (1994), the inclusion of a constant and seasonal dummies appears to be a prudent decision in testing for seasonal unit roots. Ghysels *et al.* (1994: p. 436) further conclude that 'it was found that when the data-generating processes have seasonal dummies, the regression without seasonal dummies seriously distorts the test result (i.e., it leads to a large bias in the size or too low power). Hence, although inclusion of too many lags or irrelevant deterministic terms (i.e., a constant, seasonal dummies, and/or a trend) tends to reduce the power of the tests, the safe strategy in empirical applications is the inclusion of these (possibly irrelevant) terms in the model'.

To test for a unit root at zero frequency (i.e. $x_t \sim I_0(1)$) we simply perform a *t*-test on $\pi_1=0$. To test for root -1 (the biannual frequency unit root) that is, $x_t \sim I_{1/2}(1)$, a test on $\pi_2=0$ is performed. For the complex roots (an annual frequency unit root) or $x_t \sim I_{1/4}(1)$, we can perform either a joint *F*-test of $\pi_3=\pi_4=0$, or two sequential *t*-tests of $\pi_4=0$ and then $\pi_3=0$. For a series to contain no seasonal unit roots, if $\pi_2=0$ and the joint *F*-test of

$\pi_3=\pi_4=0$ must both be rejected. On the other hand, for a series to be stationary, it must have no unit roots, hence, it must established that each of the t-test of $\pi_1=\pi_2=0$ and the joint F-test of $\pi_3=\pi_4=0$ are rejected. The critical values can be found in Hylleberg et al. (1990).

Seasonal Cointegration and Error-Correction Model

According to Hylleberg et al. (1990: p. 220), 'a pair of series each of which are integrated at frequency ω are said to be cointegrated at that frequency if a linear combination of the series is not integrated at ω'. For a two variable case consisting of X and Y, where y_t and $x_t \sim I_\omega(1)$, ω=0, 1/4, 1/2, 3/4, there may exist one or no cointegrating vector at each frequency. Engle et al. (1993) have proposed a way to test for non-cointegration at frequencies zero (0), biannual (1/2) and annual (1/4 or 3/4) by estimating the following cointegrating equations (5.4), (5.5) and (5.6) respectively.

$$y_{1t} = a_1 + \alpha_1 x_{1t} + \mu_t \qquad (5.4)$$
$$y_{2t} = a_2 + \alpha_2 x_{2t} + \upsilon_t \qquad (5.5)$$
$$y_{3t} = a_3 + \alpha_3 x_{3t} + \alpha_4 x_{3t-1} + \omega_t \qquad (5.6)$$

where in each case the x_{it} and y_{it} (i=1,2,3) represent the zero, biannual and annual frequencies which are estimated with an intercept, a_i (i=1,2,3). Furthermore, y's and x's are transformed variables such that, y_{1t} and x_{1t} equal $(1+B+B^2+B^3)y_t$ and $(1+B+B^2+B^3)x_t$ respectively; y_{2t} and x_{2t} equal -$(1-B+B^2-B^3)y_t$ and $-(1-B+B^2-B^3)x_t$ respectively; y_{3t} and x_{3t} equal $-(1-B^2)y_t$ and $-(1-B^2)x_t$ respectively.

Following the Engle and Granger (1987) two-step procedure, the test for seasonal non-cointegration at a particular frequency is based on a test for a unit root at that frequency in the residuals from a first step regression. The test for non-cointegration at the zero (long run) frequency is a test for a unit root at the zero frequency in the residuals, μ_t, from the following equation

$$\Delta\mu_t = \pi_1 \mu_{t-1} + \sum_{i=1}^{k} \delta_i \Delta\mu_{t-i} + \tau_{1t} \qquad (5.7)$$

Likewise, a test of non-cointegration at the biannual frequency (1/2) is a test of there being a unit root at that frequency in the residuals, υ_t, from running the following auxiliary regression

$$\upsilon_t + \upsilon_{t-1} = \pi_2(-\upsilon_{t-1}) + \sum_{i=1}^{k} \delta_i(\upsilon_{t-i} + \upsilon_{t-i-1}) + \tau_{2t} \qquad (5.8)$$

Similarly to the above tests, the test for seasonal non-cointegration at the annual frequency (i.e. 1/4 and 3/4) can be performed by estimating the following equation

$$\omega_t + \omega_{t-2} = \pi_3(-\omega_{t-2}) + \pi_4(-\omega_{t-1})$$
$$+ \sum_{i=1}^{k} \delta_i(\omega_{t-i} + \omega_{t-i-2}) + \tau_{3t} \qquad (5.9)$$

The t-values of the test statistics of π's can be used for inference for non-cointegration at zero, biannual and annual frequencies. However, for testing for non-cointegration at the annual frequency, the F-values of the joint test $\pi_3=\pi_4=0$ is computed together with the t-values for $\pi_3=0$ and $\pi_4=0$. The critical values for π_1 and π_2 are tabulated in Engle and Yoo (1987). On the other hand, the critical values for the F-statistic for $\pi_3 \cap \pi_4 = 0$ are tabulated in Engle et al. (1993). Engle et al. (1993) show that the general form of the error-correcting mechanism which allows for cointegration (at one cointegrating vector) at all frequencies, $\omega=0$, 1/4, 1/2, 3/4, is shown to be

$$\Delta_4 y_t = c_0 + \sum_{i=1}^{q} \phi_i \Delta_4 y_{t-i} + \sum_{j=1}^{p} \lambda_j \Delta_4 x_{t-j} + \gamma_1 \mu_{t-1}$$
$$+ \gamma_2 \upsilon_{t-1} + \gamma_3 \omega_{t-2} + \gamma_4 \omega_{t-3} + \eta_{1t} \qquad (5.10)$$

where μ_{t-1}, υ_{t-1}, ω_{t-2} and ω_{t-3} are lagged residuals from the above cointegrating equations (5.4), (5.5) and (5.6) respectively.

Description and Sources of Data Used

In this study, monetary data for ten Asian countries will be used in the analysis. The Asian countries are Indonesia, Malaysia, Myanmar, Nepal, Philippines, Singapore, South Korea, Sri Lanka, Taiwan and Thailand. Monetary data used in the analysis are the various monetary aggregates employed by the central bank of each country for monetary indicator purposes, particularly, the narrow money M1 and broader M2. Usually M1 comprises currency in circulation and demand deposits held by the private sector. Broad money M2 includes M1 plus saving and fixed (time) deposits at the commercial banks.[13]

In this study, we emphasis on the potential role of Divisia monetary aggregates as the intermediate indicators in the Asian region. The reason for considering the Divisia aggregate is that the traditional Simple-sum monetary aggregate is not a good measure of monetary services of a country. According to Barnett (1980), Simple-sum aggregates are calculated on the assumption that their components receive equal weights of one and are therefore considered to be perfect substitutes. This is contrary to the voluminous studies existing in the literature which indicate that each monetary asset has a certain degree of 'moneyness' associated with it.[14] Therefore, according to the proponents of the Divisia approach, it is not which assets are to be included in the measure of money stock which is important, but rather how much of each monetary asset is to be included. This points to the conclusion that each component should be given a different weight when adding the various components of financial assets to arrive at the official monetary aggregates.[15]

The income data used in the analysis is gross domestic product (GDP). The study employed quarterly time series data ranges from 1981:1 to 1994:4. All data are collected from various issues of the *SEACEN Financial Statistics-Money and Banking* published by the SEACEN Training Centre, Kuala Lumpur, Malaysia. Another important source of data was the *International Financial Statistics* published by International Monetary Fund. Except for Singapore, South Korea and Taiwan, the GDP series for other Asian countries are only available in annual form, thus, we have used total exports as a proxy for nominal income for these countries.[16] All variables were transformed into natural logarithms and the estimation for long-run relationship between money and income is based on equation (5.10).

Discussions on Empirical Results

Results of Seasonal Unit Root Tests

The results of applying the HEGY test for seasonal unit roots are presented in Table 5.1. The optimal lag length, p, was determined using the LM test for fourth-order autoregression criterion.[17] A series of autoregressions are estimated for equation (5.3) by varying the lag order p from 0 to 10. The highest lag orders, that is, 10 quarters was determined using Schwert's (1987) ℓ_{12} rule. According to Schwert, with 56 observations, the maximum lag length for the series are determined as the integer portion of the expression, int$\{12(56/100)^{1/4}\}$. Thus, starting from 10 quarters, we pare down the model until the LM test signalled white noise residuals.

Results of the HEGY test on the level of the series clearly show that none of the test statistics indicate that the series are stationary. This imply that the level of the Divisia money and income series in the ten Asian countries are seasonally integrated of order (1,1). Next we test whether the filter Δ_4 or $\Delta\Delta_4$ is appropriate to render the series stationary. Franses (1996) notes that in some cases, seasonal differencing by applying the filter Δ_4 is adequate to achieve stationarity in an I(1,1) variable. However, this is an empirical question. Empirical studies have shown that for developing countries, Hurn (1993) and Moosa (1997) found that money and income series in South Africa and India respectively, are adequately represented by the filter $\Delta\Delta_4$ to achieve stationarity.

Nevertheless, in Table 5.1 we have reported the HEGY tests for the series in Δ_4 and $\Delta\Delta_4$. Results of the seasonal unit root test on Δ_4 series clearly indicate that in all cases, the series are non-stationary. Whereas, the HEGY tests results on $\Delta\Delta_4$ series suggest that all test statistics are significantly different from zero at the five percent level, implying that $\Delta\Delta_4 y_t \sim I(0,0)$. In other words, this implies that one-period differencing of the seasonal differences is adequate to make the series stationary.

Results of Seasonal Cointegration Tests

The results of the above unit root tests indicate that income and Divisia money series are integrated of order one but at some specific frequencies. Having established that income and Divisia money series are seasonally integrated, our next attempt is to investigate whether income and Divisia money series are seasonally cointegrated along the lines suggested by Engle *et al.* (1993). In our case, in the quarterly series, cointegration between Divisia money and income integrated at the biannual frequency is said to exist if there is at least one linear combination of the series that is stationary at that frequency. For the annual frequency case, cointegration is said to exist if there is at least one linear combination of the series, all integrated at the annual frequency and the series lagged one quarter which is stationary at that particular frequency.

Following Engle and Granger's two-step procedure, the test for seasonal non-cointegration at a particular frequency is based on a test for a unit root at that frequency in the residuals from a first step regression. The first step regression is a regression of one of the series on the other, but after proper transformations so that no unit roots exist at other frequencies. As mentioned earlier, a test of non-cointegration at the long-run frequency is a test for a unit root at the zero frequency in the residuals, μ_t, from a regression y_{1t} on m_{1t} where y_{1t} is $(1+B+B^2+B^3)y_t$, that is the sum of four consecutive values of the log of income series while m_{1t} is defined analogously for the log of the Divisia money series. Likewise, a test of non-cointegration at the biannual frequency is a test of there being a unit root at that frequency in the residuals, v_t, from a regression of $y_{2t} = -(1-B+B^2-B^3)y_t$ on $m_{2t} = -(1-B+B^2-B^3)m_t$. And for the annual frequency the first step regression is $y_{3t} = -(1-B^2)y_t$ on $m_{3t} = -(1-B^2)m_t$ and m_{3t-1} and the test for a unit root at the annual frequency in the residuals w_t is based on the F-value for $\pi_3=\pi_4=0$ in the regression $(w_t+w_{t-2}) = \pi_3(-w_{t-2}) + \pi_4(-w_{t-1})$. In testing for cointegration, we allow for augmentation of the lagged dependent variable so as to induce white noise following the LM(4) procedure mentioned earlier.

The results of testing for seasonal cointegration at the long-run, biannual and annual frequencies are presented in Tables 5.2, 5.3 and 5.4 respectively. In testing for seasonal cointegration at zero frequency, we include an intercept (I), seasonal dummies (SD) and time trend (Tr) as the deterministic components. In the auxiliary regression equations, the deterministic components are an intercept and seasonal dummies. Looking through Table 5.2, the results suggest that income and money series are not cointegrated at the zero frequency for all Asian countries at the five percent significance level. Hurn (1993) has pointed earlier that this result is expected because there is reason to believe that cointegration at the seasonal cycles is present.

For the biannual frequency case, the cointegrating and auxiliary regressions are run with an intercept and seasonal dummies. The results are tabulated in Table 5.3 and the ADF tests based on the residuals indicate that a unit root cannot be rejected for all countries except for Indonesia and Malaysia. In the former, the ADF tests suggest that unit root at biannual frequency can be rejected for Divisia M1, while for the latter only in the case of Divisia M2 that unit root can be rejected at the five percent level. Generally the above results indicate that non-cointegration at the biannual frequency for all Asian countries can be rejected at the five percent significance level.

Results of test for cointegration at the annual frequency are shown in Table 5.4. The results of F-tests on $\pi_3 \cap \pi_4 = 0$ in Table 5.4 clearly indicate that in majority of the Asian countries the null hypothesis of no cointegration at the annual frequency cannot be rejected at the five percent level. It is only in the cases of Indonesia, Malaysia, the Philippines and Sri Lanka that the null hypothesis of no cointegration at the annual frequency can be rejected. For Indonesia, both monetary aggregates exhibit long-run relationship at the annual cycle with income during the period under study. In Malaysia, only in the case of Divisia M2 that seasonal cointegration at frequency 1/4 with income is found. In the Philippines, broad monetary aggregate - Divisia M2 is found to be cointegrated with income, while in Sri Lanka, Divisia monetary aggregates (both M1 and M2) exhibit long-run relationship with income at the annual cycle.

Results of the Seasonal Error-Correction Models

The results of estimating the full seasonal error-correction models for the ten Asian countries are presented in Tables 5.5 through 5.8. When we estimate equation (5.10), the ECM terms at different frequencies are first derived by estimating the cointegrating regressions (5.4), (5.5) and (5.6) for allowing cointegration at zero, biannual and annual frequencies respectively. In estimating the cointegrating regression at zero frequency, we include an intercept, seasonal dummies and time trend as additional variables. For cointegration at biannual and annual frequencies, the cointegrating regressions include the intercept and seasonal dummies. The lagged residuals from these cointegrating regressions are then added to equation (5.10). For all error-correction models estimated, we allow for cointegration at all frequencies. However, the final seasonal error-correction models presented in Tables 5.5 through 5.8 were derived according to the Hendry's 'general-to-specific' specification search and the congruency of the model with the data generating process (see Hendry, 1987) are observed from a battery of diagnostic tests which include the test for serial correlation, heteroskedasticity, normality and functional form. The diagnostic tests, namely; the LM(4) test for serial correlation, Arch (4) test for autoregressive conditional heteroskedasticity, Jarque-Bera test for normality of the residuals and Ramsey Reset test to test whether the original functional form is incorrect; show that the estimated error-correction models for all Asian countries estimated passes these tests at the five percent significance level. Thus, the above diagnostic tests indicate well-fitting seasonal error-correction models for each country that fulfills the conditions of serial non-correlation, homoskedasticity, normality of residuals and no specification errors.

Generally, the results of estimating the seasonal error-correction models show that in all cases except three (in the cases of Singapore, South Korea and Thailand), the error-corrections at all seasonal cycles in the parsimonious models are significantly different from zero at five percent level and correctly signed. In seven Asian countries, namely, Indonesia, Malaysia, Myanmar, Nepal, Philippines, Sri Lanka and Taiwan, the results strongly suggest that the existence of a long-run relationships between Divisia money and income at the frequencies other than zero, implying that the income-Divisia money relationship should be modelled as a seasonal error-correction model. Failure to do this, the estimated Divisia money-income equation will subject to mis-specification error.

In six of the Asian countries, namely; Malaysia, Nepal, Philippines, Singapore, South Korea and Taiwan (except for Divisia M2) the results exhibit long-run relationships at the frequencies zero and 1/4. Only in the cases of Myanmar (for both Divisia monetary aggregates) and Taiwan for Divisia M2 can a long-run relationship between money and income at all frequencies be established. For Indonesia and Sri Lanka, Divisia money and income are cointegrated at both zero and biannual frequencies. For Thailand, the results indicate that for Divisia M1, cointegration exist at the zero and biannual frequencies. However, for broad money - Divisia M2 and income are cointegrated at the zero frequency.

For comparison, we have included the summary of the results of the long-run relationships between Divisia money and income using both approaches - the Engle-Granger two-step and the ECM procedures in Table 5.9. We can observe that there is a great contrast between the two results. In general, the results of the error-correction models provide support for seasonal cointegration between money and income, while the results of the Engle-Granger procedure do not. The contradictions in the results clearly suggest the low power of the Engle-Granger two-step procedure in testing for seasonal cointegration.

Conclusions

More recently, the work of Hylleberg *et al.* (1990) and Engle *et al.* (1993) has enabled researchers to investigate the time series properties of an economic series when they contain seasonal components not only at the zero frequency but also possibly at the biannual and annual frequencies. The fact that a time series is integrated at seasonal frequencies implies that it possesses long memory properties so that shocks tend to last permanently and moreover they tend to alter the seasonal pattern permanently. The finding that time series exhibit seasonal unit roots at different frequencies suggest that some series may be cointegrated at the seasonal frequencies. Cointegration established at different frequencies will lead to an interesting seasonal error-correction model. Moosa (1995) points out that an error-correction model will be misspecified if cointegration at the seasonal frequencies is present but is not accounted for.

In this chapter we have endeavoured to investigate the seasonal properties of Divisia money and nominal income series for ten Asian countries. The three variables - Divisia M1, Divisia M2 and nominal income were first tested for seasonal unit roots using the test procedure proposed by Hylleberg *et al.* (1990). Having established that these series are seasonally integrated of the same order, it is possible to proceed to test for seasonal cointegration using the Engle-Granger (EG) two-step procedure.

The results of this study can be summarised as follows. First, our seasonal unit root test for the three series for all the Asian countries indicate that the variables are integrated of order, $x_t \sim I(1,1)$. This implies that one-period differencing of the seasonal differences ($\Delta\Delta_4$) is adequate to make the series stationary, i.e. $\Delta\Delta_4 x_t \sim I(0,0)$. Second, since all the variables are seasonally integrated of the same order, we proceed using the EG two-step procedure to test for cointegration at the zero (long-run), biannual and annual frequencies. Our results suggest that Divisia money and income are not cointegrated in the majority of the Asian countries. This means that there is no long-run relationship between money and income in these countries, thus implying that the use of Divisia money for monetary policy purposes would prove ineffective. However, results from the EG two-step procedure do suggest that for Sri Lanka, Divisia money and income is cointegrated at the annual frequency. Similar results are also suggested for the Philippines in the case of Divisia money M1, and for Indonesia in the case of Divisia M2. This implies that money and income for these countries exhibit a long-run relationship at some seasonal cycles.

Third, as an indirect test for seasonal cointegration between Divisia money and income, we have estimated the seasonal error-correction model and examined the significance of the various error-correction terms that represent cointegration at the long-run, biannual frequency and annual frequency. Contrary to our earlier results using the EG two-step procedure, we discovered that for all of the Asian countries, Divisia money and income are cointegrated not only at the long-run, but also at the seasonal cycles. In the cases of Indonesia and Sri Lanka, Divisia money and income are cointegrated at the zero and biannual frequencies. A similar relationship between Divisia money M1 and income is also obtained for Thailand. However, for majority of the Asian countries (Malaysia, Nepal, the Philippines, Singapore, South Korea and Taiwan (for Divisia money M1)), money and income are cointegrated at the long-run and annual cycle. It is only in the cases of Myanmar and Taiwan (for Divisia money M2) that cointegration between money and income was obtained at all frequencies. These results suggest that the money-income relationship in the Asian developing countries should be modelled as a seasonal error-correction model, except in the case of Divisia money M2 for Thailand in which the standard error-correction model is more appropriate.

Fourth, our results further suggest that given the low power of the unit root test derived using the EG two-step procedure, there is a strong case for estimating the seasonal error correction model directly to infer seasonal cointegration between variables. Thus, it does seem that results of many of the influential studies on seasonal cointegration based on the EG two-step procedure are questionable and should be re-considered.

Nevertheless, the results of this study indicate that the monetary authorities of the Asian countries should monitor Divisia monetary aggregates as additional intermediate indicators for their monetary policy action purposes. However, whether Divisia monetary aggregate is superior to its counter-part Simple-sum monetary aggregate is an empirical question that needs to be addressed in the future.

Notes

1. Silber (1983) provides a list of new financial products and practices (financial innovations) in the United States for the period 1970-82. According to Silber, the important sources that induced financial innovations in the United States are financial constraints (external and internal), high level of interest rates, legislation and technological breakthrough.
2. Akhtar (1983) surveys empirical evidence on five industrial countries including the United States, United Kingdom, Canada, Japan and Italy. He concludes that there is considerable evidence of shifts or instability in the money demand function in these countries.
3. The nine Asian countries include Indonesia, Malaysia, Myanmar, Nepal, Philippines, Singapore, South Korea, Sri Lanka and Thailand.
4. See Chapter 1 for discussions on financial deepening and monetisation in the Asian countries.
5. Other financial indicators that could serve such purpose includes interest rate, exchange rate, credit aggregates etc. However, addressing the issue of whether these indicators are better candidates than a monetary aggregate is beyond the scope of this study. Federal Reserve Bank of New York (1990) provides a collection of empirical studies on alternatives intermediate indicators for monetary policy for the United States.
6. According to Christelow (1981), the main forms of financial innovations in Japan include the introduction of flexibility into interest rates on bank and postal deposits and on new issue rates for bonds, the advent of sogo accounts and the successive introduction of new short-term instruments bearing market rates of interest.
7. These countries include United States, Canada, United Kingdom, Sweden and Norway. Bordo and Jonung (1987) used the share of the labour force in nonagricultural pursuits as a proxy for monetisation, and the ratio of total nonbank financial assets to financial assets as a proxy for financial development.
8. See for example Barnett (1980) and Barnett *et al.* (1984). Judd and Scadding (1982) and Stone and Thornton (1987) have also highlighted the potential problems using Simple sum aggregate as opposed to the Divisia aggregate.

9. Barnett *et al.* (1992) provide evidence from other developed countries which support the superiority of Divisia aggregate compared to the Simple sum aggregate.
10. See Chapter 3 for further discussions on brief survey, empirical evidences and derivation of a Divisia monetary aggregate.
11. See Franses (1996) for a more recent survey and treatment of seasonality in economics.
12. This probably explains why McDougall (1994) found an 'unexpected' result when money (m1) and income (py) are cointegrated although both series have different order of seasonal integration.
13. A detailed discussion on alternative monetary aggregates used by the central banks of different countries all over the world are given by Kumah (1989).
14. Barnett *et al.* (1992) provide theoretical background and a survey on divisia approach in measuring money.
15. The computation of the Divisia aggregates for the Asian countries investigated are provided in Chapter 3.
16. Furthermore, the use of export will minimise any spurious results that will arise when using income that had been generated using some interpolation technique. Nevertheless, one has to be cautious when interpreting the results.
17. See Schlitzer (1995, 1996) for similar approach. However, instead of using the Box-Ljung test, we follow Harvey's (1985) recommendation in using the LM principle for testing for serial correlation as it yield a more satisfactory test compared to the former.

Table 5.1
Results of HEGY tests for seasonal unit roots

Country	Series in level	π_1	π_2	π_3	π_4	$\pi_3 \cap \pi_4$	p	LM(4)
Indonesia	dm1	-0.60	-2.88	-2.71	-0.58	3.93	4	4.42
	dm2	-1.44	-2.77	-2.75	-1.39	5.26	4	5.22
	income	-2.05	-2.54	-3.07	-1.44	5.89	3	6.44
Malaysia	dm1	-1.82	-1.58	-3.33	-0.85	6.24	4	2.62
	dm2	-0.77	-1.31	-3.30	-1.11	6.28	7	5.35
	income	-1.96	-2.44	-2.30	-0.68	3.11	10	6.10
Myanmar	dm1	-1.06	-2.06	-3.48	-0.70	6.35	5	1.27
	dm2	-0.86	-1.92	-3.19	-0.82	5.45	5	1.46
	income	-0.22	-2.32	-2.57	-0.74	3.62	10	1.27
Nepal	dm1	-1.74	-2.84	-1.26	-1.87	2.47	5	4.06
	dm2	-1.31	-2.63	-2.12	-0.61	2.38	3	0.67
	income	-1.89	-1.58	-3.60	0.01	6.53	7	2.80
Philippines	dm1	-1.52	-1.78	-3.39	-1.08	6.34	7	8.95
	dm2	-3.42	-0.82	0.06	-1.61	1.31	10	2.73
	income	-2.20	-2.32	-3.17	-0.31	5.06	9	8.72
Singapore	dm1	-2.61	-1.73	-2.63	-1.07	3.98	5	4.17
	dm2	-3.47	-1.82	-2.18	-2.26*	5.51	5	7.16
	income	-3.23	-1.84	-2.52	-0.55	3.42	10	3.87
South Korea	dm1	-2.55	-2.27	-2.37	-1.27	3.68	5	2.88
	dm2	-2.66	-2.10	-2.53	-2.04	5.43	5	4.87
	income	-1.59	-1.27	-2.19	0.38	2.49	8	4.20
Sri Lanka	dm1	-1.62	-2.59	-3.26	-1.26	6.50	6	2.20
	dm2	-1.33	-2.50	-1.64	-1.80	3.30	6	3.75
	income	-0.68	-2.73	-3.05	1.45	5.75	5	6.45
Taiwan	dm1	-1.60	-2.60	-0.96	-2.77*	4.58	6	1.23
	dm2	-1.34	-2.83	-1.07	-2.87*	5.07	6	1.23
	income	-1.41	-1.91	-1.69	-1.84	3.14	7	1.78
Thailand	dm1	-2.17	-2.15	-2.34	-1.52	4.37	6	3.81
	dm2	-2.48	-1.55	-1.79	-1.36	2.51	7	4.86
	income	-1.90	-2.46	-1.70	-1.39	2.40	5	4.28

Notes: All regressions were estimated with intercept, seasonal dummies and trend as deterministic components. The 5 percent critical value are $t:\pi_1 = -3.71$, $t:\pi_2 = -3.08$, $t:\pi_3 = -3.66$, $t:\pi_4 = -1.91/1.97$, $F:\pi_3 \cap \pi_4 = 6.55$ (see Tables 1a and 1b in Hylleberg et al. (1990)). The LM Chi-square statistic for serial correlation with 4 lags is 9.48 with four degree of freedom (5 percent). Asterisk (*) denotes statistically significant at 5 percent level.

Table 5.1 (continued)

Country	Series in Δ_4	π_1	π_2	π_3	π_4	$\pi_3 \cap \pi_4$	p	LM(4)
Indonesia	dm1	-2.59	-4.00*	-5.20*	-0.85	14.50*	4	3.58
	dm2	-2.36	-3.46*	-5.22*	-1.20	16.19*	4	3.24
	income	-2.85	-2.83*	-4.41*	-1.59	11.23*	3	0.85
Malaysia	dm1	-1.41	-3.36*	-5.60*	-2.29*	18.19*	5	1.61
	dm2	-1.82	-3.66*	-4.77*	-2.93*	16.28*	5	1.15
	income	-2.81	-3.55*	-5.27*	-1.04	15.68*	4	5.05
Myanmar	dm1	-2.21	-3.21*	-4.58*	-1.61	14.16*	4	2.58
	dm2	-1.78	-2.89*	-4.43*	-1.59	13.17*	4	2.68
	income	-2.02	-3.62*	-5.29*	-1.53	18.27*	4	4.68
Nepal	dm1	-1.94	-4.41*	-3.46*	-3.37*	11.68*	5	1.55
	dm2	-2.08	-5.88*	-5.85*	-4.34*	26.57*	1	2.31
	income	-2.80	-3.29*	-5.77*	-1.25	19.47*	4	1.23
Philippines	dm1	-2.45	-4.80*	-8.16*	-2.34*	37.35*	5	6.37
	dm2	-2.31	-3.43*	-5.14*	-2.68*	17.65*	5	5.84
	income	-2.75	-2.58*	-4.67*	-0.37	10.94*	9	2.14
Singapore	dm1	-2.37	-2.34*	-2.58*	-2.21*	8.08*	8	3.39
	dm2	-2.61	-3.03*	-2.08*	-2.37*	5.88*	8	5.17
	income	-1.83	-2.42*	-3.04*	-1.78*	6.23*	5	1.21
South Korea	dm1	-1.63	-2.11*	-1.52	-1.27	2.32	8	3.12
	dm2	-1.90	-1.86	-1.56	-2.12*	4.18*	8	1.04
	income	-1.28	-1.68	-2.31*	-0.48	2.85	8	0.22
Sri Lanka	dm1	-1.95	-3.57*	-5.45*	-1.69	16.38*	5	4.14
	dm2	-1.41	-3.54*	-3.63*	-3.45*	12.37*	5	6.80
	income	-2.22	-3.28*	-5.84*	2.18*	19.21*	3	3.12
Taiwan	dm1	-2.11	-3.77*	-2.09*	-2.77*	7.42*	6	5.16
	dm2	-1.61	-3.57*	-3.84*	-2.85*	11.43*	5	5.58
	income	-1.38	-2.47*	-3.71*	-1.77*	10.31*	6	2.39
Thailand	dm1	-1.91	-2.36*	-5.36*	-2.29*	23.89*	4	1.07
	dm2	-2.24	-3.30*	-2.20*	-2.95*	8.68*	6	2.53
	income	-2.53	-4.51*	-2.32*	-2.73*	6.75*	3	1.02

Notes: All regressions were estimated with an intercept as deterministic component. The 5 percent critical value are $t:\pi_1 = -2.96$, $t:\pi_2 = -1.95$, $t:\pi_3 = -1.90$, $t:\pi_4 = -1.72/1.68$, $F:\pi_3 \cap \pi_4 = 3.04$ (see Tables 1a and 1b in Hylleberg et al. (1990)). The LM Chi-square statistic for serial correlation with 4 lags is 9.48 with four degree of freedom (5 percent). Asterisk (*) denotes statistically significant at 5 percent level.

Table 5.1 (continued)

Country	Series in $\Delta\Delta_4$	π_1	π_2	π_3	π_4	$\pi_3 \cap \pi_4$	p	LM(4)
Indonesia	dm1	-3.86*	-3.43*	-3.77*	2.27*	12.20*	2	8.79
	dm2	-3.76*	-3.15*	-4.69*	1.84*	15.33*	2	6.58
	income	-4.38*	-4.21*	-5.33*	0.73	15.09*	4	7.21
Malaysia	dm1	-3.17*	-2.82*	-5.44*	2.29*	17.53*	1	7.29
	dm2	-3.67*	-4.05*	-6.08*	0.51	19.12*	4	3.52
	income	-4.11*	-3.04*	-5.85*	1.94*	19.09*	1	5.33
Myanmar	dm1	-3.41*	-3.71*	-5.02*	0.97	14.29*	4	1.45
	dm2	-3.40*	-3.45*	-4.88*	0.99	13.77*	4	0.86
	income	-5.10*	-3.71*	-6.98*	1.22	25.09*	1	4.90
Nepal	dm1	-4.24*	-4.68*	-5.10*	-0.30	13.15*	4	2.98
	dm2	-3.61*	-3.74*	-4.04*	0.72	8.76*	4	1.98
	income	-4.35*	-3.64*	-7.55*	2.30*	32.82*	1	1.93
Philippines	dm1	-5.38*	-5.76*	-8.24*	1.31	39.55*	4	6.22
	dm2	-3.48*	-3.78*	-6.19*	0.27	19.53*	4	2.23
	income	-4.22*	-3.60*	-7.38*	2.00*	29.14*	1	6.68
Singapore	dm1	-3.59*	-3.78*	-5.70*	0.04	16.24*	4	1.72
	dm2	-5.31*	-5.52*	-7.19*	-1.09	29.29*	0	3.93
	income	-3.74*	-3.16*	-4.38*	0.41	9.64*	2	0.87
South Korea	dm1	-3.61*	-4.45*	-7.64*	0.61	31.17*	1	4.97
	dm2	-3.30*	-3.41*	-4.82*	0.78	12.08*	5	8.31
	income	-4.59*	-3.56*	-5.11*	1.05	14.15*	0	5.04
Sri Lanka	dm1	-4.36*	-3.47*	-6.91*	1.84*	25.48*	1	5.86
	dm2	-3.51*	-4.80*	-8.47*	-0.35	35.91*	1	4.02
	income	-6.39*	-3.62*	-2.57*	6.33*	34.83*	2	4.74
Taiwan	dm1	-3.49*	-5.56*	-7.73*	0.47	30.76*	0	3.08
	dm2	-3.19*	-3.83*	-5.08*	0.15	12.94*	4	5.67
	income	-4.72*	-3.87*	-4.81*	0.39	11.75*	4	3.34
Thailand	dm1	-4.78*	-3.24*	-8.36*	1.65	36.63*	1	8.43
	dm2	-3.28*	-3.85*	-4.95*	-0.61	13.05*	4	1.31
	income	-4.24*	-4.18*	-4.77*	-0.62	11.52*	4	1.89

Notes: All regressions were estimated with an intercept as deterministic component. The 5 percent critical value are $t:\pi_1 = -2.96$, $t:\pi_2 = -1.95$, $t:\pi_3 = -1.90$, $t:\pi_4 = -1.72/1.68$, $F:\pi_3 \cap \pi_4 = 3.04$ (see Tables 1a and 1b in Hylleberg et al. (1990)). The LM Chi-square statistic for serial correlation with 4 lags is 9.48 with four degree of freedom (5 percent). Asterisk (*) denotes statistically significant at 5 percent level.

Table 5.2
Tests for cointegration at frequency zero: The long-run

Country	Money series	Cointegrating regressions			Auxiliary regression - tests for unit roots in residuals		
		Coefficient on regressor	R^2	DW	Dickey-Fuller test π_1	p	LM(4)
Indonesia	dm1	0.169	0.964	0.16	-2.96	2	4.55
	dm2	0.493	0.972	0.21	-2.87	6	6.22
Malaysia	dm1	1.185	0.990	0.19	-3.24	6	2.12
	dm2	1.980	0.981	0.13	-1.71	7	1.24
Myanmar	dm1	1.421	0.870	0.58	-1.68	10	1.49
	dm2	1.942	0.891	0.54	-2.30	9	2.53
Nepal	dm1	3.389	0.961	0.20	-3.27	6	1.22
	dm2	3.767	0.958	0.18	-3.31	6	1.38
Philippines	dm1	1.457	0.992	0.32	-2.13	8	1.60
	dm2	0.759	0.978	0.18	-1.63	9	3.36
Singapore	dm1	1.374	0.993	0.22	-1.58	9	1.95
	dm2	0.871	0.988	0.10	-1.66	9	2.41
South Korea	dm1	0.098	0.996	0.09	-1.49	9	2.40
	dm2	0.364	0.997	0.12	-1.36	9	2.47
Sri Lanka	dm1	-1.41	0.975	0.20	-3.11	7	2.02
	dm2	0.577	0.961	0.16	-0.86	8	3.05
Taiwan	dm1	0.106	0.998	0.23	-1.65	6	4.48
	dm2	0.129	0.998	0.24	-1.65	6	4.30
Thailand	dm1	1.193	0.983	0.11	-1.60	6	2.36
	dm2	0.705	0.971	0.08	-1.59	7	5.71

Notes: All cointegrating regressions were estimated with intercept, seasonal dummies and trend as deterministic components. All auxiliary regressions were estimated with intercept and seasonal dummies as deterministic components. The 5 percent critical value is $t:\pi_1 = -3.29$ (T=50). The t-statistic for π_1 is distributed as described in Engle and Granger (1987) and Engle and Yoo (1987). The LM Chi-square statistic for serial correlation with four lags is 9.48 with four degree of freedom (5 percent).

Table 5.3
Tests for cointegration at frequency ½: Biannual cycle

Country	Money series	Cointegrating regressions			Auxiliary regression - tests for unit roots in residuals		
		Coefficient on regressor	R^2	DW	Dickey-Fuller test π_1	p	LM(4)
Indonesia	dm1	-0.840	0.284	2.63	-4.60*	7	2.13
	dm2	-0.734	0.260	2.50	-2.73	1	3.58
Malaysia	dm1	0.945	0.481	1.75	-2.65	9	0.22
	dm2	0.694	0.421	1.78	-3.54*	10	2.99
Myanmar	dm1	0.367	0.534	2.60	-2.57	10	2.59
	dm2	0.607	0.537	2.63	-2.50	10	2.76
Nepal	dm1	-0.534	0.101	1.96	-1.63	8	0.98
	dm2	-0.219	0.095	2.01	-1.63	8	0.91
Philippines	dm1	0.599	0.122	2.76	-2.12	5	6.15
	dm2	0.194	0.026	2.39	-2.12	5	5.28
Singapore	dm1	0.223	0.627	0.99	-1.90	6	1.04
	dm2	0.376	0.664	1.07	-1.62	5	2.50
South Korea	dm1	-0.201	0.909	3.59	-1.33	9	1.73
	dm2	-0.417	0.907	3.56	-1.28	9	1.75
Sri Lanka	dm1	0.737	0.054	3.12	-3.00	6	2.72
	dm2	1.196	0.059	3.17	-2.09	7	3.71
Taiwan	dm1	0.226	0.389	3.30	-1.99	10	2.07
	dm2	0.243	0.374	3.29	-1.96	10	1.16
Thailand	dm1	0.245	0.029	1.49	-1.65	9	2.42
	dm2	-0.171	0.017	1.48	-1.61	9	2.75

Notes: All cointegrating and auxiliary regressions were estimated with intercept and seasonal dummies as deterministic components. The 5 percent critical value is $t:\pi_2 = -3.29$ (T=50). The t-statistic for π_2 is distributed as described in Engle and Granger (1987) and Engle and Yoo (1987). The LM Chi-square statistic for serial correlation with four lags is 9.48 with four degree of freedom (5 percent). Asterisk (*) denotes statistically significant at 5 percent level.

Table 5.4
Tests for cointegration at frequency ¼ (and ¾): Annual cycle

Country	Money series	Cointegrating regressions			Auxiliary regressions - Tests for unit roots in residuals				
		Coefficient on regressors					HEGY tests		
		x_{3t}	x_{3t-1}	R^2	π_3	π_4	$\pi_3 \cap \pi_4$	p	LM(4)
Indonesia	dm1	-0.561	1.045	0.251	-3.98	-1.37	10.01*	2	3.24
	dm2	-0.669	1.110	0.255	-4.41*	-1.49	10.79*	3	3.38
Malaysia	dm1	-0.359	1.343	0.515	-4.08*	0.38	8.45	5	2.26
	dm2	0.028	0.896	0.471	-4.82*	-0.61	12.00*	2	1.11
Myanmar	dm1	0.143	-0.105	0.382	-2.98	-0.28	4.53	6	2.41
	dm2	0.151	0.017	0.380	-2.94	-0.16	4.35	6	2.34
Nepal	dm1	0.337	-0.053	0.188	-3.79	-1.24	8.47	4	0.95
	dm2	0.780	-0.347	0.201	-3.89	-1.19	8.76	4	1.61
Philippines	dm1	0.485	0.899	0.579	-3.96	-0.67	8.09	4	1.52
	dm2	0.124	0.689	0.220	-5.59*	-0.23	15.73*	3	2.90
Singapore	dm1	0.118	0.346	0.649	-1.04	-1.01	1.05	5	1.68
	dm2	0.397	0.186	0.704	-2.32	-1.97	4.68	3	0.74
South Korea	dm1	-0.075	-0.101	0.875	-2.62	-0.70	3.74	5	1.58
	dm2	-0.099	-0.031	0.871	-2.21	0.28	2.51	9	1.73
Sri Lanka	dm1	-1.279	0.184	0.478	-4.98*	2.26*	14.97*	3	1.19
	dm2	-0.249	-0.145	0.436	-5.58*	2.16*	17.95*	3	1.62
Taiwan	dm1	0.209	-0.085	0.285	-1.56	-1.71	3.10	8	2.90
	dm2	0.220	-0.098	0.263	-0.93	-1.31	0.46	10	3.32
Thailand	dm1	0.881	-0.117	0.097	-1.41	-1.59	2.40	5	2.57
	dm2	0.021	0.131	0.020	-0.84	-2.83*	4.50	7	1.22

Notes: All cointegrating and auxiliary regressions were estimated with intercept and seasonal dummies as deterministic components. The 5 percent critical value are $t:\pi_3 = -4.00$, $t:\pi_4 = -2.01/2.00$, $F:\pi_3 \cap \pi_4 = 9.78$ (See Table A.3 in Engle *et al.* (1993)). The LM Chi-square statistic for serial correlation with four lags is 9.48 with four degree of freedom (5 percent). Asterisk (*) denotes statistically significant at 5 percent level.

Table 5.5
Results of seasonal error-correction models

Independent variables	Indonesia Divisia M1	Indonesia Divisia M2	Malaysia Divisia M1	Malaysia Divisia M2	Myanmar Divisia M1	Myanmar Divisia M2
Constant	-0.0060 (0.4186)	-0.0006 (0.0494)	0.0050 (0.8095)	0.0017 (0.2454)	0.0130 (0.3346)	0.0236 (0.6090)
μ_{t-1}	-0.1919 (5.5729)*	-0.2620 (7.3942)*	-0.2047 (6.0215)*	-0.1042 (3.9922)*	-0.2333 (3.5193)*	-0.2893 (3.9394)*
v_{t-1}	-0.8451 (5.7017)*	-0.8416 (6.4734)*			-0.4371 (2.3024)*	-0.4168 (2.2109)*
ω_{t-2}			-0.3532 (3.4350)*	-0.2956 (2.3946)*	-0.3288 (2.2627)*	-0.3120 (2.2007)*
ω_{t-3}			0.2969 (2.6912)*	0.2966 (2.3741)*	0.4502 (3.2545)*	0.3891 (2.8430)*
$\Delta\Delta_4 M_{t-1}$				0.4178 (1.6436)		
$\Delta\Delta_4 M_{t-5}$					-0.4283 (2.3063)*	-0.5778 (1.9381)
$\Delta\Delta_4 Y_{t-1}$	-0.7508 (6.2473)*	-0.8371 (7.6137)*			-0.4433 (3.3739)*	-0.4817 (3.6046)*
$\Delta\Delta_4 Y_{t-2}$	-0.2341 (2.5541)*	-0.2927 (3.5647)*	-0.4148 (3.7161)*	-0.3049 (2.2610)*	-0.3300 (2.7013)*	-0.3409 (2.8685)*
$\Delta\Delta_4 Y_{t-3}$	-0.3682 (3.3771)*	-0.3999 (4.1118)*				
$\Delta\Delta_4 Y_{t-4}$	-0.3294 (3.5208)*	-0.2976 (3.5999)*				
$\Delta\Delta_4 Y_{t-5}$	-0.3051 (2.9657)*	-0.3162 (3.4618)*		-0.2937 (2.4389)*		
$\Delta\Delta_4 Y_{t-10}$					-0.2406 (2.4076)*	-0.2177 (2.1934)*
R-squared	0.681	0.751	0.573	0.498	0.710	0.714
SER	0.097	0.085	0.043	0.048	0.242	0.240
DW	1.876	1.805	2.582	2.256	2.149	2.155
LM $\chi^2(4)$	2.168 [0.705]	4.316 [0.364]	7.258 [0.123]	5.941 [0.203]	4.753 [0.313]	3.305 [0.508]
Arch $\chi^2(4)$	2.615 [0.624]	2.851 [0.582]	3.883 [0.422]	2.001 [0.735]	1.243 [0.870]	0.849 [0.931]
Norm $\chi^2(2)$	0.472 [0.789]	1.576 [0.455]	0.916 [0.632]	0.092 [0.954]	0.934 [0.627]	0.782 [0.676]
Reset $\chi^2(2)$	0.355 [0.837]	2.650 [0.266]	0.312 [0.855]	1.292 [0.524]	1.244 [0.536]	2.133 [0.344]

Notes: Numbers in parentheses (.) are t-statistics and numbers in the square brackets [.] are p-values. Asterisk (*) denotes statistically significant at 5 percent level. Others are as previously defined.

Table 5.6
Results of seasonal error-correction models

Independent variables	Nepal Divisia M1	Nepal Divisia M2	Philippines Divisia M1	Philippines Divisia M2	Singapore Divisia M1	Singapore Divisia M2
Constant	0.0162 (0.9502)	0.0083 (0.5281)	-0.0066 (0.7210)	0.0029 (0.2835)	0.0007 (0.3756)	-0.0007 (0.3830)
μ_{t-1}	-0.1525 (5.7396)*	-0.1556 (6.2826)*	-0.1540 (3.4365)*	-0.1750 (5.7913)*	-0.0977 (4.4902)*	-0.0393 (2.5267)*
v_{t-1}						
ω_{t-2}	-0.5252 (5.4124)*	-0.5729 (6.2649)*	-0.7142 (5.8031)*	-0.3575 (3.1238)*	-0.2408 (2.2407)*	-0.4272 (3.3114)*
ω_{t-3}	0.4079 (3.1309)*	0.3382 (2.8918)*	0.7506 (5.6039)*	0.3392 (2.4609)*	0.3617 (3.2509)*	0.5203 (3.9487)*
dum84:3			0.2859 (4.5043)*	0.3497 (4.5989)*		
dum89:2	-0.5500 (4.6371)*	-0.5325 (4.9133)*				
dum90:1&2			0.2516 (5.7824)*	0.3039 (6.0809)*		
$\Delta\Delta_4 M_t$			0.6488 (6.1490)*		0.2114 (2.8398)*	0.2615 (2.6530)*
$\Delta\Delta_4 M_{t-1}$		0.9989 (1.8899)	0.7311 (6.5840)*			0.2894 (2.7022)*
$\Delta\Delta_4 M_{t-7}$			-0.2801 (2.6911)*			
$\Delta\Delta_4 M_{t-9}$	-0.7913 (1.6824)				-0.0604 (0.7992)	
$\Delta\Delta_4 Y_{t-2}$	-0.5374 (6.0302)*	-0.5248 (6.4317)*	-0.3371 (4.3508)*	-0.2850 (3.3578)*		
$\Delta\Delta_4 Y_{t-4}$	-0.2780 (2.7835)*	-0.3850 (4.1221)*		-0.3272 (3.6064)*		
$\Delta\Delta_4 Y_{t-5}$						-0.2260 (1.7655)
$\Delta\Delta_4 Y_{t-6}$					-0.2632 (2.1178)*	
$\Delta\Delta_4 Y_{t-9}$						-0.1476 (1.4837)
R-squared	0.776	0.802	0.876	0.817	0.635	0.615
SER	0.111	0.104	0.059	0.070	0.012	0.013
DW	2.496	2.511	2.069	1.774	2.134	1.815
LM $\chi^2(4)$	3.844 [0.427]	4.056 [0.398]	2.112 [0.715]	2.680 [0.612]	2.521 [0.641]	4.002 [0.406]
Arch $\chi^2(4)$	1.831 [0.766]	2.462 [0.651]	1.520 [0.823]	4.322 [0.364]	3.331 [0.504]	1.216 [0.875]
Norm $\chi^2(2)$	0.506 [0.776]	1.454 [0.483]	1.302 [0.521]	0.663 [0.717]	1.039 [0.595]	2.145 [0.342]
Reset $\chi^2(2)$	2.763 [0.251]	2.766 [0.251]	1.505 [0.471]	0.729 [0.694]	1.083 [0.581]	0.441 [0.801]

Notes: Numbers in parentheses (.) are t-statistics and numbers in the square brackets [.] are p-values. Asterisk (*) denotes statistically significant at 5 percent level. Others are as previously defined.

Table 5.7
Results of seasonal error-correction models

Independent variables	South Korea Divisia M1	South Korea Divisia M2	Sri Lanka Divisia M1	Sri Lanka Divisia M2	Taiwan Divisia M1	Taiwan Divisia M2
Constant	-0.0007 (0.1804)	-0.0008 (0.1948)	0.0048 (0.2786)	-0.0139 (0.6956)	-0.0043 (1.2207)	-0.0037 (1.2805)
μ_{t-1}	-0.1261 (3.0361)*	-0.1481 (3.2297)*	-0.2098 (4.6163)*	-0.1715 (3.8882)*	-0.1513 (2.3303)*	-0.1537 (2.6126)*
v_{t-1}			-0.4617 (4.6596)*	-0.4481 (4.0368)*		-0.1820 (1.8337)
ω_{t-2}	-0.1121 (1.6804)	-0.1155 (1.7812)			-0.2513 (2.3453)*	-0.2795 (2.4165)*
ω_{t-3}	0.0491 (0.7077)	0.0477 (0.6945)			0.4734 (4.0363)*	0.5649 (5.6220)*
dum88:3					0.1210 (4.8686)*	0.1080 (5.2194)*
$\Delta\Delta_4 M_t$			-1.6179 (3.9727)*	-2.4152 (2.8076)*		
$\Delta\Delta_4 M_{t-1}$						0.1960 (2.3641)*
$\Delta\Delta_4 M_{t-2}$	0.0735 (1.7460)	0.2081 (1.8793)				
$\Delta\Delta_4 M_{t-8}$						-0.1726 (2.1690)*
$\Delta\Delta_4 M_{t-9}$					-0.1668 (2.3765)*	
$\Delta\Delta_4 Y_{t-1}$	-0.3577 (2.6155)*	-0.3635 (2.7007)*	-0.8900 (8.0858)*	-0.8138 (6.7650)*	-0.1691 (1.7421)	-0.3212 (3.4130)*
$\Delta\Delta_4 Y_{t-2}$	-0.1998 (1.5219)	-0.2152 (1.6804)				-0.2150 (1.8957)
$\Delta\Delta_4 Y_{t-5}$			-0.5127 (4.7068)*	-0.4557 (4.0845)*		
$\Delta\Delta_4 Y_{t-6}$			-0.1448 (1.4390)			-0.2006 (2.0657)*
$\Delta\Delta_4 Y_{t-7}$						0.1563 (1.8623)
R-squared	0.351	0.376	0.730	0.635	0.704	0.818
SER	0.029	0.029	0.116	0.134	0.022	0.018
DW	2.050	2.099	2.138	1.824	2.034	1.679
LM $\chi^2(4)$	3.082 [0.544]	3.719 [0.445]	1.241 [0.871]	0.598 [0.963]	7.326 [0.119]	6.553 [0.161]
Arch $\chi^2(4)$	5.690 [0.223]	6.377 [0.173]	5.059 [0.281]	1.738 [0.783]	2.713 [0.607]	0.926 [0.921]
Norm $\chi^2(2)$	0.378 [0.827]	0.725 [0.695]	0.230 [0.891]	0.805 [0.668]	0.934 [0.627]	0.464 [0.793]
Reset $\chi^2(2)$	5.541 [0.063]	5.401 [0.067]	3.360 [0.186]	2.187 [0.701]	4.924 [0.085]	2.948 [0.229]

Notes: Numbers in parentheses (.) are *t*-statistics and numbers in the square brackets [.] are *p*-values. Asterisk (*) denotes statistically significant at 5 percent level. Others are as previously defined.

Table 5.8
Results of seasonal error-correction models

Independent variables	Thailand Divisia M1	Divisia M2
Constant	-0.0005	-0.0014
	(0.0819)	(0.2076)
μ_{t-1}	-0.0787	-0.0555
	(2.9976)*	(2.7513)*
ν_{t-1}	-0.3436	
	(2.5273)*	
ω_{t-2}		
ω_{t-3}		
$\Delta\Delta_4 M_{t-3}$		-0.3965
		(2.2486)*
$\Delta\Delta_4 M_{t-4}$		0.3451
		(1.9624)
$\Delta\Delta_4 M_{t-8}$	-0.5672	
	(2.8449)*	
$\Delta\Delta_4 Y_{t-4}$		-0.2859
		(2.8742)*
$\Delta\Delta_4 Y_{t-6}$	-0.2323	-0.2282
	(2.1237)*	(2.6134)*
$\Delta\Delta_4 Y_{t-10}$	0.2884	
	(3.1044)*	
R-squared	0.490	0.465
SER	0.040	0.042
DW	2.132	2.243
LM $\chi^2(4)$	5.363	7.848
	[0.251]	[0.097]
Arch $\chi^2(4)$	1.933	4.161
	[0.748]	[0.385]
Norm $\chi^2(2)$	0.026	2.104
	[0.986]	[0.349]
Reset $\chi^2(2)$	1.842	4.950
	[0.398]	[0.084]

Notes: Numbers in parentheses (.) are *t*-statistics and numbers in the square brackets [.] are *p*-values. Asterisk (*) denotes statistically significant at 5 percent level. Others are as previously defined.

Table 5.9
Summary of results of long-run relationships between Divisia money and income at different frequencies

Country	Money series	Engle-Granger procedure			Seasonal error-correction model		
		Zero	Biannual	Annual	Zero	Biannual	Annual
Indonesia	Divisia M1	√	√		√	√	
	Divisia M2		√		√	√	
Malaysia	Divisia M1				√		√
	Divisia M2		√	√	√		√
Myanmar	Divisia M1				√	√	√
	Divisia M2				√	√	√
Nepal	Divisia M1				√		√
	Divisia M2				√		√
Philippines	Divisia M1			√	√		√
	Divisia M2				√		√
Singapore	Divisia M1				√		√
	Divisia M2				√		√
South Korea	Divisia M1				√		√
	Divisia M2				√		√
Sri Lanka	Divisia M1			√	√	√	
	Divisia M2		√		√	√	
Taiwan	Divisia M1				√		√
	Divisia M2				√	√	√
Thailand	Divisia M1				√	√	
	Divisia M2				√		

Note: The symbol '√' indicate cointegration between two variables.
Sources: Tables 5.2, 5.3, 5.4 and 5.5

Bibliography

Adhikary, G.P. 1989a. *Deregulation in the Financial System of the SEACEN Countries*. Kuala Lumpur: The South East Asian Central Banks (SEACEN) Research and Training Centre.

Adhikary, G.P. 1989b. *Non-Bank Financial Institutions [NBFIs]: Their Impact on the Effectiveness of Monetary Policy in the SEACEN Countries*. Kuala Lumpur: The South East Asian Central Banks (SEACEN) Research and Training Centre.

Agell, J. and L. Berg. 1996. Does Financial Deregulation Cause a Consumption Boom? *Scandinavian Journal of Economics* 98(4): 579-601.

Akhtar, M.A. 1983. Financial Innovations and their Implications for Monetary Policy: An International Perspective. BIS Economic Papers No. 9. Basle: Bank for International Settlement.

Allen, C. and S. Hall. 1991. Money as a Potential Anchor for the Price Level: A Critique of the P* Approach. *Economic Outlook* 15: 45-49.

Arestis, P. and P. Demetriades. 1996. Finance and Growth: Institutional Considerations and Causality. Department of Economics Working Paper No. 5. University of East London.

Arestis, P. and P. Demetriades. 1993. Financial Liberalisation and Economic Development: A Critical Exposition. In P. Arestis (ed.). *Money and Banking: Issues for the Twenty-First Century*. Basingstoke and London: MacMillan.

Argy, V., A. Brennan and G. Stevens. 1989. Monetary Targeting: The International Experience. In I. Macfarlane and G. Stevens (Eds.). *Studies in Money and Credit: Proceedings of a Conference*. Australia: Reserve Bank of Australia.

Atta-Mensah, J. 1996. A Modified P*-Model of Inflation Based on M1. Bank of Canada Working Paper 96-15. Bank of Canada.

Bahmani-Oskooee, M. 1986. Determinants of International Trade Flows. *Journal of Development Economics* 20: 107-123.

Bailey, R.W., M.J. Driscoll, J.L. Ford and A.W. Mullineux. 1982. The Information Content of Monetary Aggregates in the U.K. *Economics Letters* 9: 61-67.

Banerjee, A., J.J. Dolado, D.F. Hendry and G.W. Smith. 1986. Exploring Equilibrium Relationship in Econometric through Static Models: Some Monte Carlo Evidence. *Oxford Bulletin of Economics and Statistics* 48: 253-277.

Bank Negara Malaysia. 1994. *Money and Banking in Malaysia*. Kuala Lumpur: Bank Negara Malaysia.

Bank Negara Malaysia. 1985. *Quarterly Economic Bulletin* 18(4): 118-125.

Barnett, W.A. 1997. Which Road Leads to Stable Money Demand? *Economic Journal* 107: 1171-1185.

Barnett, W.A. 1983. Understanding the New Divisia Monetary Aggregates. *Review of Public Data Use* 11: 349-355.

Barnett, W.A. 1982. The Optimal Level of Monetary Aggregation. *Journal of Money, Credit and Banking* 14(4): 687-710.

Barnett, W.A. 1980. Economic Monetary Aggregates: An Application of Index Number and Aggregation Theory. *Journal of Econometrics* 14: 11-48.

Barnett, W.A. 1978. The User Cost of Money. *Economics Letters* 1: 145-149.

Barnett, W.A. 1991. A Reply to Julio J. Rotemberg. In M.T. Belongia (ed.). *Monetary Policy on the 75th Anniversary of the Federal Reserve System*. Boston: Kluwer Academic Publishers.

Barnett, W.A. 1990. Developments in Monetary Aggregation Theory. *Journal of Policy Modeling* 12(2): 205-257.

Barnett, W.A., D. Fisher and A. Serletis. 1992. Consumer Theory and the Demand for Money. *Journal of Economic Literature* 30: 2086-2119.

Barnett, W.A., E.K. Offenbacher and P.A. Spindt. 1984. The New Divisia Monetary Aggregates. *Journal of Political Economy* 92: 1049-1085.

Barnett, W.A., E.K. Offenbacher and P.A. Spindt. 1981. New Concepts of Aggregated Money. *Journal of Finance* 36(2): 497-505.

Barnett, W.A. and P.A. Spindt. 1982. Divisia Monetary Aggregates: Their Compilation, Data and Historical Behavior. Federal Reserve Board Staff Study No. 116. Washington, D.C.: Federal Reserve Board.

Batchelor, R. 1988. Monetary Developments. *City University Business School Economic Review* 6(1): 17-22.

Bayoumi, T. 1993. Financial Deregulation and Household Saving. *Economic Journal* 103: 1432-1443.

Bayoumi, T. and P. Koujianou. 1990. Consumption, Liquidity Constraints and Financial Deregulation. *Greek Economic Review* 12: 195-210.

Belongia, M.T. 1996. Measurement Matters: Recent Results from Monetary Economics Reexamined. *Journal of Political Economy* 104(5): 1065-1083.

Belongia, M.T. and J.A. Chalfant. 1990. Alternative Measures of Money as Indicators of Inflation: A Survey and Some New Evidence. *Federal Reserve Bank of St. Louis, Review* 72(6): 20-33.

Belongia, M.T. and K.A. Chrystal. 1991. An Admissible Monetary Aggregate for the United Kingdom. *Review of Economics and Statistics* 73: 497-503.

Ben-Horim, M. and W.L. Silber. 1977. Financial Innovation: A Linear Programming Approach. *Journal of Banking and Finance* 1: 277-296.

Binner, J.M. 1990. The Construction, Intepretation and Analysis of Divisia Monetary Aggregates for the U.K. Unpublished PhD Thesis, The University of Leeds.

Blundell-Wignall, A., F. Browne and A. Tarditi. 1995. Financial Liberalization and the Permanent Income Hypothesis. *The Manchester School* 63(2): 125-144.

Blundell-Wignall, A., F. Browne and P. Manasse. 1990. Monetary Policy in Liberalised Financial Markets. OECD Economic Studies No. 15. Paris: OECD.

Bordes, C., E. Girardin and V. Marimoutou. 1993. An Evaluation of the Performance of P-Star as an Indicator of Monetary Conditions in the Perspective of EMU: The Case of France. In P. Aretis (Ed.). *Money and Banking: Issues for the Twenty-First Century*. Basingstoke and London: MacMillan.

Bordo, M.E. and L. Jonung. 1987. *The Long-Run Behaviour of the Velocity of Circulation: The International Evidence*. Cambridge: Cambridge University Press.

Bordo, M.E. and L. Jonung. 1990. The Long-Run Behaviour of Velocity: The Institutional Approach Revisited. *Journal of Policy Modeling* 12(2): 165-197.

Boughton, J.H. 1981. Money and Its Substitutes. *Journal of Monetary Economics* 8: 375-386.

de Brouwer, G. 1995. The Liberalization and Integration of Domestic Financial Markets in Western Pacific Economies. Research Discussion Paper 9506, Reserve Bank of Australia.

Box, G.E.P. and G.M. Jenkins. 1970. *Time Series Analysis Forecasting and Control*. San Francisco: Holden-Day.

Breusch, T.S. 1978. Testing for Autocorrelation in Dynamic Linear Models. *Australian Economic Papers* 17: 334-355.

Bullard, J.B. 1994. Measures of Money and the Quantity Theory. *Federal Reserve Bank of St. Louis Review* 76(1): 19-30.

Cameron, R (ed.). 1972. *Banking and Economic Development: Some Lessons of History*. New York: Oxford University Press.

Campbell, J.Y. and N.G. Mankiw. 1991. The Response of Consumption to Income: A Cross-Country Investigation. *European Economic Review* 35: 723-767.

Campbell, J.Y. and N.G. Mankiw. 1990. Permanent Income, Current Income and Consumption. *Journal of Business and Economic Statistics* 8(3): 265-279.

Campbell, J.Y. and N.G. Mankiw. 1989. Consumption, Income and Interest Rates: Reinterpreting the Time Series Evidence. In O.J. Blanchard and S. Fischer (eds.). *NBER Macroeconomics Annual 1989*. Cambridge: The MIT Press.

Caruso, M. 1996. Stock Prices and Money Velocity: A Multi-Country Analysis. Discussion Paper No. 264. Bank of Italy.

Chandavarkar, A.G. 1977. Monetization of Developing Economies. *IMF Staff Papers* 24(3): 665-721.

Charemza, W.W. and D.F. Deadman. 1992. *New Direction in Econometric Practice*. England: Edward Elgar.

Chetty, V.K. 1969. On Measuring the Nearness of Near-Moneys. *American Economic Review* 59: 270-281.

Cho, Y.J. and D. Khatkhate. 1989a. Financial Liberalisation: Issues and Evidence. *Economic and Political Weekly* 20: 1105-1114.

Cho, Y.J. and D. Khatkhate. 1989b. Lessons of Financial Liberalization in Asia: A Comparative Study. World Bank Discussion Papers No. 50. Wshington, D.C.: The World Bank.

Chong, Y.Y. and D.F. Hendry. 1986. Econometric Evaluation of Linear Macro-Economic Models. *Review of Economic Studies* 53: 671-690.

Chou, N.T. 1991. An Alternative Monetary Policy Target: The New Benchmark Divisia Monetary Index. *Applied Economics* 23: 1699-1705.

Choudhry, T. 1996. Real Stock Prices and the Long-Run Money Demand Function: Evidence from Canada and the USA. *Journal of International Money and Finance* 15(1): 1-17.

Chow, G.C. and A.L. Lin. 1976. Best Linear Unbiased Estimation of Missing Observations in an Economic Time Series. *Journal of the American Statistical Association* 71: 719-722.

Chowdhury, A.R. 1989. Financial Innovations and the Interest Elasticity of Money Demand in Canada. *Economics Letters* 31: 43-48.

Christelow, D.B. 1981. Financial Innovations and Monetary Indicators in Japan. *Federal Reserve Bank of New York, Quarterly Review* 6(1): 42-53.

Chrystal, K.A. and R. MacDonald. 1994. Empirical Evidence on the Recent Behavior and Usefulness of Simple-sum and Weighted Measures of the Money Stock. *Federal Reserve Bank of St. Louis Review* 76(2): 73-109.

Chyi, Y.L. and C.H. Huang. 1997. An Empirical Study of the 'Rule of Thumb' Consumption Model in Five East Asian Countries. *Applied Economics* 29: 1271-1282.

Clements, K.W. and P. Nguyen. 1980. Economic Monetary Aggregates - Comment. *Journal of Econometrics* 14: 49-53.

Cogley, T. and J. Nason. 1995. Effects of the Hodrick-Prescott Filter on Trend and Difference Stationary Time Series: Implications for Business Cycles. *Journal of Economic Dynamics and Control* 19: 235-278.

Corker, R.J. and R.D. Haas. 1991. Price Pressure Gaps: An Application of P* Using Korean Data. IMF Working Paper WP/91/26. Washington, D.C.: International Monetary Fund.

Cuthbertson, K., S.G. Hall and M.P. Taylor. 1992. *Applied Econometric Techniques*. New York: Harvester Wheatsheaf.

Davidson, J., D.F. Hendry, F. Sbra and S. Yeo. 1978. Econometric Modelling of Aggregate Time Series Relationship between Consumers' Expenditure and Income in the United Kingdom. *Economic Journal* 88: 661-692.

Deaton, A. 1992. *Understanding Consumption*. Oxford: Clarendon Press.

Demetriades, P.O. and K.A. Hussein. 1996. Does Financial Development Cause Economic Growth? Time-Series Evidence from 16 Countries. Department of Economics Working Paper No. 4. University of East London.

Dewald, W.G. 1997. Inflation: Always a Monetary Phenomenon!. *Federal Reserve Bank of St. Louis Monetary Trends* (October): 1.

Dewald, W.G. 1988. Monetarism is Dead; Long Live the Quantity Theory. *Federal Reserve Bank of St. Louis Review* 70(4): 3-18.

Diaz-Alejandro, C. 1985. Good-Bye Financial Repression, Hello Financial Crash. *Journal of Development Economics* 19: 1-24.

Dickey, D.A. and W.A. Fuller. 1981. Likelihood Ratio Statistics for Autoregressive Time Series with a Unit Root. *Econometrica* 49: 1057-1072.

Dickey, D.A., D.W. Jansen and D.L. Thronton. 1991. A Primer on Cointegration with an Application to Money and Income. *Federal Reserve Bank of St. Louis Review* 73: 58-78.

Dickey, D.A., H.P. Hasza and W.A. Fuller. 1984. Testing for Unit Roots in Seasonal Time Series. *Journal of the American Statsitical Association* 79: 355-367.

Dickey, D.A. and S.G. Pantula. 1987. Determining the Order of Differencing in Autoregressive Processes. *Journal of Business and Economic Statistics* 5: 455-461.

Diebold, F.X. and M. Nerlove. 1990. Unit Roots in Economic Time Series: A Selective Survey. In T.B. Fomby and Rhodes (eds.). *Advances in Econometrics: Cointegration, Spurious Regressions and Unit Roots*. Greenwich, C.T.: JAI Press.

Diewert, E.W. 1976. Exact and Superlative Index Numbers. *Journal of Econometrics* 4: 115-145.

Donovan, D.J. 1978. Modeling the Demand for Liquid Assets: An Application to Canada. *IMF Staff Papers* 25(4): 676-704.

Dooley, M.P. and F. Spinelli. 1989. The Early Stages of Financial Innovation and Money Demand in France and Italy. *The Manchester School* 57(2): 107-124.

Dornbusch, R. and A. Reynoso. 1989. Financial Factors in Economic Development. *American Economic Review, Papers and Proceedings* 79: 204-209.

Driscoll, M.J., J.L. Ford and A.W. Mullineux. 1985. Monetary Aggregates, their Information Content and their Aggregation Error: Some Preliminary Findings for Austria, 1965-1980. *Empirical Economics* 10: 13-25.

Duck, N.W. 1993. Some International Evidence on the Quantity Theory of Money. *Journal of Money, Credit and Banking* 25(1): 1-12.

Dutt, S.D. and D. Ghosh. 1996. The Export Growth-Economic Growth Nexus: A Causality Analysis. *Journal of Developing Areas* 30: 167-182.

Dutt, S.D. and D. Ghosh. 1994. An Empirical Investigation of the Export Growth-Economic Growth Relationship. *Applied Economics Letters* 1: 44-48.

Dwyer, G.P. and R.W. Hafer. 1988. Is Money Irrelevant? *Federal Reserve Bank of St. Louis Review* 70(3): 3-17.

Engelhardt, G.V. 1996. Consumption, Down Payments and Liquidity Constraints. *Journal of Money, Credit and Banking* 28(2): 255-271.

Engle, R.F. 1982. Autoregressive Conditional Heteroscedasticity with Estimates of the Variance of United Kingdom Inflations. *Econometrica* 50: 987-1007.

Engle, R.F. and C.W.J. Granger. 1987. Cointegration and Error Correction: Representation, Estimation and Testing. *Econometrica* 55: 251-276.

Engle, R.F., C.W.J. Granger, S. Hylleberg and H.S. Lee. 1993. Seasonal Cointegration: The Japanese Consumption Function. *Journal of Econometrics* 55: 275-298.

Engle, R.F. and B.S. Yoo. 1987. Forecasting and Testing in Cointegrated Systems. *Journal of Econometrics* 35: 143-159.

Enzler, J., L. Johnson and J. Paulus. 1976. Some Problems of Money Demand. *Brookings Paper on Economic Activity* 1: 261-280.

Fackler, J.S., W.D. McMillin and J.W. Silver. 1990. Are Monetary Services Indexes Superior to Conventional Monetary Aggregates as Intermediate Targets? *Applied Economics* 22: 1751-1759.

Fase, M.M.G. 1985. Monetary Control: The Dutch Experience. In C. van Ewijk and J.J. Klant (eds). *Monetary Conditions for Economic Recovery*. Dordrecht: Martinus Nijhoff Publishers.

Fase, M.M.G. and C.C.A. Winder. 1996. Wealth and the Demand for Money: Empirical Evidence for the Netherlands and Belgium. *De Economist* 144(4): 569-589.

Favero, C.A. 1993. Error Correction and Forward Looking Models for UK Consumers' Expenditure. *Oxford Bulletin of Economics and Statistics* 55(4): 453-472.

Feder, G. 1983. On Export and Economic Growth. *Journal of Development Economics* 12: 59-73.

Federal Reserve Bank of New York (ed.). 1990. *Intermediate Targets and Indicators for Monetary Policy: A Critical Survey*. New York: Federal Reserve Bank of New York.

Field, A.J. 1984. Asset Exchanges and the Transaction Demand for Money, 1919-1929. *American Economic Review* 74(1): 43-59.

Fisher, I. 1922. *The Making of Index Numbers: A Study of Their Varieties, Tests and Reliability*. Boston: Houghton Mifflin.

Fisher, P., S. Hudson and M. Pradhan. 1993. Divisia Indices for Money: An Appraisal of Theory and Practice. Working Paper Series No. 9. London: Bank of England.

Ford, J.L., W.S. Peng and A.W. Mullineux. 1992. Financial Innovation and Divisia Monetary Aggregates. *Oxford Bulletin of Economics and Statistics* 54(1): 87-102.

Franses, P.H. 1996. Recent Advances in Modelling Seasonality. *Journal of Economic Surveys* 10(3): 299-345.

Freedman, C. 1983. Financial Innovation in Canada: Causes and Consequences. *American Economic Review, Papers and Proceedings* 73(2): 101-106.

Friedman, B.M. 1997. The Rise and Fall of Money Growth Targets as Guidelines for US Monetary Policy. In I. Kuroda (ed.). *Towards More Effective Monetary Policy*. Basingstoke and London: MacMillan Press Ltd.

Friedman, B.M. 1988. Monetary Policy Without Quantity Variables. *American Economic Review* 78: 440-445.

Friedman, B.M. and K.N. Kuttner. 1996. A Price Target for U.S. Monetary Policy? Lessons from the Experience with Money Growth Targets. *Brookings Papers on Economic Activity* 1: 77-125.

Friedman, M. 1988. Money and the Stock Market. *Journal of Political Economy* 96(2): 221-245.

Friedman, M. 1984. Lessons from the 1979-82 Monetary Policy Experiment. *American Economic Review* 74: 397-400.

Friedman, M. and A.J. Schwartz. 1970. *Monetary Statistics of the United States: Estimates, Sources, Methods*. New York: Columbia University Press.

Frisch, H. (ed.). 1976. *Inflation in Small Countries*. Berlin: Springer-Verlag.

Fry, M.J. 1997. In Favour of Financial Liberalisation. *Economic Journal* 107: 754-770.

Fry, M.J. 1996. Saving, Growth and Financial Distortions in Pacidif Asia and Other Developing Areas. Department of Economics Discussion Paper No. 96-23. The University of Birmingham.

Fry, M.J. 1989. Financial Development: Theories and Recent Experience. *Oxford Review of Economic Policy* 5: 13-27.

Fry, M.J. 1988. *Money, Interest and Banking in Economic Development*. Baltimore, MD.: John Hopkins.

Fuller, W.A. 1976. *Introduction to Statistical Time Series*. New York: John Wiley & Sons.

Funke, M. and S. Hall. 1994. Is the Bundesbank Different from Other Central Banks: A Study Based on P*. *Empirical Economics* 19: 691-707.

Furey, K. 1993. The Effect of Trading in Financial Markets on Money Demand. *Eastern Economic Journal* 19(1): 83-90.

Ghysels, E. 1992. On the Economics and Econometrics of Seasonility. In C.A. Sims (ed.). *Advances in Econometrics: Sixth World Congress, Volume I*. Cambridge: Cambridge University Press.

Ghysels, E. 1990. Unit Root Tests and the Statistical Pitfalls of Seasonal Adjustment: The Case of US Postwar Real Gross National Product. *Journal of Business and Economic Statistics* 8: 145-152.

Ghysels, E. 1988. A Study Towards a Dynamic Theory of Seasonility for Economic Time Series. *Journal of the American Statistical Association* 83: 168-172.

Ghysels, E., H.S. Lee and P.L. Siklos. 1994. On the (Mis)Specification of Seasonality and Its Consequences: An Empirical Investigation with US Data. In J.M. Dufour and B. Raj (eds.). *New Developemnts in Time Series Econometrics*. New York: Springer-Verlag.

Godfrey, L.G. 1978. Testing for Higher Order Serial Correlation in Regression Equations When the Regressors Include Lagged Dependent Variables. *Econometrica* 46: 1303-1310.

Goldfeld, S.M. 1976. The Case of the Missing Money. *Brookings Paper on Economic Activity* 3: 683-730.

Goldfeld, S.M. 1982. Comment on the Optimal Level of Monetary Aggregation. *Journal of Money, Credit and Banking* 14(4): 716-720.

Goldsmith, R.W. 1969. *Financial Structure and Development*. New Haven, Conn.: Yale University Press.

Granger, C.W.J. 1994. Some Comments on Empirical Investigations Involving Cointegration. *Econometric Reviews* 13(3): 345-350.

Granger, C.W.J. 1988. Some Recent Development in a Concept of Causality. *Journal of Econometrics* 36: 199-211.

Granger, C.W.J. 1986. Developments in the Study of Cointegrated Economic Variables. *Oxford Bulletin of Economics and Statistics* 48: 213-228.

Granger, C.W.J. 1981. Some Properties of Time Series Data and Their Use in Econometric Model Specification. *Journal of Econometrics* 16: 121-130.

Granger, C.W.J. 1969. Investigating Causal Relations by Econometric Models and Cross-Spectral Methods. *Econometrica* 37: 424-438.

Granger, C.W.J. and P. Newbold. 1977. *Forecasting Economic Time Series*. New York: Academic Press.

Granger, C.W.J. and P. Newbold. 1974. Spurious Regression in Econometrics. *Journal of Econometrics* 2: 111-120.

Gupta, K.L. 1984. *Finance and Economic Growth in Developing Countries*. London: Croom Helm.

Gurley, G.J. and S.E. Shaw. 1960. *Money in a Theory of Finance*. Washington, D.C.: Brookings Institution.

Habibullah, M.S. and P. Smith. 1999. Liquidity Constraints and Financial Liberalisation: The Case for Asian Developing Countries. *Applied Economics Letters (forthcoming)*.

Habibullah, M.S. and P. Smith. 1997. Financial Liberalization and Economic Development: Lessons from ASEAN Countries. Paper presented at the Sixth Tun Razak Conference on 'Industrialization and Development in Southeast Asia.' Ohio, Athens, U.S.A.

Hagger, A.J. 1977. *Inflation: Theory and Policy*. London and Basingstoke: The MacMillan Press Ltd.

Hall, R.E. 1978. Stochastic Implications of the Life Cycle-Permanent Income Hypothesis: Theory and Evidence. *Journal of Political Economy* 86: 971-987.

Hall, R.E. and F.S. Mishkin. 1982. The Sensitivity of Consumption to Transitory Income: Estimates from Panel Data on Households. *Econometrica* 50: 461-481.

Hall, S.G., S.G.B. Hendry and J.B. Wilcox. 1990. The Long-Run Determination of the U.K. Monetary Aggregates. In S.G.B. Hendry and K.D. Patterson (eds.). *Economic Modelling at the Bank of England*. London: Chapman and Hall.

Hallman, J.J., R.D. Porter and D.H. Small. 1991. Is the Price Level Tied to the M2 Monetary Aggregate in the Long Run? *American Economic Review* 81(4): 841-858.

Hallman, J.J., R.D. Porter and D.H. Small. 1989. M2 per Unit of Potential GNP as an Anchor for the Price Level. Staff Study No. 157. Washington, D.C,: Board of Governors of the Federal Reserve System.

Hansen, L.P. and K.J. Singleton. 1983. Stochastic Consumption, Risk Aversion and the Temporal Behavior of Asset Returns. *Journal of Political Economy* 91: 249-265.

Harvey, A.C. 1985. Trends and Cycles in Macroeconomic Time Series. *Journal of Business and Economic Statistics* 3(3): 216-227.

Hasza, D.P. and W.A. Fuller. 1982. Testing for Nonstationary Parameter Specification in Seasonal Time Series Models. *Annals of Statistics* 10: 1209-1216.

Hataiseree, R. 1993. The Demand for Money in Thailand: Cointegration and Error-Correction Approaches. *Singapore Economic Review* 38: 195-230.

Hataiseree, R. 1991. Financial Developments in Thailand: Causes, Changes and Consequences. *Bank of Thailand Quarterly Bulletin* 31(1): 29-45.

Hendry, D.F. 1987. Econometric Methodology: A Personal Perspective. In T.F. Bewley (ed.). *Advances in Econometrics,* Volume II. Cambridge: Cambridge University Press.

Hendry, D.F. 1983. Econometric Modelling: The Consumption Function in Retrospect. *Scottish Journal of Political Economy* 30: 193-220.

Hendry, D.F. 1979. Predictive Failure and Econometric Modelling in Macroeconomics: The Transactions Demand for Money. In P. Omerod (ed.). *Economic Modelling.* London: Heinemann.

Hermann, H., H.E. Reimers and K.H. Toedter. 1994. Weighted Monetary Aggregates for Germany. Unpublished Preliminary Discussion Paper, Deutsche Bundesbank.

Hester, D.D. 1981. Innovations and Monetary Control. *Brookings Paper on Economic Activity* 1: 141-189.

Hoeller, P. and P. Poret. 1991. Is P-Star a Good Indicator of Inflationary Pressure in OECD Countries? *OECD Economic Studies* 17 (Autumn): 7-29.

Hoggarth, G. and H. Pill. 1992. The Demand for M0 Revisited. *Bank of England Quarterly Bulletin* 32(3): 305-313.

Horne, J. and V.L. Martin. 1989. Weighted Monetary Aggregates: An Empirical Study Using Australian Monetary Data, 1969-1987. *Australian Economic Papers* 28: 181-200.

Huang, G. 1995. Modelling China's Demand for International Reserves. *Applied Financial Economics* 5: 357-366.

Huang, C.J., J.C. Cheng, C.S. Chou and S.Y.C. Lin. 1992. The Substitutability of Monetary Assets in Taiwan. *Southern Economic Journal* 58(4): 975-987.

Humphrey, T.M. 1989. Precursors of the P-Star Model. *Federal Reserve Bank of Richmond Economic Review* 75 (July/August): 3-9.

Hurn, A.S. 1993. Seasonality, Cointegration and Error Correction: An Illustration Using South African Monetary Data. *Scottish Journal of Political Economy* 40(3): 311-322.

Hylleberg, S., R.F. Engle, C.W.J. Granger and B.S. Yoo. 1990. Seasonal Integration and Cointegration. *Journal of Econometrics* 44: 215-238.

Hylleberg, S., C. Jorgensen and N.K. Sorensen. 1993. Seasonality in Macroeconomic Time Series. *Empirical Economics* 18: 321-335.

International Monetary Fund. *International Financial Statistic Yearbook 1979 & 1996*. Washington, D.C.: IMF.

Ishida, K. 1984. Divisia Monetary Aggregates and the Demand for Money: A Japanese Case. *Bank of Japan Monetary and Economic Studies* 2: 49-80.

Issing, O., K.-H. Todter, H. Herrmann and H.-E. Reimers. 1993. Zinsgewichtete Geldmengenaggregate und M3- ein Vergleich. *Kredit and Kapital* 26(1): 1-21.

Jaeger, A. 1994. Mechanical Detrending by Hodrick-Prescott Filtering: A Note. *Empirical Economics* 19: 493-500.

Jappelli, T. and M. Pagano. 1989. Consumption and Capital Market Imperfections: An International Comparison. *American Economic Review* 79(5): 1088-1105.

Jarque, C.M. and A.K. Bera. 1980. Efficient Tests of Normality, Homoskedasticity and Serial Independence of Regression Residuals. *Economics Letters* 6: 255-259.

Johansen, S. 1988. Statistical Analysis of Cointegration Vectors. *Journal of Economic Dynamics and Control* 12: 231-254.

Journal of Financial Services Research. 1997. Volume 11.

Judd, J.P. and J.L. Scadding. 1982. The Search for a Stable Money Demand Function: A Survey of the Post-1973 Literature. *Journal of Economic Literature* 20: 993-1023.

Judd, J.P. and B. Trehan. 1988. Portfolio Substitution and the Reliability of M1, M2 and M3 as Monetary Policy Indicators. *Federal Reserve Bank of San Francisco, Economic Review* (Summer): 5-29.

Jung, W.S. 1986. Financial Development and Economic Growth: International Evidence. *Economic Development and Cultural Change* 34: 333-346.

Kavoussi, R.M. 1984. Export Expansion and Economic Growth: Further Empirical Evidence. *Journal of Development Economics* 14: 241-250.

Kimball, R.C. 1980. Wire Transfer and the Demand for Money. *New England Economic Review* (March/April): 5-22.

King, R.G. and R. Levine. 1993. Finance, Entrepreneurship and Growth. *Journal of Monetary Economics* 32: 513-542.

King, R.G. and S.T. Rebelo. 1993. Low Frequency Filtering and Real Business Cycles. *Journal of Economic Dynamics and Control* 17: 207-231.

Kitchen, T. 1985. A Comparison of the Velocities of Monetary Aggregates Using UK Data for the Period 1963:1-1982:1. *Economics Letters* 18: 931-949.

Klein, B. 1974. Competitive Interest Payments on Bank Deposits and the Long-Run Demand for Money. *American Economic Review* 64: 931-949.

Kole, L.S. and M.P. Leahy. 1991. The Usefulness of P* Measures for Japan and Germany. International Finance Discussion Papers No. 414. Board of Governors of the Federal Reserve System.

Kool, C.J.M. and J.A. Tatom. 1994. The P-Star Model in Five Small Economies. *Federal Reserve Bank of St. Louis Review* 76(3): 11-29.

Kremers, J.J.M., N.R. Ericsson and J.J. Dolado. 1992. The Power of Cointegration Tests. *Oxford Bulletin of Economics and Statistics* 54(3): 325-348.

Kumah, E.O. 1989. Monetary Concept and Definitions. IMF Working Paper WP/89/92. Washington, D.C.: International Monetary Fund.

Kunst, R.M. 1994. Seasonal Cointegration, Common Seasonals and Forecasting Seasonal Series. In J.M. Dufour and B. Raj (eds.). *New Developments in Time Series Econometrics*. New York: Springer-Verlag.

Laidler, D. 1997. Inflation Control and Monetary Policy Rules. In I. Kuroda (ed.). *Towards More Effective Monetary Policy*. Basingstoke and London: MacMillan Press Ltd.

Laumas, G.S. 1968. The Degree of Moneyness of Saving Deposits. *American Economic Review* 58: 501-503.

Laumas, P.S. and S. Porter-Hudak. 1986. Monetization, Economic Development and the Exogeneity of Money. *Journal of Development Economics* 21: 25-34.

Lee, S.Y. 1992. *Money and Finance in the Economic Development of Taiwan*. London and Basingstoke: MacMillan.

Lee, H.S. and P.L. Siklos. 1991. Unit Roots and Seasonal Unit Roots in Macroeconomic Time Series. *Economic Letters* 35: 273-277.

Lehmussaari, O.P. 1990. Deregulation and Consumption: Saving Dynamics in the Nordic Countries. *IMF Staff Papers* 37(1): 71-93.

Levi, M.D., I. Venezia and Y. Zhang. 1996. The Velocity Puzzle Revisited: The Effects of the Housing and Stock Markets. *Journal of Economics and Business* 48: 23-32.

Lewis, W.A. 1955. *Theory of Economic Growth*. London: Unwin University Books.

Lieberman, C. 1979. Structural and Technological Change in Money Demand. *American Economic Review, Papers and Proceedings* 69(2): 324-329.

Lwin, T. 1993. Monetary Policy in Myanmar: An Update (1979-1990). In A. Talib (ed.). *Monetary Policy in the SEACEN Countries: An Update*. Kuala Lumpur: The South East Asian Central Banks (SEACEN) Research and Training Centre.

MacKinnon, J.G. 1991. Critical Values for Cointegration Tests. In R.F. Engle and C.W.J. Granger (eds.). *Long-Run Economic Relationships: Readings in Cointegration*. Oxford: Oxford University Press.

Mayer, T. 1993. Monetarism in a World without 'Money'. In S.F. Frowen (ed.). *Monetary Theory and Monetary Policy: New Tracks for the 1990s*. Basingstoke and London: St Martin Press.

McCandles, G.T. and W.E. Weber. 1995. Some Monetary Facts. *Federal Reserve Bank of Minneapolis Quarterly Review* 19(3): 2-11.

McCann, E. and D. Giles. 1989. Divisia Monetary Aggregates and the Real User Cost of Money. *Journal of Quantitative Economics* 5: 127-141.

McCornac, D.C. 1991. Money and the Level of Stock Market Prices: Evidence from Japan. *Quarterly Journal of Business and Economics* 30(4): 42-51.

McDougall. R.S. 1995. The Seasonal Unit Root Structure in New Zealand Macroeconomic Variables. *Applied Economics* 27: 817-827.

McDougall, R.S. 1994. The Stability of Velocity: A Test for Seasonal Cointegration. Applied *Economics Letters* 1: 152-157.

McGiven, A. 1996. Trade with Newly Industrialised Economies. *Bank of England Quarterly Bulletin* 36(1): 69-78.

McKinnon, R.I. 1988. Financial Liberalization in Retrospect: Interest Rate Policies in LDCs. In G. Ranis and T.P. Schultz (eds.). *The State of Development Economics: Progress and Perspectives.* New York: Basil Blackwell.

McKinnon, R.I. 1973. *Money and Capital in Economic Development.* Washington, D.C.: Brookings Institution.

Melvin, M. and C.D. Shiau. 1990. Property Rights, Development and Velocity in Developing Countries. *Economic Development and Cultural Change* 38(4): 821-832.

Miller, M.H. 1986. Financial Innovations: The Last Twenty Years and the Next. *Journal of Financial and Quantitative Analysis* 21: 459-471.

Mills, T.C. and A.G. Mills. 1992. Modelling the Seasonal Patterns in UK Macroeconomic Time Series. *Journal of the Royal Statistical Society, Series A* 155(Part 1): 61-75.

Minsky, H.P. 1957. Central Banking and Money Market Changes. *Quarterly Journal of Economics* 71: 171-187.

Miron, J.A. 1992. The Economics of Seasonal Cycles. In C.A. Sims (ed.). *Advances in Econometrics: Sixth World Congress, Volume I.* Cambridge: Cambridge University Press.

Moosa, I.A. 1997. Testing the Long-Run Neutrality of Money in a Developing Economy: The Case of India. *Journal of Developing Economics* 53: 139-155.

Moosa, I.A. 1995. On the Specification of the Australian Consumption Function. *Australian Economic Papers* 34(65): 263-276.

Moroney, J.R. and B.J. Wilbratte. 1976. Money and Money Substitutes. *Journal of Money, Credit and Banking* 8(1): 181-198.

Moschos, D. 1989. Export Expansion, Growth and the Level of Economic Development: An Empirical Analysis. *Journal of Development Economics* 30: 93-102.

Mullineux, A. (ed.). 1996. *Financial Innovation, Banking and Monetary Aggregates*. Cheltenham: Edward Elgar.

Murinde, V. and F.S.H. Eng. 1994. Financial Development and Economic Growth in Singapore: Demand-Following or Supply-Leading? *Applied Financial Economics* 4: 391-404.

Musi, A.S. 1989. Construction of New Monetary Aggregates: The Case of Mexico. Unpublished PhD Dissertation, The University of Texas at Austin.

Nurkse, R. 1962. *Problems of Capital Formation in Underdeveloped Countries*. London: Basil Blackwell.

Odedokun, M.O. 1996. Alternative Econometric Approaches for Analysing the Role of the Financial Sector in Economic Growth: Time Series Evidence for LDCs. *Journal of Development Economics* 50(1): 119-146.

Odedokun, M.O. 1991. Differential Impacts of Export Expansion on Economic Growth in the LDCs: A Comparison of Evidences Across Regional Income Groups and Between the Decades of 1970s and 1980s. *Eastern Africa Economic Review* 7: 69-93.

Offenbacher, E.K. 1980. Economic Monetary Aggregates: Comment. *Journal of Econometrics* 14: 55-56.

Olekalns, N. 1994. Testing for Unit Roots in Seasonally Adjusted Data. *Economics Letters* 45: 273-279.

Osborn, D.R. 1990. A Survey of Seasonality in UK Macroeconomic Variables. *International Journal of Forecasting* 6: 327-336.

Osborn, D.R., A.P.L. Chui, J.P. Smith and C.R. Birchenhall. 1988. Seasonality and the Order of Integration for Consumption. *Oxford Bulletin of Economics and Statistics* 50: 361-377.

Osterwald-Lenum, M. 1992. A Note with Quantiles of the Asymptotic Distribution of the Maximum Likelihood Cointegration Rank Test Statistics. *Oxford Bulletin of Economics and Statistics* 54: 461-472.

Otto, G. and T. Wirjanto. 1990. Seasonal Unit-Root Tests on Canadian Macroeconomic Time Series. *Economics Letters* 34: 117-120.

Palley, T.I. 1996. The Demand for Money and Non-GDP Transactions. *Economics Letters* 48: 145-154.

Patrick, H.T. 1966. Financial Development and Economic Growth in Underdeveloped Countries. *Economic Development and Cultural Change* 14: 174-189.

Patterson, K.D. and B. Pesaran. 1992. The Intertemporal Elasticity of Substitution in Consumption in the United States and the United Kingdom. *Review of Economics and Statistics* 74: 573-584.

Payne, J.E. 1995. Velocity and the Variability of Yields on Financial and Other Assets. *American Economist* 39: 89-94.

Perman, R. 1991. Cointegration: An Introduction to the Literature. *Journal of Economic Studies* 18: 3-30.

Phillips, A.W. 1954. Stabilisation Policy in a Closed Economy. *Economic Journal* 64: 290-323.

Raj, B. 1995. Institutional Hypothesis of the Long-Run Income Velocity of Money and Parameter Stability of the Equilibrium Relationship. *Journal of Applied Econometrics* 10: 233-253.

Ram, R. 1987. Exports and Economic Growth in Developing Countries: Evidence from Time Series and Cross-Section Data. *Economic Development and Cultural Change* 36: 51-72.

Ramsey, J.B. 1969. Tests for Specification Errors in Classical Linear Least Squares Regression Observations. *Journal of the Royal Statistical Society*, Series B, Part 2: 350-371.

Razzak, W. and R. Dennis. 1996. The Output Gap Using the Hodrick-Prescott filter with a Non-Constant Smoothing Parameter: An Application to New Zealand. Discussion Paper No. G95/8. Reserve Bank of New Zealand.

Roper, D.E. and S.J. Turnovsky. 1980. The Optimum Monetary Aggregate for Stabilization Policy. *The Quarterly Journal of Economics* 95: 333-355.

Rotemberg, J.J. 1991. Commentary: Monetary Aggregates and Their Uses. In M.T. Belongia (ed.). *Monetary Policy on the 75th Anniversary of the Federal Reserve System.* Boston: Kluwer Academic Publishers.

Rotemberg, J.J., J.C. Driscoll and J.M. Poterba. 1995. Money, Output and Prices: Evidence from a New Monetary Aggregate. *Journal of Business and Economic Statistics* 13(1): 67-83.

Said, S.E. and D.A. Dickey. 1984. Testing for Unit Roots in Autoregressive-Moving Average Models with Unknown Order. *Biometrika* 71: 599-607.

Sargan, J.D. 1964. Wages and Prices in the United Kingdom: A Study of Econometric Methodology. In P.E. Hart, G. Mills and J.K. Whittakers (eds.). *Econometric Analysis for National Planning.* London: Butterworths.

Schlitzer, G. 1996. Testing the Null of Stationarity Against the Alternative of a Unit Root: An Application to the Italian Post-War Economy. *Applied Economics* 28: 327-331.

Schlitzer, G. 1995. Testing the Stationarity of Economic Time Series: Further Monte Carlo Evidence. *Ricerche Economiche* 49: 125-144.

Schwert, G.W. 1987. Effects of Model Specification Tests for Unit Root in Macroeconomic Data. *Journal of Monetary Economics* 20: 73-103.

Schwert, G.W. 1979. Tests of Causality: The Message in the Innovations. In K. Brunner and A.H. Meltzer (eds.). *Three Aspect of Policy and Policymaking: Knowledge, Data and Institutions*. Amsterdam: North-Holland.

Schmidt-Hebbel, F., L. Serven and A. Solimano. 1996. Saving and Investment: Paradigms, Puzzles, Policies. *The World Bank Research Observers* 11(1): 87-117.

SEACEN Centre. *SEACEN Financial Statistics-Money and Banking*. Kuala Lumpur: The South East Asian Central Bank (SEACEN) Research and Training Centre.

Sek, D. and Y.H.E. Nil. 1993. Financial Liberalization in Africa. *World Development* 21(11): 1867-1881.

Serletis, A. 1990. Velocity Effects of Anticipated and Unanticipated Money Growth and its Variability. *Applied Economics* 22: 775-783.

Serletis, A. And M. King. 1993. The Role of Money in Canada. *Journal of Macroeconomics* 15(1): 91-107.

Shannon, C. 1948. A Mathematical Theory of Communication. *Bell System Technical Journal* 27: 379-452.

Shaw, E.S. 1973. *Financial Deepening in Economic Development*. New York: Oxford University Press.

Shin, S. 1986. Monetary Aggregates and Economic Activity in Korea. *The Bank of Korea, Quarterly Economic Review* (March): 20-30.

Siklos, P.L. 1993. Income Velocity and Institutional Change: Some New Time Series Evidence, 1870-1986. *Journal of Money, Credit and Banking* 25(3), Part 1: 377-392.

Silber, W.L. 1983. The Process of Financial Innovation. *American Economic Review, Papers and Proceedings* 73(2): 89-95.

Simpson, T.D. 1979. A Proposal for Redefining the Monetary Aggregates. *Federal Reserve Bulletin* 65(1): 13-42.

Simpson, T.D. and R.D. Porter. 1980. Some Issues Involving the Definition and Interpretation of the Monetary Aggregates. In Federal Reserve Bank of Boston (ed.). *Controlling the Monetary Aggregates III, Conference Series No. 23*. Boston: Federal Reserve Bank of Boston.

Sims, C.A. 1972. Money, Income and Causality. *American Economic Review* 62: 540-555.

Speight, A.E.H. 1990. *Consumption, Rational Expectations and Liquidity: Theory and Evidence*. London: Harvester Wheatsheaf.

Speight, A.E.H. and M.J. White. 1995. Private Consumption, Public Consumption and Liquidity Constraints in Developing Countries: Some Empirical Evidence. *Applied Economics* 27: 925-933.

Spencer, P. 1994. Portfolio Disequilibrium: Implications for the Divisia Approach to Monetary Aggregation. *The Manchester School* 62(2): 125-150.

Spindt, P.A. 1985. Money is What Money Does: Monetary Aggregation and The Equation of Exchange. *Journal of Political Economy* 93(1): 175-204.

Stone, C.C. and D.L. Thornton. 1987. Solving the 1980s' Velocity Puzzle: A Progress Report. *Federal Reserve Bank of St. Louis, Review* 69(7): 5-23.

Subrahmanyam, G. And S.B. Swami. 1991. Simple Sum Versus Superlative Monetary Aggregates for India. *Journal of Quantitative Economics* 7(1): 79-92.

Suzuki, Y. 1987. Financial Innovation in Japan: Its Origins, Diffusion and Impacts. In M. De Cecco (ed). *Changing Money: Financial Innovation in Developed Countries*. Oxford: Basil Blackwell.

Swamy, P.A.V.B. and G.S. Tavlas. 1989. Financial Deregulation, the Demand for Money, and Monetary Policy in Australia. *IMF Staff Papers* 36(1): 63-101.

Swofford, J.L. and G.A. Whitney. 1991. The Composition and Construction of Monetary Aggregates. *Economic Inquiry* 29: 752-761.

Talib, A. (ed). 1993. *Monetary Policy in the SEACEN Countries: An Update*. Kuala Lumpur: The South East Asian Central Banks (SEACEN) Research and Training Centre.

Tatom, J.A. 1990. The P-Star Approach to the Link Between Money and Prices. Working Paper No. 90-008. Federal Reserve Bank of St. Louis.

Theil, H. 1967. *Economics and Information Theory*. Amsterdam: North-Holland.

Thornton, D.L. 1983. Why does Velocity Matter? *Federal Reserve Bank of St. Louis, Review* 65(10): 5-13.

Thornton, J. 1996. Financial Deepening and Economic Growth in Developing Economies. *Applied Economics Letters* 3: 243-246.

Thornton, J. 1991. The Financial Repression Paradigm: A Survey of Empirical Research. *Savings and Development* 15(1): 5-17.

Thornton, J. and P. Molyneux. 1996. Unanticipated Income and Consumption in ASEAN Countries. *Applied Economics Letters* 3: 247-249.

Thornton, D.L. and P. Yue. 1992. An Extended Series of Divisia Monetary Aggregates. *Federal Reserve Bank of St. Louis Review* 74(6): 35-52.

Timberlake, R.H. and J. Forston. 1967. Time Deposits in the Definition of Money. *American Economic Review* 57(1): 190-194.

Tinsley, P.A., P.A. Spindt and M.E. Friar. 1980. Indicator and Filter Attributes of Monetary Aggregates: A Nit-Picking Case for Dissaggregation. *Journal of Econometrics* 14: 61-91.

Todter, K.H. and H.E. Reimers. 1994. P-Star as a Link between Money and Prices in Germany. *Weltwirtschaftliches Archiv* 130: 273-289.

Tornqvist, L. 1936. The Bank of Finland's Consumption Price Index. *Bank of Finland Bulletin* 10: 1-8.

Tseng, W. and R. Corker. 1993. SEACEN Study on Monetary Policy and Financial Reform. In A. Talib (ed). *Monetary Policy in the SEACEN Countries: An Update*. Kuala Lumpur: The South East Asian Central Banks (SEACEN) Research and Training Centre.

Tseng, W. and R. Corker. 1991. Financial Liberalization, Money Demand, and Monetary Policy in Asian Countries. Occasional Paper 84, Washington, D.C.: International Monetary Fund.

Tyler, W.G. 1981. Growth and Export Expansion in Developing Countries: Some Empirical Evidence. *Journal of Development Economics* 15: 349-363.

Vaidyanathn, G. 1993. Consumption, Liquidity Constraints and Economic Development. *Journal of Macroeconomics* 15: 591-610.

Villagomez, F.A. 1997. Private Saving, Interest Rates and Liquidity Constraints in LDCs: Recent Evidence. *Applied Economics* 29: 607-615.

Villanueva, D. and A. Mirakhor. 1990. Strategies for Financial Reforms: Interest Rate Policies, Stabilization and Bank Supervision in Developing Countries. *IMF Staff Papers* 37(3): 509-536.

Vogel, R.C. 1974. The Dynamics of Inflation in Latin America, 1950-1969. *American Economic Review* 64(1): 102-114.

Wilcox, J.A. 1989. Liquidity Constraints on Consumption: The Real Effects of "Real" Lending Policies. *Federal Reserve Bank of San Francisco Economic Review* (Fall): 39-52.

World Bank. 1995. *World Development Report 1995*. Washington, D.C.: The World Bank.

World Bank. 1993. *The East Asian Miracle: Economic Growth and Public Policy*. New York: Oxford University Press.

World Bank. 1989. *World Development Report 1989*. Washington, D.C.: The World Bank.

Yue, P. and R. Fluri. 1991. Divisia Monetary Services Indexes for Switzerland: Are they Useful for Monetary Targeting? *Federal Reserve Bank of St. Louis Review* 73: 19-33.